Expert Shell Scripting

Ron Peters

Apress®

Lead Editor: Frank Pohlmann
Technical Reviewer: Brian Culp
Editorial Board: Clay Andres, Steve Anglin, Mark Beckner, Ewan Buckingham, Tony Campbell, Gary Cornell, Jonathan Gennick, Michelle Lowman, Matthew Moodie, Jeffrey Pepper, Frank Pohlmann, Ben Renow-Clarke, Dominic Shakeshaft, Matt Wade, Tom Welsh
Project Manager: Sofia Marchant
Copy Editor: Candace English
Associate Production Director: Kari Brooks-Copony
Production Editor: Liz Berry
Compositor: Pat Christenson
Proofreader: Lisa Hamilton
Indexer: Julie Grady
Artist: April Milne
Cover Designer: Kurt Krames
Manufacturing Director: Tom Debolski

Distributed to the book trade worldwide by Springer-Verlag New York, Inc., 233 Spring Street, 6th Floor, New York, NY 10013. Phone 1-800-SPRINGER, fax 201-348-4505, e-mail orders-ny@springer-sbm.com, or visit http://www.springeronline.com.

For information on translations, please contact Apress directly at 2855 Telegraph Avenue, Suite 600, Berkeley, CA 94705. Phone 510-549-5930, fax 510-549-5939, e-mail info@apress.com, or visit http://www.apress.com.

Apress and friends of ED books may be purchased in bulk for academic, corporate, or promotional use. eBook versions and licenses are also available for most titles. For more information, reference our Special Bulk Sales–eBook Licensing web page at http://www.apress.com/info/bulksales.

The source code for this book is available to readers at http://www.apress.com. You will need to answer questions pertaining to this book in order to successfully download the code.

Contents at a Glance

PART 1 ▪▪▪ Basic Scripting Techniques

PART 2 ▪▪▪ System Interaction and Advanced Techniques

PART 3 ■■■ Useful Scripts

Contents

PART 1 ▪▪▪ Basic Scripting Techniques

PART 2 ▪▪▪ System Interaction and Advanced Techniques

PART 3 ▪▪▪ Useful Scripts

About the Author

RON PETERS has worked as a system administrator for most of the last 15 years. He was a senior administrator at Intel in a 24/7 production environment and was the primary administrator of a large compute cluster dedicated to design work. He is now a Linux/ UNIX administrator for Columbia Sportswear. He enjoys spending time with his family, restoring his Dodge Challenger, and playing racquetball.

About the Technical Reviewer

BRIAN CULP has worked professionally in the information-services industry for 20 years. Throughout those years he has worked with startups and small businesses, and spent a dozen years employed by a leading company in the IT industry. Brian has spent time on service desks, as a UNIX systems admin, a project manager, an e-commerce/business web site administrator, and a solutions developer.

Brian's development and use of UNIX shell scripts has always grown out of specific needs, as he always seems to be in some stage of trying to solve a technical problem. He hopes you will find the scripts and methods described in this book useful in building your own problem-solving toolkit.

Acknowledgments

For most things in this world, we depend on others. This book is no exception; this project is larger than most I have taken on, and I could not have done it alone. I would firstly and most importantly like to thank my God for the free gift of life as well as the skills and abilities that enabled me to write this book. I would also like to thank my wife, Kathleen, and my two boys, Austin and Grant, for enduring the seemingly endless hours and evenings I've been spending with my laptop.

I want to express my gratitude to the two Brians: to Brian Grell for giving me ideas and discussing many topics that have found their way into this book, and to Brian Culp for reviewing the whole book and keeping me focused on what I was trying to say, and asking the right questions so I could maintain clarity.

Finally, I want to thank all the other editors who have had a hand in helping me remove the Englilsh[1] from my writing.

---

1. http://www.homestarrunner.com/sbemail64.swf

Introduction

I learned the basics of programming when I was in school; I learned how to shell-script by example.

I've met and worked with many system administrators and other *NIX folks, each of whom has their own bag of tricks when it comes to managing a system, interacting with their environment, or coding a script. It's always very useful to have conversations and interact with people like this because you invariably gain some tidbits that you can throw into your own collection of tricks. I decided to collect all the useful shell-scripting and interaction techniques I have learned through the years and combine them into one beneficial reference guide. In fact, I used some of my own notes about those techniques while writing this book. Since I haven't memorized everything present in this book, I would periodically look up items when I was working on various tasks. I want this book to be the beginning of a higher-level reference library that can be added to and can grow continually.

You might be aware of the large number of shell-scripting books and online resources aiding in the mastery of shell scripting. Many are excellent and cover a wide range of topics. The main purpose of this book is to combine some of the most unique tools, code snippets, and scripts that go beyond the level of basic scripts. I wanted to create a cookbook of sorts—lesser-known recipes and fairly advanced algorithms that have proved useful to me.

I have included scripts you can use as is, and sample scripts illustrating a specific algorithm. I also demonstrate a few complex commands that may be useful on the command line. I have tried to tailor the scripts to be useful at multiple levels. Most times, however, there is little or no error-checking since that is not necessarily the point of a specific script. You must be prepared to make modifications to fit your local environment.

How This Book Came About

My friend Brian Culp and I have worked together as UNIX system administrators for many years. Periodically, Brian or I will be working on some script and run into a problem. One of us will stop, walk over to the other, and say something like, "Do you have any code that does X?" The answer may be no, in which case we'll launch into a discussion on how we might tackle the problem, or come up with a few different solutions. However, many times it might be something like, "Hmm, yeah, I think I remember doing something like that in a script that does X on system Y. Let me look for a minute." A few carefully chosen grep commands, and the solution is at hand.

Although finding the solution we want is great, it's not the most efficient use of our time. To go from having a place to store and organize all of our (and, of course, other programmers') gems and having them in a heavily documented form, to writing a book on the subject was only a short step. Even though it is possible to search online references quickly for specific code, there were many occasions when I just wanted to pull a book off my shelf. It's not always obvious what to search for when you have a specific itch that needs scratching, so you're not sure exactly to what search for online.

This is to some extent an expression of my own limitations: my family and friends think I'm a computer guru, but rest assured, I know better. There are many programmers out there who are much more adept at shell coding than I am. I mainly intended to collect, order, and explain code that I have found to be highly useful in my professional experience as a system administrator, and share that information with others.

Who Should Read This Book

The book is meant for the intermediate shell coder up to the advanced shell-code hacker, because I don't explain many basic programming structures. If you're looking for that type of book, you should look to the resources mentioned in Appendix C.

This is not to say that the beginner won't find this book useful; it may work well as a supplementary reference to a more traditional shell-scripting training guide. But there is a difference between learning English as a second language and learning how to apply sarcasm. This book is like sarcasm in that example; it assumes some basic shell-code literacy.

I go into great detail about how and why the scripts were written in their present form, and I include some explanation of how to avoid certain problems. Much of my learning came from sources heavy in obfuscation and light on clarity, so I tried to be as explicit as possible, and favored explaining too much rather than too little. You can think of many chapters I included as shell scripts with extremely detailed commentary.

The book is divided into three parts: "Basic Scripting Techniques," "System Interaction and Advanced Techniques," and "Useful Scripts." Most chapters serve as stand-alone discussions, although they may refer to other chapters on some minor points.

Issues and Ideas

I have made every effort to test the code that I included in this book to validate that it works. With a project of this size, however, even with the number of eyes that have reviewed it, there may be mistakes. I would like to know about the mistakes as well as, and more importantly, any other ideas and scripts that could be used for future revisions of this book. Please drop me a note at rbpeters@peterro.com.

PART 1

Basic Scripting Techniques

## CHAPTER 1

Shell Script Debugging

Even though this book isn't a "how to script" manual, some concepts that are fundamental to writing successful scripts should be discussed. Debugging is one of them. Debugging code is a significant part of writing code. No matter how disciplined you are or how skilled you become at coding, you will have bugs in your code, in the form of either syntax or logic errors. The syntactical problems tend to be simpler to resolve since many times they show up when the code throws an error when it is run. The logical bugs, on the other hand, may be more difficult to track down since the code may run without error, but the resulting output does not match the design of the program. The more complex your code becomes as your skill increases, the more difficult these types of problems will be to detect.

Since writing bug-free code is nearly impossible, you need a few techniques up your sleeve that will help you finish, diagnose, repair, and clean up your code. This chapter presents a few ways to debug code that I have used consistently and that help me extract details from the inner workings of my scripts. These techniques validate that the code is living up to my expectations and demonstrate where the code needs more work to perform the intended task.

Shell Trace Options

The first technique—using the set command—is the simplest to implement and can give you great amounts of detail about how the logic is progressing and the values of variables internal to your script. Using the set command is really just using shell options to display verbose output when the script is running. One of the functions of the set command is to turn on and off the various options that are available in the shell. In this case, the option being set is -x, or xtrace. This is where the running script will, in addition to any normal output, display the expanded commands and variables of a given line of code before the code is run. With this increased output, you can easily view what is happening in the running script and possibly determine where your problem lies.

When you put the instruction set -x into your script, each of the commands that execute after that set instruction will be displayed, together with any arguments that were supplied to the command, including variables and their values. Each line of output will be preceded by a plus-sign (+) prompt to designate it as part of the trace output. Traced commands from the running shell that are being executed in a subshell are denoted by a double plus sign (++).

To demonstrate what the use of set -x can do for you, consider this script:

```
#!/bin/sh
#set -x
echo -n "Can you write device drivers? "
read answer
answer=`echo $answer | tr [a-z] [A-Z]`
if [ $answer = Y ]
then
  echo "Wow, you must be very skilled"
else
  echo "Neither can I, I'm just an example shell script"
fi
```

Note that the set -x line is currently commented out. When this script is entered in the file example and run, the behavior is as expected.

```
$ ./example
Can you write device drivers? y
Wow, you must be very skilled
```

or

```
$ ./example
Can you write device drivers? n
Neither can I, Im just an example shell script
```

This is the output when the set -x line is uncommented:

```
$ ./example
+ echo -n 'Can you write device drivers? '
Can you write device drivers? + read answer
y
++ tr '[a-z]' '[A-Z]'
++ echo y
+ answer=Y
+ '[' Y = Y ']'
+ echo Wow, you must be very skilled
Wow, you must be very skilled
```

or

```
$ ./example
+ echo -n 'Can you write device drivers? '
Can you write device drivers? + read answer
n
++ echo n
++ tr '[a-z]' '[A-Z]'
+ answer=N
+ '[' N = Y ']'
+ echo Neither can I, Im just an example shell script
Neither can I, Im just an example shell script
```

The output is a verbose trace of the script's execution. Note that the lines without the plus sign are the output of the script that would be displayed if the script were run without tracing enabled. As you can see, this type of trace is highly useful in determining the value that variables contain during the execution of a script, as well as the route that the code took based on the conditions satisfied.

A shell option that is a slight variation of this output can also be used for troubleshooting. The -v option to the shell enables verbose mode and outputs the script code (as it is being executed) to the standard error file handle (often abbreviated as stderr). More specifically, in the case of a shell script, each line of code that is encountered during execution is output to stderr along with any other output from the script. (Chapter 9 contains more discussion of file handles.) The following is the output from the same script when the set -v line is implemented:

```
$ ./example
echo -n "Can you write device drivers? "
Can you write device drivers? read answer
y
answer=`echo $answer | tr [a-z] [A-Z]`
echo $answer | tr [a-z] [A-Z]if [ $answer = Y ]
then
  echo "Wow, you must be very skilled"
else
  echo "Neither can I; I'm just an example shell script"
fi
Wow, you must be very skilled
```

or

```
$ ./example
echo -n "Can you write device drivers? "
Can you write device drivers? read answer
n
answer=`echo $answer | tr [a-z] [A-Z]`
echo $answer | tr [a-z] [A-Z]if [ $answer = Y ]
then
  echo "Wow, you must be very skilled"
else
  echo "Neither can I; I'm just an example shell script"
fi
Neither can I; I'm just an example shell script
```

The verbose (-v) option to the shell is more useful if you simply want to see the running code of the script that you're working with (as opposed to the expanded values of variables) to make sure the code is working as designed with the xtrace (-x) option. Both options can be employed together by using set -xv, and you'll see both types of output at the same time, although it may be difficult to wade through.

Both the verbose and xtrace options are valuable in their own way for troubleshooting both logical and syntactical problems. As with all options to the shell, they can be turned on and off. The syntax for disabling an option is the opposite of that for turning on an option. Instead of using a minus (-) sign as you did before to enable an option such as in -x, you would use a plus sign, as in +x to disable the option. This will disable the option from that point on. This is very useful if you want to debug only a small portion of the script. You would enable the option just prior to the problem area of code, and disable it just after the problem area so you aren't inundated with irrelevant output.

Simple Output Statements

The next debugging technique—the use of echo or print commands in the code—is also very simple, but it is used frequently to gather specific variable values from a running script rather than displaying potentially large amounts of data using the set -x option. Typically these commands are used for simple output of a script to some type of display or file. In this case, however, they will be used as a checkpoint in the code to validate variable assignments.

These additional output instructions are used regularly in at least a couple of ways. The first way is to output the value of a specific variable at a specific time. Sometimes variables get changed when you aren't expecting them to be, and adding a simple output line will show this. The main advantage of this type of output compared to set -x is that you have the ability to format your output for ease of reading. While set -x has a valid use and is valuable in tracing through the running of a script, it can be cumbersome to isolate the exact piece of data that you're looking for. With an echo or print statement, you can display a single line of output with multiple variables that include some headings for easy reading. The following line is an example of the code you might use:

```
echo Var1: $var1 Var2: $var2 Var3: $var3
```

The output doesn't need to be polished since it is simply for your validation and troubleshooting, but you will want it to be meaningful so you can see the exact data you're looking for at its exact spot in the code.

The second way is to output a debugging line to verify that the logic is correct for known input data. If you are running a script that should have known results but does not, it may contain a logical error where what you've designed and what you've coded don't quite match. Such errors can be difficult to find. Adding some echo statements in key positions can reveal the flow of control through the script as it executes, and so validate whether you are performing the correct logical steps.

I've modified the script slightly to add echo statements at two key positions, but only one of the statements in each echo-statement pair will be executed because of the if statement. This way you not only see the output of the statement itself, but you know which condition of the if statement the code executed. In the following very simple example code, you can see that there is an echo statement as part of the original code. When there are many conditions and comparisons without output, these types of statements are very valuable in determining if your logic is correct.

```
#!/bin/sh
echo -n "Can you write device drivers? "
read answer
answer=`echo $answer | tr [a-z] [A-Z]`
if [ $answer = Y ]
then
  echo Wow, you must be very skilled
echo this is answer: $answer
else
  echo Neither can I, Im just an example shell script
echo this is answer: $answer
fi
```

Tip I tend not to format these debugging echo statements with the traditional indentation because they are usually temporary additions while I'm troubleshooting. Indenting them with the normal code makes them more difficult to find when I want them removed.

Controlling Output with Debug Levels

The problem with using echo statements as I described previously is that you have to comment or remove them when you don't want their output displayed. This is fine if your program is working to perfection and will not need further modification. However, if you're constantly making changes to a script that is actually being used, the need to add back or uncomment echo statements each time you debug can be tiresome. This next debugging technique improves on the basic echo statement by adding a debugging level that can be turned on or off. After you've prepped your script once, enabling or disabling debugging output is as simple as changing a single variable.

The technique is to set a debug variable near the beginning of the script. This variable will then be tested during script execution and the debug statements will be either displayed or suppressed based on the variable's value.

The following is our original example, modified once again for this technique:

```
#!/bin/sh
debug=1
test $debug -gt 0 && echo "Debug is on"
echo -n "Can you write device drivers? "
read answer
test $debug -gt 0 && echo "The answer is $answer"
answer=`echo $answer | tr [a-z] [A-Z]`
if [ $answer = Y ]
then
  echo Wow, you must be very skilled
  test $debug -gt 0 && echo "The answer is $answer"
else
  echo Neither can I, Im just an example shell script
  test $debug -gt 0 && echo "The answer is $answer"
fi
```

This idea can be expanded to include many debug statements in the code, providing output of varying levels of detail during execution. By varying the value to which $debug is compared in the test (e.g., $debug -gt 2), you can, in principle, have an unlimited number of levels of debug output, with 1 being the most simple and the highest-numbered level of your choosing being the most complex. You can, of course, create any debug-level logic you wish. In the example here, I am checking if the debug variable is greater than some specified value. If it is, the debug output is displayed. With this model, if you have various debug output levels and your debug variable is assigned a value higher than the highest debug level, all levels below that one will be displayed. Here are a few lines of code to illustrate the point:

```
debug=2
test $debug -gt 0 && echo "A little data"
test $debug -gt 1 && echo "Some more data"
test $debug -gt 2 && echo "Even some more data"
```

If these three lines were executed in a script, only the output from the first two would be displayed. If you were to change the logic of the test from "greater than" (-gt) to "equal to" (-eq), only the output of the last debug statement would be displayed.

My mind works best when things are simple. For simple scripts I usually set the debug value to either on or off. Multilevel debugging is more valuable for larger scripts, since the code can become quite complex and difficult to track. Using multiple debug levels in a complex script allows you to follow the code's logic as it executes, selecting the level of detail desired.

A further improvement to this technique is to design the script to accept a debug switch when the script is called. You can then use the switch to specify whatever value of debug level you desire for the information you're looking for, without having to modify the code every time you would like to view debugging output. See Chapter 5 for more information on how to process command-line switches passed to a script.

Simplifying Error Checking with a Function

The last debugging approach I'll discuss is an error-checking technique. Instead of simply checking the values of variables and debug statements, this method is more proactive. You evaluate the final condition of an executed command and output a notification if the command was unsuccessful.

The code is a very simple function that I include in a standard function library I use. (You can find information on function libraries in Chapter 2.) This function uses the $? shell internal variable. The shell sets this variable automatically to the value of the previous command's return code. This function uses that value and alerts you of the command's success or failure. A command's return code is a numeric value that defines the exit status of the most recently executed command. Traditionally, a successful completion of a command will yield a value of 0 for the $? shell variable. Error checking is an important part of all types of coding. Not only do you need to get the commands, logic, and functionality of the program correct along the desired path of execution, you should also check for problem conditions along the way. Anticipating potential problems will make your code more robust and resilient.

The function that is included here is called alert since it notifies you of any issues. A function is something like a mini-program within the main code, and it can be called like any other regular command. A good use for a function is to reduce duplication of code if you're going to perform a given task many times throughout the script. The alert function, like all others, needs to be included in the code (that is, defined) prior to it being called by the script. Once the function has been defined, it should be called following any critical commands. By *critical*, I mean those that are most important to the success of the script. For instance, if you have a script that does some file manipulation (such as finding files that match certain criteria and moving them around or modifying them), there will be plenty of lines of code, but the key commands might be find, mv, sed, and a few others. These are the commands that are performing real action, and I would consider them critical.

When you identify a line of code that you want to check, you should call the alert function directly following the execution of that command because that is when you can first retrieve the value of the $? shell variable and thus determine the effect of the executed command.

The alert function's code is simple. The function is called with $? as its first argument, and a string describing what is being reported as its second argument. If the value of $? is 0, the function echoes that the operation succeeded; otherwise it echoes that it didn't.

```
alert () {
  # usage: alert <$?> <object>
  if [ "$1" -ne 0 ]
  then
    echo "WARNING: $2 did not complete successfully." >&2
    exit $1
  else
    echo "INFO: $2 completed successfully" >&2
  fi
}
```

The following is an example of a command followed by a call to the alert function. The command simply mails the contents of a log file specified in the environment variable LOG to a predefined recipient specified in the variable TO.

```
cat $LOG | mail -s "$FROM attempting to get $FILE" $TO
alert $? "Mail of $LOG to $TO"
```

Depending on the success or failure of the cat and mail commands, the output of the call to alert would look like this:

```
INFO: Mail of $LOG to $TO completed successfully
```

or like this:

```
INFO: Mail of $LOG to $TO did not complete successfully
```

with the LOG and TO variables expanded to their values.

The following code is a more advanced form of the previous alert function. It is simpler to call and has a couple of additional features. First, it has been combined with a global DEBUG variable so that it will only report issues if that variable is set. It has also been combined with a global STEP_THROUGH variable. When that variable is set to 1, the code pauses for input on any error it encounters. If the STEP_THROUGH variable is set to 2, the function pauses every time it has been called.

```
alert () {
local RET_CODE=$?
if [ -z "$DEBUG" ] || [ "$DEBUG" -eq 0 ] ; then
  return
fi
```

We first set the RET_CODE variable to the last command's return code and then determine if the DEBUG variable is either undefined or set to 0. The -z test determines if a variable has a zero length. If either of these conditions are true, the function will return to the main code from which it was called.

```
if [ "$RET_CODE" -ne 0 ] ; then
  echo "Warn: $* failed with a return code of $RET_CODE." >&2
  [ "$DEBUG" -gt 9 ] && exit "$RET_CODE"
```

The next step is to determine if the return code of the command was nonzero, which implies a failure of some kind. If it is zero, the code echoes out a warning that states what the command was attempting to do and the return code that it received. The $* shell internal variable holds all the positional parameters that were passed to the function itself. If it was called with something like alert creating the archive of last months records and there was a problem, the output would look like this: Warn: creating the archive of last months records failed with a return code of 1. In a real case, the return-code value will vary.

The last line in this code segment determines if the DEBUG variable is greater than 9. If this is the case, the script will exit with the most recent failure's return code.

```
  [ "$STEP_THROUGH" = 1 ] && {
    echo "Press [Enter] to continue" >&2; read x
  }
fi
  [ "$STEP_THROUGH" = 2 ] && {
    echo "Press [Enter] to continue" >&2; read x
  }
}
```

This last bit of code is where the function allows you to pause, either at only nonzero return codes or any time the alert function was called. You could improve the function by sending output to an optional log file for later review.

Manual Stepping

My final comments on debugging code stem from an interaction I had recently with a friend who was trying to debug an issue with her script. The code attempted to move around some files on the local disk as well as on a Network File System (NFS)–mounted file system. It was receiving a puzzling "permission denied" error. Nothing was obviously wrong with the code, and the permissions on the directories seemed correct. It wasn't until we started performing the steps in the script manually that we found the problem. A file move was attempting to overwrite a preexisting file in the destination directory with read-only permissions and obviously (hindsight, you know) this was what triggered the "permission denied" errors. When we initially looked at the code and the directories involved, we were focusing on the directory permissions and the user that needed to write to the directory. We failed to notice the permissions on the files in the directory.

I'm not suggesting that all problems are this easy to find. Debugging code can take hours, days, or even longer when the code is complex, but a few lessons can be learned from this simple example.

First, before you start writing a program, attempt to perform the code's steps manually where appropriate. This won't always be feasible, but when it is you may be able to weed out some trouble spots before they are mixed in with all the script's other tasks.

Second, try out the code with sample input and attempt to follow it through by performing the loops and conditionals as they are written. It is not an easy task, but attempt to look at the code as objectively as possible without making assumptions, and ask the too-obvious-to-ask questions about what is happening.

Last, seek out another set of eyes. Using a third party is an excellent way of finding problems, especially when you've been working on the same issue for a long time. Sometimes a peer with a fresh viewpoint is able to solve the problem right away.

CHAPTER 2

■ ■ ■

Standard Function Library

After writing many scripts, I realized there were several functions and routines I was using repeatedly. Sometimes I would write the code for these duplicated functions again, and other times I would copy and paste the code from an earlier script. But the best coding practice is to keep a file around that contains all of your already tested and working functions. This creates a scriptwriter's toolbox, or, in programming speak, a library. With a library in place, many of the tools you need often are close at hand and you don't have to code the functions anew each time you need them. This chapter shows you how to set up a standard function library and how to utilize the library in your scripts.

The Library File

The library itself is simply a collection of functions held in a single file. When the library is brought into your script's environment, you can call any of the library functions as if they were in your original code. You could create a single library that contains all of your functions or, if you have a large and varied number of them, create a set of libraries where each one is specific to a category of coding.

Libraries are not only handy to have around; they eliminate redundant coding as well as provide a common environment for all programmers involved to work from. Function libraries reduce redundant code and speed up the development process, plus they can reduce debugging and code-hardening time. If there are bugs in any of the functions, fixes will positively impact all scripts that rely on those bits of code. Function libraries can also level the programming field when working with many and varied system types by adding a layer of abstraction between system differences and the programmer writing the code.

The following example library is very simple and contains only a single function. To keep things organized, especially when files get large, you should write the functions with good indenting form as well as comments about what the code does. Include in the library file a header that lists all the functions and gives a brief description of each, along with any variables that get defined. With the header you could include a list of revisions and owners. This is especially useful when working in a team where other members may be making changes.

```
#!/bin/echo Warning: this library should be sourced!
# ostype(): Define OSTYPE variable to current operating system
ostype() {
  osname=`uname -s`
  # Assume we do not know what this is
  OSTYPE=UNKNOWN
  case $osname in
    "FreeBSD") OSTYPE="FREEBSD"
    ;;
    "SunOS") OSTYPE="SOLARIS"
    ;;
    "Linux") OSTYPE="LINUX"
    ;;
  esac
  return 0
}
```

The first line of the library is an excellent method of ensuring that the library is sourced rather than executed as a regular script. With this line, error output will be generated if someone attempts to run the library instead of sourcing it into the environment. The output would look like this:

```
Warning: this library should be sourced! /path_to_library
```

Another way to avoid execution of libraries is to make them nonexecutable.

The first function, ostype(), determines the operating system of the computer on which the library is running. Because there are subtle differences between operating systems, knowing what OS your script is running on will help you take the differences into account. There are, of course, many more operating systems than we are able to list here.

Some Useful Functions

The code in this section comes from a few utility functions that I find very useful. You will probably come up with many more that are specifically geared toward the systems you work with. Gentoo Linux provides an excellent example of a library of shell functions. If you're running this Linux distribution, you can find the library under the filename /etc/init.d/functions.sh. Even if you're not a Gentoo user, you should be able to get a copy of this library and use it by performing an Internet search for Gentoo and functions.sh, making sure that you follow the applicable usage guidelines contained within the file.

The following are a few functions that I've found particularly useful to include in my standard library. The first function is fairly straightforward, but it contains a cool trick. Pass this function any number, and it will determine whether the number is even or odd. This function was originally used in a moderately large environment where various tasks needed to be load-balanced. We chose a simple method of splitting the environment in half based on the numeric value of the system name. The cool trick is the use of the sed command to determine the last character of a string. Once the last digit is found, the function returns a true value of 1 if the digit is an even number and a false of 0 if it is not. I will discuss this command and others like it in Chapter 24.

```
evenodd() {
  # determine odd/even status by last digit
  LAST_DIGIT=`echo $1 | sed 's/\(.*\)\(.\)$/\2/'`
  case $LAST_DIGIT in
  0|2|4|6|8 )
    return 1
  ;;
  *)
    return 0
  ;;
  esac
}
```

This second function is one I have used many times. It determines whether a remote system is running and connected to the network. It works by pinging the specified machine three times and sending the output to /dev/null. Success is based on the value of $? that is returned following the ping command. If the value of $? is 0, then the machine is alive. The usage of the ping command is encapsulated in the setupenv() function, which I'll present next. The switches and usage of the ping command varies among operating systems. The usage presented here will work on Linux systems. HP-UX machines would use the command ping $NODE 3 for the same functionality.

```
isalive() {
  NODE=$1
  $PING -c 3 $NODE >/dev/null 2>&1
  if [ $? -eq 0 ]
  then
    return 1
  else
    return 0
  fi
}
```

The final function is one you'll find useful if you need to run your scripts on multiple hosts, some for which you don't know the exact configuration. It sets the path to an executable based on the operating-system type, in this case the path to ping, and stores its value as a variable. Your scripts can then call this variable when they need to utilize the executable without you needing to hand-code the exact path for each unique host. You can use this function as a template for storing the location of other executables.

You can see how this script uses the ostype() function covered earlier to determine your OS and thus the executable path.

```
setupenv() {
  if [ "$OSTYPE" = "" ]
  then
    ostype
  fi
  NAME=`uname -n`
  case $OSTYPE in
    "LINUX" )
      PING=/usr/sbin/ping
    ;;
    "FREEBSD" )
      PING=/sbin/ping
    ;;
    "SOLARIS" )
      PING=/usr/sbin/ping
    ;;
    *)
    ;;
  esac
}
```

Using Your Library

Once you've included a library in your shell scripting environment, all functions it contains become available to your scripts. There are several ways to incorporate the library into the environment.

You can make the library available by entering the source command at the shell prompt, as shown here. This command evaluates the commands in a file, which in the case of our library places its resources inside the current shell environment.

```
source std_lib
```

Another way of sourcing a library file is with dot syntax. This is a shorthand way of performing the same task as the source command by replacing the command with a dot (.). This is a built-in function included in both ksh and bash.

```
. std_lib
```

If you work with a large number of networked systems, keeping a copy of your library on every machine promotes consistency. It is very important to be able to count on the environment you are working in to be the same on all machines. An excellent method for this is to store your libraries on a central NFS server to which all machines in the environment have access. This also lets you make library changes in one place that will update the whole environment. A somewhat less desirable method would be to keep the source copies of your libraries in one place for editing and propagate any changes to the remote machines through some utility, such as rsync. The worse case would be to manually copy the libraries to each machine when changes are made. This is viable only if you have an environment with only a few systems.

If you have a heterogeneous environment, you will always have to cope with minor differences from OS to OS or even between different versions of the same OS. A standard library is a good way of dealing with those differences and keeping your scripts portable.

CHAPTER 3

■ ■ ■

Date and Time Manipulation

On occasion, the need for date math arises, such as when you're trying to calculate a time interval between events. The calculations seem easy enough because there are precise numbers of seconds, minutes, and hours in a day. It gets tricky, though, when you consider the fact that values have to roll over when, for example, Monday turns into Tuesday or June becomes July.

For instance, calculating the difference in minutes between 6:53 am and 7:04 am is easy enough: you can multiply the hours (6 and 7) by 60 for each value, add the minutes that do not make up the next full hour, then subtract to find the difference. But what if you want the difference in minutes between 11:57 pm and 1:13 am? This calculation is more complex because it involves a change in day. And the complexity only increases when the date interval spans months or years.

Date in Days

The following script shows one way to make date and time calculations much easier. Because UNIX and Linux calculate time based on a starting point of January 1, 1970, the script measures time in seconds since that date.

Although the use of seconds may seem cumbersome, the math is simple, as you'll see in the bit of code in the "Days Since Epoch" section of this chapter. You reduce the date and time values to numbers of seconds elapsed since the base date then manipulate these values. All of the issues that arise when spanning across calendar increments, such as days or months, simply disappear.

You might use this type of calculation when determining the age of a user's password. The third field of an account entry in a system /etc/shadow file contains the day value on which the password was changed for a particular account, as counted from 1/1/1970 (the epoch). This number can be used for various purposes—for example, to determine when passwords are about to expire so as to facilitate user notifications. You can find an example of this in Chapter 36 in connection with password aging.

Converting all temporal quantities to elapsed time also reduces the complexity of making time comparisons. Suppose, for example, that you would like to monitor time synchronization between multiple network nodes. When you convert the time on a system to seconds elapsed since the beginning of the UNIX epoch, the calculation becomes a simple subtraction.

■**Caution** Yes, the Network Time Protocol (NTP) keeps system clocks in sync. However, not all systems run NTP implementations. Also, clocks on some aging hardware keep such poor time that even NTP can't keep them in sync. NTP implementations can generally keep system clocks synchronized, but if a particular clock drifts beyond the panic threshold, NTP will not update the clock. Additionally, even where NTP is ubiquitous, systems can fail.

The following "Days Since Epoch" script calculates the number of days between two dates. The valid dates for this equation (taken from the Gregorian calendar) range from October 15, 1582 to December 31, 9999. Dates outside this range (or dates from different calendars) require a different equation. This script is a fairly longhand way of getting these values, but the benefit is that it will run on most any system using ksh or bash. The alternatives may not.

The script is based on the following formula. When the program runs, it calculates and displays the number of days that have elapsed since January 1, 1970 by determining the number for 1/1/1970 and subtracting that from the number for the current date.

```
(Year*365)+(Year/4)-(Year/100)+(Year/400)+(Month*306001/10000)+(Day)
```

There are a couple of caveats to using this formula to account for dates that land on a number line. In that case, before you perform the calculation, the values of Month and Year may need to be altered: for the months of January (1) and February (2), you must add 13 to Month and subtract 1 from Year; for all other months you simply add 1 to Month to return the correct value. The Day value to be used is always the day of the month. Thus, the equation applied to January 1, 1970, is as follows:

```
(1969*365)+(1969/4)-(1969/100)+(1969/400)+(14*306001/10000)+1
```

Days Since Epoch

The start of the script sets the variables for the current time and date. Since the epoch (1/1/1970) is fixed, its value can be calculated once and the constant 719591 used in its place, thus saving some CPU cycles.

```
#!/bin/sh
epoch_days=719591
second=`date +'%S'`
minute=`date +'%M'`
hour=`date +'%k'`
day=`date +'%d'`
month=`date +'%m' | sed 's/0*//'`
year=`date +'%Y'`
```

You could improve the script's performance as follows, although it reduces readability. Instead of performing a date call to set each time and date variable, you could make one date call that outputs space-delimited values, then place those values into an array.

To initialize the array in ksh, use

```
set -A DATE `date +"%S %M %k %d %m %Y"
```

In bash, use

```
declare -a DATE=( `date +"%S %M %k %d %m %Y"` )
```

For example, to access the third array element in either bash or ksh, use something like

```
echo ${DATE[2]}
```

where 2 is referencing the third element in the DATE array. Note that the first element in an array would be accessed with a subscript of 0.

The following code makes the initial changes to the month and year variables the equation needs:

```
if [ $month -gt 2 ]
then
  month=$(($month+1))
else
  month=$(($month+13))
  year=$(($year-1))
fi
```

If the month is not January or February (greater than 1 or 2), you have to add 1 to the month. Otherwise you have to add 13 to the month and subtract 1 from the year.

The following code calculates the day value for today. Once you know this, you subtract the epoch value from that value to get the number of days since the start of the epoch. The script then outputs that value. The output is left unformatted in case you want to use the number as input for another command or process.

```
today_days=$((($year*365)+($year/4)-\ ($year/100)+($year/400)+\

  ($month*306001/10000)+$day))
days_since_epoch=$(($today_days-$epoch_days))
echo $days_since_epoch
```

You may find it useful to have two versions of this script: one that outputs the elapsed time in days and the other that outputs it in seconds.

```
seconds_since_epoch=`echo "($days_since_epoch*86400)+\
  ($hour*3600)+($minute*60)+$second" | bc`
```

The calculation to convert from days to seconds is fairly trivial. It may also be useful to turn the code for the calculations into functions and put them in your central library as discussed in Chapter 2. You then would need only to source this library into your current environment and call the function whenever needed.

Alternatives for Finding the Date in Seconds

There are two other ways to calculate the number of seconds since the epoch. Both of them are much simpler than the preceding script, but they require system utilities that you may not have installed, such as Perl and the latest GNU utilities. Most administrators would probably install whatever is needed to get the job done, but there are controlled production environments where it's not that simple—sometimes many requirements must be met and testing must be performed before any changes are made to a system. In those cases, it is simpler to come up with a solution that utilizes existing resources as opposed to installing more-advanced tools.

The first alternative uses the GNU version of the date command. If you have this version, you can produce output that is almost identical to that of the script discussed in the section "Days Since Epoch" except that, because the number of seconds since epoch in that script is calculated based on GMT, it may be out of sync with your local time zone. If so, you may want to add the appropriate number of seconds for your local time zone. (This may not be necessary if you're using the values to simply calculate the difference between two arbitrary dates/times in which the local time zone information is irrelevant.)The following date command is much simpler than deriving the calculations manually. This returns the number of seconds since epoch directly.

```
gnu_seconds_since_epoch=`date +%s`
```

There is also a Perl function for performing the same task. You can access it like this:

```
perl_seconds_since_epoch=`perl -e 'print time'`
```

Evaluating for the Current Day and Time

Say you want to schedule a job, such as a system monitor, to run at particular times or on certain days. You want to know whether there are issues on the system, but you don't necessarily want to be jarred awake by your pager simply to learn that the message is non-critical; you'd like to get those routine notices by page during the day and by e-mail at other times.

The following script determines whether the current day and hour are within a certain time frame that you set. This code would be called from another script, which actually performs the notifications.

Two sets of day and hour parameters (for a total of four) are passed to the script when it is called. These parameters specify a range of days (Sunday through Monday) and a range of hours when pages may be sent during those days. The script returns a 0 if the current day and hour are within those parameters and gives the user a message stating the same. If the current day and hour values do not lie within the given range, a different message is output and the function returns a 1 (representing failure).

```
#!/bin/sh
if [ $# -ne 4 ]
then
  echo Usage: $0 {day begin} {day end} {hour begin} {hour end}
  echo " Days are 0-6 where 0 is Sunday."
  echo " Hours are 0-23."
  exit
fi
```

The script starts by determining how many parameters have been sent to the script. Recall that four is the expected number. If four parameters haven't been sent, such as if the script calling this code were written incorrectly, you should output a usage message containing some explanation of how the script should be invoked. The usage explanation provided here shows that the four parameters that should be passed are DAY_BEGIN, DAY_END, HOUR_BEGIN, and HOUR_END. All of these values are integers in which the day values range from 0–6 where Sunday is 0, and the hours range from 0–23.

If the parameter count is correct, the code assigns the parameters to variables with more meaningful names, such as DAY_BEGIN and DAY_END instead of 1 and 2. Making this change helps the readability and it is easier to see what is happening.

```
DAY_BEGIN=$1
DAY_END=$2
HOUR_BEGIN=$3
HOUR_END=$4
```

Next, the variables for the current day and hour need to be set.

```
DAY=`date +%w`
HOUR=`date +%H`
```

The code here is the main check to determine whether it is time to notify the administrator. The large if statement compares the current DAY and HOUR values with the values that were passed to the script.

```
if [ $DAY -ge $DAY_BEGIN -a $DAY -le $DAY_END\
  -a $HOUR -ge $HOUR_BEGIN -a $HOUR -le $HOUR_END ]
then
  echo "It is time to notify"
  return 0
else
  echo "It is not time to notify"
  return 1
fi
```

Note The valid day and hour ranges include the end points specified by the parameters. That is, if the script was invoked with DAY values of 1 and 5, the test should succeed on Monday, Friday, and on the days in between.

In a real-world implementation, you would probably replace the echo lines with code for performing actual notification, such as a call to a paging utility such as QuickPage.[1]

As mentioned earlier, I've assumed for simplicity that the actual notification is handled by the code that calls this script. That script might be an exhaustive monitoring utility that performs many types of monitoring tasks. Each monitor could call this script with different parameters based on the level of criticality. The calling script would then evaluate the return code by accessing the $? variable to determine whether to send a notification.

To simplify this script, you could hard-code the DAY_BEGIN/DAY_END and HOUR_BEGIN/HOUR_END ranges instead of assigning them the values of the passed parameters. You would then remove the validation check for the number of parameters passed.

---

1. QuickPage is an application that allows you to send messages to an alphanumeric pager. More information can be found at http://www.qpage.org.

CHAPTER 4

■■■

Comparisons and Tests

Two of the fundamental types of operations in any programming language are the comparison and the test. They are the building blocks of conditional statements (if/ then and case) and iteration statements (while). They give you the ability to examine relationships between data items, such as files, variables, strings, and numeric values, and to take action based on the result. You can also carry out actions based on the attributes of a particular item, such as a file's type, whether a variable has been assigned a value, and the return code of a command.

The examples in this chapter illustrate various ways to compare items or to check their properties, and use the results. I have used all of these techniques throughout this book, although some are used more frequently than others. Here I want to present a diverse set of examples that demonstrate the many uses of the test shell programming structure.

The Basics of Comparisons

In UNIX shell scripting there are both internal operators that allow you to test attributes or to compare values, and a /usr/bin/test system call. Please refer to Appendix A for more specific information.

The following two comparison examples are among the most common forms:

```
if [ "$string" = "some_string" ];then...
if [ $integer -eq 15 ];then...
```

The first example represents a string comparison and the second an integer test. The quotation marks are required only for an explicit string. Quotation marks around the name of a string variable are not required. It is wise, however, to always quote your string variables to gracefully handle an undefined variable or white space within the string. A comparison involving an unquoted, undefined string variable in the bash shell will return a "unary operator expected" error, whereas ksh will return an "argument expected" message. A comparison involving an unquoted string that contains white space will result in a "too many arguments" error in bash and an "unknown operator" in ksh. All of these errors are related to the test command finding that there are too few or too many arguments in the comparison—too few because an unquoted null variable is skipped over in the comparison, and too many because an unquoted string containing white space will be viewed as more than one argument instead of a single string.

The spaces between the values being compared and the square brackets are required syntax, but the spaces between the values being compared and the comparison operator are optional.

Note that the operators for string and numeric comparison are the opposite of what you might expect. To my mind, the equal sign (=) implies a numeric comparison and the -eq operator suggests a string operation, but this is not the case. The other conditional operators mirror this distinction. The operators =, !=, >, and < used for string comparisons are direct counterparts to the numeric comparison operators -eq, -ne, -gt, and -lt. There are still more operators that can be found in both the test man page and the man pages for specific shells.

The square brackets in the previous examples contain the enclosed expressions to create a statement that represents the logical result (true or false) of the test described by the enclosed expressions. To be more accurate, the left square bracket ([) is both a command internal to the shell and a system command (/usr/bin/[) that can be thought of the same as the test command. The [command has specific syntax that must be followed; for instance, the comparison is completed with a closing right square bracket (]), and this command's return code determines if the comparison is true. In the following example, the square brackets have been replaced with the test command to illustrate another method of forming a comparison statement. The square brackets can be used interchangeably with the test command.

```
if test $string = "some_string" ;then...
```

All examples so far have used the if/then structure for comparing values. Usually, if the expression given to the test command or enclosed in the square brackets evaluates to true, then we perform some task. The syntax of this example is slightly different. In this code pattern, the test on the left of the && operator is performed as in previous comparison examples and based on the result (true or false); the code on the right is executed or skipped. Here, if the debug variable is set to 1, the left-hand expression evaluates to true and the echo command will be run. The line of code can also be read as "test the condition AND execute the additional code if the test evaluates as true."

```
test $debug -eq 1 && echo some_debug_output
```

An alternative is available. If the logical AND (&&) is replaced with a logical OR (||), the additional code is executed only if the test returns false. This example can be read as "test the condition OR execute the additional code (if the test evaluates as false)."

```
test $debug -eq 1 || echo some_debug_output
```

Both the logical AND (&&) and logical OR (||) sequences are simply shortcut versions of the more verbose syntax presented here.

```
test $debug -eq 1 && {
  echo some_debug_output
  echo some_more_debug_output
}
```

In both of the previous examples, the additional code following the logical AND or OR to be run was a single command. Compound commands can be formed by surrounding the individual commands with curly braces. Such groupings can contain any amount of code, including output statements, control structures, assignments, or all of the above.

As you've seen before, the `test` command can be replaced with square brackets; the two forms of syntax are equivalent. This segment of code evaluates the expression within the square brackets and runs the compound statement if the expression evaluates as true. I have not noticed any significant performance differences between these two syntax types.

```
[ $debug -eq 1 ] && {
  echo some_debug_output
  echo some_more_debug_output
}
```

Conditional logic can become quite complex. The following example demonstrates two `test` expressions that must each evaluate as true before the additional code will run. In this case, the logical AND (&&) characters are used to perform two separate functions. The first instance of && is used to require both the first and second expressions to be true. The second instance is used to indicate the additional code that should be run if they both evaluate as true. The use of a logical OR (||) in both places is also valid, and specifies that both of the tests would need to be false to execute the additional code.

```
[ "$txt" ] && [ "$txt" != "$txt2" ] && some_text="$txt $txt2"
```

The following example adds another layer of complexity to the previous example. Not only are there two expressions to evaluate, but the first expression of the two contains two additional expressions of its own. Note that the two main expressions are surrounded by square brackets and are separated by a logical OR (||). The use of the OR indicates that the entire test evaluates as true whenever either one of the two expressions is true. The -a operator inside the first expression is also a logical AND. You can string multiple expressions together with the -a or the logical OR (-o) operator, as you can with the && and || syntax.

```
if [ "$txt" != "$txt2" -a $num -eq $num2 ] || [ $num2 -eq 100 ];then...
```

When such expressions become very complex, it is easy to make logic mistakes that can be difficult to track down. In the following examples, the complexity has been toned down.

```
if [ -n $string ];then...
if [ $any_variable ];then...
```

You can use this code to determine whether variables have been defined. The first example of the two applies to string variables, since the -n operation evaluates to true if the length of the supplied string variable is nonzero. However, this method also works for determining whether a numeric variable has been defined, as its value is then treated as a string.

The second example simply tests a variable. Once the variable has been assigned a value, the expression will evaluate to true. Thus, both expressions determine if a variable has been assigned a value.

The following expressions are similar to the previous ones; they determine if a variable is undefined:

```
if [ -z $string ];then...
if [ ! $any_variable ];then...
```

These conditional statements are simply the negations of the corresponding expressions in the previous examples (-z tests whether a string has zero length, and ! is the logical NOT symbol).

The next example uses a couple of features, one of which we have already seen.

```
if [ "`grep nodename /etc/hosts`" ];then...
```

The test here evaluates to true if the quoted expression is not null. You saw one example of this earlier, in connection with quoted string variables. In this case, however, you are not looking at the value of a variable, but rather running an external command, and you're capturing its output to be tested within the square brackets as if it were a string. An expression enclosed in reverse single quotes (`) is evaluated by the shell and substituted with the resulting output. Here, if the grep command returns a match from /etc/hosts, then there is output and the test evaluates as true because the quoted expression is non-null. If grep returns nothing, the quoted expression would then be null and the test would evaluate as false.

A test can be performed on more than just a variable or a value, such as a number or a string. In the following example, the test examines the return code of a command:

```
if ping -c 3 node.mydomain.com > /dev/null 2>&1;then
```

As I mentioned earlier, all of these comparisons are really commands that have their return code evaluated. If the command returns a 0 code (indicating successful termination), its execution, in the context of a test, evaluates as true. You can take advantage of this with the ping command, as shown here, because you don't need to know the actual output of the command to determine whether a system is responsive, which is why all the output is being redirected to /dev/null. The return code will tell you that. If a system is unresponsive to a ping, the return code will be nonzero. This is a much simpler method than retrieving and analyzing the output of the command.

The last example uses the -l switch to the test system command.

```
/usr/bin/test -l "hello" -gt 4 && echo some_message
```

Here you are testing if the length of the string hello is greater than 4. If it is, the code will echo a message. I have included this example because the syntax for this switch is not obvious from the test man page. There is a brief comment about the -l switch, and no example. This example also emphasizes that there is both an internal shell test command and a system test command. The internal test is called unless the system command is specified using the executable's fully qualified filename (including the path). If you don't specify the full path to the system test as shown here, the shell's internal test will return a "unary operator expected" error if you run bash. An "unknown operator" error will appear using ksh. Neither shell's internal test command uses the -l switch to specify a length comparison.

CHAPTER 5

. . .

Accepting Command-Line Options, Switches, and Parameters

Sometimes you may want to pass optional parameters to your script, allowing its behavior to be controlled more precisely. For example, the tar archiving utility uses optional parameters. It creates archives and restores directory and file trees, but it can do so in different ways. The GNU version of tar has roughly 80 different options that can be used in various combinations to tailor the ways in which the utility performs. The major benefit of this technique is that you can write a single program and have it perform multiple tasks based on the command-line input. Additionally, you're not duplicating code by writing smaller, more specific scripts tailored to each individual task.

You are unlikely to use the code demonstrated here in its current form, as it is designed to demonstrate processing of command-line options within a framework of a specific task for a specific application environment. However, it's a good basic set of simple utilities that you could give to first-level support staff for basic initial troubleshooting so they don't have to remember all the paths and commands. That could be especially helpful if that support staff is not very proficient with the command line. To modify the sample code for more general use, you could have the code view the /var/log/messages file with one switch, perform a df -k with another switch, and perform a netstat -a with yet another. This is much like creating a set of command-line aliases to save time by reducing keystrokes for commonly used commands and utilities.

Most of the scripts I have written don't use many options because they are fairly specific in their purpose. If you need a single option, you can easily have the user supply it as a command-line parameter and check the value of $1 to see if an option was in fact passed to the script. The complexity of this technique increases dramatically when you have multiple options that can be used in combination independently of each other, and the method of evaluating command-line parameters becomes unwieldy. Also consider the difficulty of accounting for users' foibles and the ways users may specify the options—sometimes erroneously.

For instance, a typical tar command might be tar -xvf file.tar. This could also be entered as tar -x -v -f file.tar. Attempting to account for all possible combinations of user-specified options using shell-script code that works with positional variables would be very problematic.

This brings us to the getopts utility, which handles command-line switches much more elegantly. You have to concern yourself only with how the script will function based on the supplied parameters, not how to read the parameters and account for their potential variability.

The following example code does not represent a full script. It is a single function that would get sourced into your environment through a login script such as /etc/profile or through a standard library of functions (see Chapter 2). To use this function, you type its name (jkl) at the command line and pass it various parameters to perform specific tasks.

The code was used in an environment where there were multiple machines, each of which had one or more versions of the same set of applications installed. Troubleshooting problems with the active application became tedious and time-consuming because you had to begin by determining which installed version was active. The one constant was a single configuration file residing in a known location that held the active version of the installed software. The following code allows users to immediately switch to the correct configuration or log directory for quick troubleshooting:

```
APPHOME=/usr/local/apphome
if [ ! -f $APPHOME/myapp.sh ]
then
  echo "Myapp is not installed on this system so jkl is not functional"
  return 1
fi
```

First you define a variable containing the top of the directory subtree where the installed applications live; then you determine if the main configuration file exists. If it does not exist, the script should exit and provide a notification. Next comes the jkl() function itself.

```
jkl () {
  Usage="Usage: \n \
  \tjkl [-lbmcdxh] [-f filename]\n \
  \t\t[-h] \tThis usage text.\n \
  \t\t[-f filename] \t cat the specified file. \n \
  \t\t[-l] \tGo to application log directory with ls. \n \
  \t\t[-b] \tGo to application bin directory. \n \
  \t\t[-c] \tGo to application config directory.\n \
  \t\t[-m] \tGo to application log directory and more log file.\n \
  \t\t[-d] \tTurn on debug information.\n \
  \t\t[-x] \tTurn off debug information.\n"
  APPLOG=myapp_log
  UNAME=`uname -n`
```

```
DATE=`date '+%y%m'`
MYAPP_ID=$APPHOME/myapp.sh
```

The start of the function sets up a number of variables, the most interesting of which is Usage. The Usage variable is being formatted manually for the output of the usage statement with tabs and carriage returns. For more information on these character combinations and definitions, consult the man page for echo on your system. Here is a more readable output of the usage statement that demonstrates the formatting:

Usage:

    jkl [-lf:bmcdxh]

        [-h] This usage text.

        [-f] cat specified file.

        [-l] Go to application log directory with ls.

        [-b] Go to application bin directory.

        [-c] Go to application config directory.

        [-m] Go to application log directory and more log file.

        [-d] Turn on debug information.

        [-x] Turn off debug information.

Then you define the software version numbers based on the information found in the application configuration file, as in the following code:

```
major=`egrep "^MAJOR_VER=" $MYAPP_ID | cut -d"=" -f2`
minor=`egrep "^MINOR_VER=" $MYAPP_ID | cut -d"=" -f2`
dot=`egrep "^DOT_VER=" $MYAPP_ID | cut -d"=" -f2`
```

This file isn't shown in this example, but you can assume that these values are in that file. The file is included in the downloadable script package in the Source Code/ Download area of the Apress web site (www.apress.com).

The names of the various application directories are formed from the combination of application names and version-number variables. Here we assign the directory variables their values.

```
APPDIR=$APPHOME/myapp.$major.$minor.$dot
LOGDIR=$APPHOME/myapp.$major.$minor.$dot/log
CFGDIR=$APPHOME/myapp.$major.$minor.$dot/config
BINDIR=$APPHOME/myapp.$major.$minor.$dot/bin
```

Then we check to see if any command-line switches were used when the function was called. If none are found, the usage statement should be displayed. Note that the echo command uses the -e switch, which enables the use of the escape sequences found in the Usage variable.

```
if [ "$#" -lt 1 ]
then
  echo -e $Usage
fi
```

If the script did not use the -e switch, it would not format the output properly, instead printing the escape sequences along with the usage information.

User-supplied options are accessed through an argument vector, or what you may think of as an array. The getopts utility uses the OPTIND environment variable to index this array. Each time the example code function is invoked, the variable needs to be reset to 1 before option processing starts in order to point at the beginning of the options that have been passed.

```
OPTIND=1
```

As the while loop in the following code snippet iterates through the passed options, the getopts utility increments the value of the OPTIND variable and processes through any parameters that were passed.

This while loop is the core of the script. It is where the passed parameters are processed and appropriate actions are taken.

```
while getopts lf:bmcdxh ARGS
do
  case $ARGS in
    l) if [ -d $LOGDIR ] ; then
         cd $LOGDIR
         /bin/ls
       fi
    ;;
    f) FILE=$OPTARG
       if [ -f $FILE ]
       then
         cat $FILE
       else
         echo $FILE not found. Please try again.
       fi
    ;;
    b) if [ -d $BINDIR ] ; then
         cd $BINDIR
       fi
    ;;
    m) if [ -d $LOGDIR ] ; then
         cd $LOGDIR
         /bin/more $APPLOG
       fi
    ;;
    c) if [ -d $CFGDIR ] ; then
         cd $CFGDIR
       fi
    ;;
    d) set -x
    ;;
```

```
        x) set +x
        ;;
        h) echo -e $Usage
        ;;
        *) echo -e $Usage
        ;;
    esac
  done
}
```

The getopts command is invoked with a list of the valid switches, which it parses to determine which switches need arguments. Each time getopts is invoked, it checks whether there are still switches to be processed. If so, it retrieves the next switch (and updates the value of OPTIND), stores it in the specified environment variable (here, ARGS), and returns true. Otherwise, it returns false. In this way, the while loop iterates through the options vector. Each time the shell executes the loop body, the case statement applies the actions that the current option requires.

In this case, most of the options take you to an application-specific directory. The three most interesting cases here are the -d, -x, and -f switches. The -d switch turns on command expansion and the -x switch turns it off. This is very useful and an easy method for debugging scripts. The -f switch is different from the rest. Note that it has a colon (:) following the f in the getopts switch list. If a switch is followed by a colon, an argument should follow the switch when it is used. In our example, the -f switch lists the contents of a file and requires the filename to follow. The case branch for -f sets the FILE variable to $OPTARG. This is another special environment variable that is set by getopts to assign the argument that is passed to the switch. If the file exists, it will be displayed; if not, the code will generate an error message.

The last two switches cause the usage statement to be displayed. A more advanced example of the getopts construct can be found in Chapter 17. Additionally, I have included another script in the download package for this chapter (at www.apress.com) that performs some basic administrative tasks, including turning on and off the set -x value.

CHAPTER 6

∎∎∎

Testing Variables and Assigning Defaults

Many scripts require a minimum set of input parameters or defined variables in order to run correctly. For example, they may contain customizable values used for configuration purposes, which are initially set to default values. In this chapter we'll look at various methods of testing variables and setting default values. The differences between many of these syntactical variants are subtle, but each is useful for working with undefined variables, setting variable defaults, and debugging.

All of the methods in this chapter check the state of a given variable and assign or substitute a value based on that assessment. The point here is to provide a variety of ways to perform these types of tasks. Whereas some are simple and will be used often, others are more specific and will be used only in specific situations.

For example, assume that you've written a script to change a machine's network name. At the very least, the script's input parameters would probably include the old and new machine names, the machine's IP address, and perhaps the machine's domain or subnet mask.

While you may want the subnet mask and domain name to be set from the command line, these values likely won't be changing often and you'll simply want to set default values for your local site and not have to worry about passing additional parameters. The techniques in this chapter will give you the tools to easily set default values when a variable has a null value or is otherwise undefined.

Setting Defaults

The following code samples demonstrate several ways to set and manage variables with default values. Although these examples all perform the same task, they do it in slightly different ways. The first example is probably the easiest to read from a human perspective, but is likely the most verbose in terms of coding efficiency. The option you choose will depend on your motives. Many times I have used the first type of code because scripts I've written need to be simple to read and support by others with varying levels of shell-scripting skill. I may want to use the more terse code types if supportability is of less concern than efficiency is.

The first code example checks to see if a variable (VAR) has been set. The -z (zero) test checks to see if the length of the string variable is zero. If it is, the code resets the value of the variable to a default value.

```
if [ -z "$VAR" ]
then
  VAR="some default"
fi
```

The next example performs the same task but it is a bit more elegant because it is contained within a single line of code instead of being spread out over four. The same test is performed against the variable, but the && (logical AND) syntax executes the code that follows if the test evaluates as true.

```
[ -z "$VAR" ] && VAR="some default"
```

The next example is streamlined (by one character). The test syntax within the square brackets can determine if the variable is set without performing the -z, or zero-length, test. The test used in this example determines whether the variable has been set by using the logical NOT modifier (!). If the variable being tested does not have a value, the use of the test ["$VAR"] will evaluate as false since there was no value to be found. With the addition of the NOT modifier, the test will evaluate to true because the combination of two negatives (! and an unassigned variable) yields a positive outcome. The extra code, assigning the default value to the VAR variable following the AND operator (&&), is then executed as before.

```
[ ! "$VAR" ] && VAR="some default"
```

Now we simplify the code one final time. If the variable is set, the simpler test evaluates as true, and we want to perform the extra code only in the opposite case. Remember that when we use the logical OR syntax (||), the extra code is run only if the test is false. So we can streamline the code even more by using the simpler test and the OR operation.

```
[ "$VAR" ] || VAR="some default"
```

Variable Substitution

Variable substitution is closely related to setting default variables, at least conceptually. In the previous examples, I set default values by testing a particular variable to see if it had been defined, and then assigning it a value if not. The following syntax uses a type of parameter expansion to perform the same kind of task.

Parameter expansion is where the parameter, such as a variable, is replaced with the value of that parameter, such as calling a simple variable in the form of echo $VAR.

However there are more features that can be accessed. Included in this syntax are some characters that won't be expanded, but have meaning of their own. The first such character performs the default variable assignment. When these characters are used, curly braces are required to surround the whole expression.

```
: ${VAR:="some default"}
```

The colon character that starts this line is a valid shell command that performs no active task. In this syntax it simply expands any arguments that may follow it on the line. In this case we simply want to expand the value contained within the braces.

The argument given to : is the interesting part of this line; it's a parameter expansion that surrounds some logic with curly braces, {}. The := syntax indicates that the VAR variable will be compared to the "some default" string.

In this expression, if the variable is unset, it is then assigned the value of the expression that follows the equal sign, which can be a number, a string, or another variable.

Your scripts may have more than one variable that you want to ensure has a default value. Instead of coding a list of variable substitutions, you can set multiple variable defaults on a single line, which makes the code more compact and readable. The following example shows various types of substitutions that you may want to perform. The first involves an explicit string, the second an explicit integer, and the third an already defined variable.

```
: ${VAR:="some default"} ${VAR2:=42} ${VAR3:=$LOGNAME}
```

Several variable-substitution types are similar to the := syntax in the previous example. Because the syntax for the different substitution types is almost identical and their meanings are so subtly different, they can be confused easily. Most of these substitutions would be used for *substituting* values of another variable into the code at the location of the substitution syntax, rather than for *setting* variables. The definitions for all of the following syntax types can be found in your shell man pages, but those explanations are often unclear. The rest of this chapter covers each substitution type with its syntax, some example code to set up the scenario, and an explanation of how the syntax works when making its comparison within the braces.

:= Syntax

For this substitution type we use the same := syntax that we used when we set a default variable in the previous example.

```
username=""
echo "${username:=$LOGNAME}"
```

When the := comparison is encountered, the username variable is defined, but its value is null. As a result, this command uses the value of the LOGNAME variable for the echo command, and sets the value of username to the value of LOGNAME.

With this particular syntax, the only time the variable username would not be set to the value of LOGNAME is when the username variable is defined and has an actual, non-null value.

The main difference between this and the previous example where a default variable was set is the use of an active command (echo) instead of the passive colon. When the active command is used, the default assignment is still performed and the resulting variable outputs to the display.

= Syntax

The following statement looks very similar to the := syntax, but the colon has been removed:

```
username=""
echo "${username=$LOGNAME}"
```

As before, the variable has been defined, but its value is null. With this syntax the command will echo the statement, but there will be no output other than a carriage return because the username variable was defined even though it was null. Only if the username variable were totally undefined would the variable be set to the value of LOGNAME.

This syntax could be useful in a login or cron script where you need to rely on certain variables being defined for the script to function. If a specific environment variable hasn't been defined, you can assign it to the value your script requires.

:- Syntax

In this command, the value of the LOGNAME variable will be used for the echo statement because username is null even though it is defined:

```
username=""
echo "${username:-$LOGNAME}"
```

The value of the username variable remains unchanged. The difference between this command and the one that uses the = syntax is that the values are only *substituted* for the ${} syntax in the code before it executes. In other words, the echo command will output the value of the LOGNAME variable, but that value will not be assigned to the username variable.

- Syntax

When the colon is removed from the previous :- statement, the output will be null because the username variable is defined. If it were undefined, the value of LOGNAME would have been used. Again, as in the :- syntax, the username variable is unchanged.

```
username=""
echo "${username-$LOGNAME}"
```

Both the :- and – syntax could be used when a script evaluates its environment. These two checks are essentially opposites; they will substitute the default value or not depending on whether the username variable is defined. If you have a list of variables that need to be defined and ones that shouldn't be defined, the combination of the two syntaxes could make sure everything is set correctly before the script performs its tasks.

:? Syntax

When using the :? syntax, if the username variable is defined and it has a non-null value, the value of the username variable is used in the echo command. If the username variable is defined but does not have a "real" value (that is, it is null) or if it is undefined, the value of LOGNAME is used in the echo command, and the script then exits.

```
username=""
echo "${username:?$LOGNAME}"
```

Changing the argument that follows the question mark to some type of error string will make this statement very useful in debugging and finding undefined variables in your code. The code will not only output the string, but it will also display the line in the script that the code came from.

? Syntax

Removing the colon from the :? syntax removes the requirement that the username variable have a non-null value in order for it to be used. If that variable is set to only a null value, then that value is used. If, however, the username variable is undefined, the script will exit and display the variable, the line of code where it exited, and its LOGNAME substitution, as with the :? syntax.

```
username=""
echo "${username?$LOGNAME}"
```

Both the :? and ? syntaxes are excellent for script debugging when variables need to be defined or have a real non-null value. The big advantage to this code is that the script will exit at the line where the problem was found, and the line number will be displayed. Changing the value of the text that is to be displayed to something like "is undefined" or "has a null value" will easily point you to the problem in the script.

:+ Syntax

This syntax has the opposite effect from the previous examples, because the alternative value will be substituted for the ${} expression if the variable is *defined* instead of undefined.

```
username="mars"
echo "${username:+$LOGNAME}"
```

Here, if the username variable is defined and not null, the value of LOGNAME will be used instead of username. If username is undefined, or defined but null, then a null value is used. In any event, the value of the username variable will not change.

+ Syntax

When the colon is removed from the previous example, the value of LOGNAME is used in place of the ${} expression whenever the username variable is defined; the username variable is not required to have an actual (non-null) value for this substitution to take place. If the username variable is undefined, a null value is substituted.

```
username=""
echo "${username+$LOGNAME}"
```

The :+ and + syntax could be used in much the same way as the :- and – syntax is used. The main difference is that the :+ and + examples check for a defined value instead of an undefined one. This is much like addition and subtraction being opposite sides of the same coin.

Experiment with these techniques to gain a clear understanding of how they work and when they are most useful. You should also refer to your shell's man page, which discusses each of these forms. In the bash shell, you can find these defined in the section on pattern expansion. In the ksh man page, they can be found in the parameter-expansion section.

■ ■ ■

## CHAPTER 7

Indirect Reference Variables

It is possible to set a normal (direct) variable in three ways:

- Directly, by assigning it a value

- By storing the output of a command

- By storing the results of some type of calculation

In all of these cases, although you might not know a variable's value in advance of any given point, you do know the name of the variable that is to receive the value.

For example, AGE=36 is a direct variable assignment. The value of 36 might change at a later stage and it may also have some calculation applied to it, but the variable *name* AGE will not change.

In some cases, however, you may need the ability to generate variable *names* on the fly. You may not know the number or names of variables you are going to need at the time of execution. These could be referred to as *variable variables*, or *variable variable names*. This chapter shows how to create and use such indirect variables.

Log File Monitoring with Indirect Variables

The following example monitors log files and notifies the user when specified string values show up in the file. The script is designed to run continuously while keeping track of where it last left off in the file; thus, it knows where to start the next time it looks. The configuration value at the beginning of the script points to the log files it needs to watch and the string values to be tracked.

This configuration value can consist of many entries, each specifying strings the script needs to watch for in all the tracked files. There may be several entries specifying different strings for the same log file. Our example script is configured in this way.

```
#!/bin/sh
#set -x
debug=0
DELAY=120
```

```
LOGCHKS="/var/log/messages:authentication%20failure:\
  rbpeters:warn /var/log/messages:recv%20failure::error"
```

This `LOGCHKS` variable configures which log files will be monitored. You could create a separate configuration file to hold this information, but to keep things straightforward, I've included the configuration variables as part of the script.

Each entry consists of four fields separated by colons (`:`). Here are the meanings of the four fields:

First: The full path to the log file being watched; nothing special here.

Second: The string or strings to watch for. Multiple strings can be specified in this field by separating each with a pipe character, `|`. Because the entries in the configuration string are themselves separated by spaces, you can't have a space within the watch string. If you want to watch for a phrase that includes spaces, the spaces need to be replaced with %20, as shown in the `LOGCHKS` variable assignment.

Third: Exception strings that are to be ignored. In our example, the script will watch for any authentication-failure messages in the `/var/log/messages` file, with the exception of those containing the string `rbpeters`. The subfields of this field, like those of the second, are pipe-separated, and any spaces should be replaced with %20.

Fourth: Notification level. The two values here are `warn` and `error`. If the notification is not an `error`, the script defaults to `warn`. The notification strings are left undefined because they will be determined by the user implementing them.

The Main Monitor Loop

To begin, start the infinite loop in which the script will be running. Then you can look at each configuration entry.

```
while :
do
  entry_count=0
  for LOGCHK in `echo $LOGCHKS`
  do
```

Now all values of the configured entry have to be parsed and then assigned to a direct variable. The script also replaces %20 characters with real spaces.

```
    logfile=`echo $LOGCHK | cut -d: -f1`
    strings="`echo $LOGCHK | cut -d: -f2`
    strings="`echo $strings | sed -e \"s/%20/ /g\"`"
    exceptions=`echo $LOGCHK | cut -d: -f3`
    exceptions="`echo $exceptions | sed -e \"s/%20/ /g\"`"
    notify=`echo $LOGCHK | cut -d: -f4`
```

entry_count represents the number assigned to the specific *entry* in the configuration string. If two log files are configured to be watched, their entry_count values will be 1 and 2, respectively. This variable will be used later to create a new variable on the fly.

```
entry_count=`expr $entry_count + 1`
```

The suffix is nothing more than the name of the log file. Slashes (/) and dots (.) are replaced with underscores (_). You'll also use the suffix value later to build indirect variable names. The combination of this suffix and the entry_count allows us to create unique variable names specific to the log files that the script is working with.

```
suffix=`echo $logfile | sed -e s/\\\// _/g`
suffix=`echo $suffix | sed -e s/\\\./_/g`
```

Next comes the first reference to an indirect variable. The shell evaluates a normal line of code within a script so that any variables are replaced with their values before any comparisons or calculations are performed.

The eval command is used when you want the shell to perform an *additional* evaluation prior to the normal evaluation. This allows you to construct names for new variables using the values of existing variables.

In this case, the line in the script is as follows:

```
if [ "`eval echo '$COUNT'${suffix}_$entry_count`" = "" ]
```

After the first explicit evaluation (in the embedded eval), to the shell, the line would look like this:

```
if [ "$COUNT_var_log_messages_1" = "" ]
```

Then, when the shell evaluates the line normally, it sees a direct variable, although we know that the direct variable has been conjured up by a prior evaluation.

Now back to the code logic: the code then checks whether the log file's base line count is null. The only time it will be null is the first time the line count is tested. If this is the case, the base line count is set to the current file length (in number of lines).

```
if [ "`eval echo '$COUNT'${suffix}_$entry_count`" = "" ]
then
  eval BASE${suffix}_$entry_count=`wc -l $logfile | awk '{ print $1 }'`
fi
```

Resetting the value of the line count the first time the loop is executed is a safe way of *not* having the monitor find any previous string entries being watched for in the log file. We don't want to see strings that were there prior to the monitor ever running.

Now the line count of the log file is set. The line count is different from the base count. Let us assume the script starts up to find 10 lines in the log file. The log's base is then set to 10. The script sets the line count of the file to 10, sees there is no difference between the line count and the base count, and completes running this script segment.

```
eval COUNT${suffix}_$entry_count=`wc -l $logfile | awk '{ print $1 }'`
```

The script then sleeps for the number of seconds specified at the beginning of the script and wakes up again. Suppose that it now finds 13 lines in the file. The difference between the file's line count and the base count is used to detect new log entries.

The following code checks to see whether the log file has grown. If it has, we use the tail command to check the newly added lines inside the log file for the desired strings. The script then resets the file's *base count* to whatever the current *line count* happens to be so you don't look at lines that have already been checked.

```
if [ `eval echo '$COUNT'${suffix}_$entry_count` -gt
   `eval echo '$BASE'${suffix}_$entry_count` ]
then
   LINES=`eval expr '$COUNT'${suffix}_$entry_count - '$BASE'${suffix}_$entry_count`
   eval \ BASE${suffix}_$entry_count='$COUNT'${suffix}_$entry_count
   if [ "$exceptions" != "" ]
   then
      MSGS=`tail -$LINES $logfile | egrep -i "\"$strings\"" | egrep -iv "$exceptions"`
      test $debug -gt 0 && echo "MSGS is $MSGS"
   else
      MSGS=`tail -$LINES $logfile | egrep -i "$strings"`
      test $debug -gt 0 && echo "MSGS is $MSGS"
   fi
```

If any messages found in the log file match what you're looking for, the script should send a notification. As mentioned earlier, there are two possible forms of notification: a warning and an error. In the environments I've worked with, both notification methods would normally result in an e-mail with a warning status message, or in an alphanumeric page if it were a more critical message. You must decide how to configure the notifications, so the code here simply echoes a message depending on the notification type.

```
if [ ! -z "$MSGS" ]
then
   if [ "$notify" != "error" ]
   then
   echo Send a warning notification...
else
   echo Send an error notification...
   fi
fi
```

If the file's line count is less than the base value (the value from the previous loop through the code), you need to reset the base value.

```
elif [ `eval echo '$COUNT'${suffix}_$entry_count` -lt
   `eval echo '$BASE'${suffix}_$entry_count` ]
then
   # This resets the tracked size of the
   # log if the log size gets smaller
   eval BASE${suffix}_$entry_count='$COUNT'${suffix}_$entry_count
```

```
        if [ "$exceptions" != "" ]
        then
          MSGS=`cat $logfile | egrep -i "\"$strings\"" | egrep -iv "$exceptions"`
          test $debug -gt 0 && echo "MSGS is $MSGS"
        else
          MSGS=`cat $logfile | egrep -i "$strings"`
          test $debug -gt 0 && echo "MSGS is $MSGS"
        fi
        if [ ! -z "$MSGS" ]
        then
          if [ "$notify" != "error" ]
          then
            echo Send a warning notification...
          else
            echo Send an error notification...
          fi
        fi
```

A likely scenario for this occurrence is when the log file is trimmed to a preset size to save disk space, such as with the logrotate utility. If this is the case, we want to check the whole file for the strings we're looking for. If we don't, we might miss something.

If there is no change in the file size, nothing needs to be done. We just complete the loop, and go back and repeat the same operations for all the other log files in the configuration string. Finally, the script should sleep for the specified amount of time before starting over again.

```
      else
        test $debug -gt 0 && echo "No change in size of $logfile"
      fi
    done
    sleep $DELAY
done
```

CHAPTER 8

■■■

Shell Process Tree

The process-tree script presented in this chapter does exactly what its name suggests: it prints out the names of some or all of the currently running processes that are present in the process table, displaying the parent/child relationships that exist among them in the form of a visual tree. There is an implementation of this functionality on some versions of Solaris (ptree) and on all flavors of Linux (pstree). These have proved very valuable to me for finding the root of a process group quickly, especially when that part of the process tree needs to be shut down.

There are some UNIX-based operating systems that don't have this functionality, such as HP-UX; hence the reason for this script. Along the way, this script also demonstrates several interesting shell programming techniques.

This script was originally a shell wrapper for an awk script[1] whose code I decided to rewrite for this book using a shell scripting language. All the versions of this script listed here use the same algorithm. The difference between them is that the first version stores data within arrays, and the second version uses indirect variables. The last version will run in the Bourne shell if that is all you have. Although the array version provides a good demonstration of arrays, it is not ideal since it requires bash. While bash may be installed on many systems, there is no guarantee that you will find it on non-Linux systems. The indirect-variable method is more useful, as it can be run in either ksh or bash with only minor modifications. You can find a more in-depth explanation of the indirect-variable technique in Chapter 7.

The following is some sample output from the script. It contains only some of the process tree of a running system, but it gives a good impression of the full output.

```
|\
|   2887 /usr/sbin/klogd -c 3 -2
|\
|   3362 /bin/sh /usr/bin/mysqld_safe
|    \
|     3425 /usr/sbin/mysqld --basedir=/usr
|      \
```

---

1. Based on an awk script that was written by Mark Gemmell and posted to the comp.unix.sco.misc Usenet newsgroup in 1996.

```
|      3542 /usr/sbin/mysqld --basedir=/usr
|      |\
|      | 3543 /usr/sbin/mysqld --basedir=/usr
|      \
|       3547 /usr/sbin/mysqld --basedir=/usr
 \
   3552 /usr/sbin/sshd
```

Process Tree Implemented Using Arrays

The concept of the script is simple enough: It can be run with no arguments, and its output is then the complete tree representation of all current entries in the process table. A process ID (pid) can also be passed to the script, and then the script will generate a tree displaying that process and its descendants.

By default, the root of the process-tree output is the init process, which has the process ID 1. The first part of the code sets the process ID to 1 if no process number has been passed to the script.

```
#!/bin/bash
if [ "$1" = "" ]
then
  proc=1
else
  proc=$1
fi
```

As its name suggests, the main() function, used in the following code, contains the main code to be executed. I have defined a main() function here because I wanted to explain this code first. Functions need to be defined before they can be called, and I would normally define functions near the beginning of a script and place the main code that calls these functions after the function definitions. Here I have used a main() function, which is invoked at the bottom of the script, and put its definition at the top of the script because it is easier to describe the main logic of the code before dealing with that of the helper function. Having a main() function is not required in shell scripts, however, (as it is in, say, C programs) and the script can easily be organized with or without one.

```
main () {
  PSOUT=`ps -ef | grep -v "^UID" | sort -n -k2`
```

First the script creates a variable containing the current process-table information. The switches passed to the ps command (here -ef) are typical, but depending on the OS you're running, different switches (such as -aux) may be more appropriate. You may also need to modify the variable assignments to properly reflect these variations. The command usage in Linux systems is a combination of these types, and ps under Linux will accept both option sets.

The following is the start of the loop that goes through the whole process table and grabs the needed information for each process:

```
while read line
do
```

My first inclination here would be to perform the ps command to generate the process table; then I would pipe the table to the while loop. That way I would not need to generate a temporary output file, which would be more efficient.

While the intention would be noble, it wouldn't work in pdksh or bash. It does, however, work in ksh. When the output from ps is piped to the loop in pdksh or bash, the loop is spawned in a subshell, so any variables defined there are not available to the parent shell after the loop completes. Instead of piping the output of ps to the while loop, the variable containing the process-table output is redirected into an input file handle from the other end of the loop, and we get to keep our variable definitions. This technique is discussed further in Chapter 10.

This loop processes each line of the redirected file one by one and gathers information about each running system and user process.

Some entries in the process table may have the greater-than (>) character in the output that displays the command being executed. Occurrences of this character (which means redirection to the shell) must be escaped, or else they may cause the script to act inappropriately. The sed command in the following code replaces the > character with the \> character combination. There are other characters, such as the pipe (|), that may occur in the ps output and present the same issue. In these cases, which are not accounted for here, additional lines similar to this one would be needed.

```
line=`echo "$line" | sed -e s/\>/\\\\\>/g`
```

Next we need to define an array, here called process, to hold the elements of the ps output line being read. I chose the bash shell to run this version of the script because its array structure does not enforce an upper bound on the number of array elements or on the subscripts used to access them. The pdksh shell limits the size of arrays to 1,024 elements, and ksh93 will allow up to 4,095 array elements. Both shells also require the subscripts that index the array elements to be integers starting from 0. This latter restriction isn't a problem when setting up the array that contains a single line from the ps output. However, the process ID will be used later as an index into other arrays, and then this limitation does become a problem. Process IDs are integers commonly greater than 1,024, and it happens quite frequently that their values reach five-digit numbers.

```
declare -a process=( $line )
```

A possible modification would be to use translation tables; that is, arrays associating smaller subscript values with the actual process ID numbers. The tree structure would then be created using these values, and it would be possible to print out the original process IDs using the translation tables. Even with this modification, you would be limited as to the number of processes the script could handle. The sample script used here doesn't have that limitation. Later in this chapter you'll see a version of this script that uses indirect variables and eval to implement pseudoarrays that allow very large sets of data items to be accessed individually using arbitrary indexes.

Here's where the arrays containing process information are populated. These arrays are indexed by process ID. First we get the pid of the process whose line of information is being read.

```
pid=${process[1]}
```

We use an owner array to hold strings specifying the owner of each process. We store the name of the current process's owner in the appropriate array location.

```
owner[$pid]=${process[0]}
ppid[$pid]=${process[2]}
command[$pid]="`echo $line | awk '{for(i=8;i<=NF;i++) {printf "%s ",$i}}'`"
```

Next we assign the process ID of the current process's parent to the appropriate element of the ppid (parent pid) array.

Then we do the same for the command array, which holds the commands being executed by each running process. The difference here is that the command being run isn't necessarily a simple value. The command could be just one word, or it could be quite long. The array-assignment statement pipes the line variable's current value to an awk script, which outputs the fields of the ps output line for this process, starting from the eighth field. This is done using a loop controlled by NF (number of fields), since it cannot be known in advance how many whitespace-separated fields the command will occupy. What is known is that the elements of the command string start at the eighth field of the ps output. Keep in mind that if you change the switches given to the ps command that generates this output, you may need to modify the awk statement to reflect the new output format.

The last assignment is a bit tricky. The children array is indexed by the pid and each of its elements contains a list of the pids of the corresponding process's children.

```
children[${ppid[$pid]}]="${children[${ppid[$pid]}]} $pid"
```

This assignment adds the current process's pid to the list of children of its parent process. An example may clarify the logic of this step. Consider a process tree consisting entirely of two processes, process 1 and process 2, where process 2 is the child of process 1. Suppose that at this line in the script, the line variable contains the information for process 2. Then the array assignment adds the current pid (2) to the list stored in the element of the children array for the process with pid 1. In this way, when the array has been populated and you want to know the children of a process with a particular pid, you can access the children array using that pid as the subscript.

The assignment appends the current pid to the children array entry because any given process may have multiple children. For example, take the process with pid 1 on any running system. This is the original system-startup process and will have many direct children. It is not necessary to explicitly track grandchildren (or further descendants), as they will be the direct children of other processes and appear elsewhere in the `children` array already.

This completes the loop. As discussed previously, the process table's file handle is redirected into the loop from the back end.

```
done <<EOF
$PSOUT
EOF
```

This is a very efficient algorithm, since it takes in the whole process table and appropriately categorizes all the data in it using only one iteration through the table.

Now that all the data has been read, you can call the function that prints it out in tree form, which completes the `main()` function.

```
  print_tree $proc ""
}
```

The `print_tree()` function is called with two parameters.

```
print_tree () {
  id=$1
```

The first is the pid of the process that should be at the root of the tree. The second is a string that will be prepended to the information about a process to form a line of displayed output. This string contains the characters that depict the tree-branch structure leading up to a tree leaf. The first time the function is called (from the `main()` function discussed earlier) the second argument is set to null because the root of the process tree has no branches leading into it.

This function is used recursively to process the tree level-by-level. As you can see by examining the sample output shown earlier, the ASCII characters needed to print out a particular process branch are determined by the branch's level in the tree and whether it is the last child of its parent. When we recursively descend one level in the tree to the next child, this adds one more straight branch symbol and an appropriate slanted branch (or space) leading into the child.

This is where the output of the process ID, owner and command are printed. You can add more information, such as parent pid or CPU time, but you would have to modify the main function.

```
  echo "$2$id" ${owner[$id]} ${command[$id]}
```

If the process has no children, the function will stop and return to the caller to process the next tree branch.

```
  if [ "${children[$id]}" = "" ]
  then
    return
```

If the process does have child processes associated with it, we loop through the list of its children so those branches of the tree can be printed.

```
else
  for child in ${children[$id]}
  do
```

Now we determine if the current child process is the last one in the `children` array. If it is, print a terminating branch character (\) to the screen. Note that the code specifies two backslash characters in succession when we only need one in the output. This is because the backslash character tells the shell to ignore any special processing of the next character, and thus we need two to get one. If the child process isn't the last one in the `children` array, print a split branch (|\), which will allow for this child process and its direct descendants on the tree.

```
if [ "$child" = "`echo ${children[${ppid[$child]}]} | awk '{print $NF}'`" ]
then
  echo "$2 \\"
  temp="$2 "
else
  echo "$2|\\"
  temp="$2| "
fi
```

When this function is called, it is assumed that the ASCII characters depicting the tree structure have already been set for the current process being displayed. The function's responsibility is to then determine what the branch structure will be for the next process to be displayed so the branches will line up appropriately.

Now we recursively call the function with the current child process ID and the new prefix string.

```
print_tree $child "$temp"
```

This is a natural way to write a `print_tree()` function, because a tree is a recursive data structure. Each branch off the main trunk will either branch again or terminate. This continues until all branches terminate. In the case of the processes running on a system, the init process will have child processes, which will in turn have children or be terminal (childless) processes.

This completes the loop and the function. It also completes the main code of the script itself, which, as discussed earlier, simply calls the `main()` function.

```
  done
  fi
}
main
```

Process Tree Implemented Using Indirect Variables

The process-tree script is interesting in its design, but it isn't particularly useful as a script because not all systems can run it, and those that can (mainly standard Linux systems using bash) already have a command that performs the same task. The following version of the script is more portable and it can be run using either bash or ksh. I've made very limited commentary on the code, as it is essentially the same as that of the previous script.

```
#!/bin/ksh
if [ "$1" = "" ]
then
  proc=1
else
  proc=$1
fi
main () {
  PSOUT=`ps -ef | grep -v "^UID" | sort -n -k2`
  while read line
  do
    line=`echo "$line" | sed -e s/\>/\\\\\\>/g`
    #declare -a process=( $line )
    set -A process $line
```

The boldface array definition is the single line that you would need to change depending on the shell under which this script will be running.

If you are using ksh, you should use the set -A command. If you are using bash, you should use the declare -a command. Since this script is written for ksh, the declare line has been commented out. The remainder of the script will work under either shell without modification.

```
    pid=${process[1]}
    eval owner$pid=${process[0]}
    eval ppid$pid=${process[2]}
    eval command$pid="\"`echo $line | awk '{for(i=8;i<=NF;i++) {printf \"%s \",$i}}'`\""
    eval parent='$ppid'$pid
    eval children$parent=\"'$children'$parent $pid\"
  done <<EOF
$PSOUT
EOF
  print_tree $proc ""
}
```

```
print_tree () {
  id=$1
  echo -n "$2$id"
  eval echo \"'$owner'$id '$command'$id\"
  if eval [ \"'$children'$id\" = \"""\" ]
  then
    return
  else
    for child in `eval echo '$children'$id`
    do
      eval parent='$ppid'$child
      if [ "$child" = "`eval echo '$children'$parent | awk '{print $NF}'`" ]
      then
        echo "$2 \\"
        temp="$2 "
      else
        echo "$2|\\"
        temp="$2| "
      fi
      print_tree $child "$temp"
    done
  fi
}
main
```

Bourne Shell Implementation of a Process Tree

The last version of the script runs under the Bourne shell. The main difference from the
other two is that the ps output stored in a temporary file is iterated through manually, one
line at a time. This eliminates the issue of undefined variables, which I discuss in detail in
Chapter 10. While not quite as elegant or speedy as the earlier versions, it does get the job
done. It once again uses the same algorithm as the original and, like the second version,
relies on indirect variables. I will limit the commentary to the differences from the previous versions.

```
#!/bin/sh
if [ "$1" = "" ]
then
  proc=1
else
  proc=$1
fi
```

Since I have written a manual counter loop, I have to initialize the counter. Then I must
determine the number of lines through which we will iterate in the file.

```
main () {
PSFILE=/tmp/duh
ps -ef | sort -n +1 | tail +2 > $PSFILE
pscount=`wc -l $PSFILE`
count=0
```

The while loop continues until the counter is equal to the number of lines in the input file.

```
while [ $count -le $pscount ]
do
  line=`tail +$count $PSFILE | head -1`
```

The assignment of the line variable is the key here. It uses the tail utility to start its output at the appropriate line number and then pipes that to the head utility to capture only the first line.

```
  line=`echo "$line" | sed -e s/\>/\\\\\\\>/g`
  pid=`echo $line | awk '{print $2}'`
  eval owner$pid=\"`echo $line | awk '{print $1}'`\"
  eval ppid$pid=\"`echo $line | awk '{print $3}'`\"
  eval command$pid="\"`echo $line | awk '{for(i=8;i<=NF;i++) {printf \"%s \",$i}}'`\""
  eval parent='$ppid'$pid
  eval children$parent=\"'$children'$parent $pid\"
  count=`echo $count+1 | bc`
done
print_tree $proc ""
}
```

The last two lines here, which were combined in the earlier versions of this script, wouldn't play well together under the Bourne shell, so I split them up.

```
print_tree () {
  id=$1
  echo "$2$id \c"
  eval echo \"'$owner'$id '$command'$id\"
```

The \c instructs the first echo command not to perform a carriage return after the output. The output of the subsequent echo of the owner and command variables completes the output.

```
  if eval [ \"'$children'$id\" = "\"\"" ]
  then
    return
  else
    for child in `eval echo '$children'$id`
    do
      eval parent='$ppid'$child
      if [ "$child" = "`eval echo '$children'$parent | awk '{print $NF}'`"]
      then
```

```
            echo "$2 \\"
            temp="$2 "
        else
            echo "$2|\\"
            temp="$2| "
        fi
        print_tree $child "$temp"
    done
  fi
}
main
```

CHAPTER 9

■■■

Data Redirection

Data redirection is when the input or output of a command is redirected using special notation. It is also used for opening and closing files for read and write operations. The forms and syntax of redirection are varied and their meanings are specific. I will cover some of the common uses here, and provide a bit more explanation than system man pages to aid you in avoiding pitfalls.

Avoiding Confusion

Data redirection is a common point of confusion among users. Problems with its usage arise most often when a user wants to set up a `cron` job that sends all its output to `/dev/null`, such as in the following `crontab` entry:

```
10 5 * * * /run/some/script > /dev/null 2>&1
```

In this example, all of the output will be sent to `/dev/null`, whether it is standard output generated by the script or error output generated by the shell or the commands in the script. This kind of `cron` job is usually created because a simple `cron` entry without any redirection will cause an e-mail containing all the output, both standard output and error output, to be sent to the job's owner. Many users don't want this type of annoying e-mail, but instead of modifying the script to output information only when useful, they set up the `cron` job to throw all of it out. This is a bad habit to develop. I have seen jobs like this run for years under the assumption that they were performing the desired tasks, when all the while they did nothing because they were broken and the error output was never sent to alert users of the problem.

As in the previous `cron` example, users will sometimes attempt to remove the output with syntax like this:

```
10 5 * * * /run/some/script 2>&1 > /dev/null
```

Even assuming that we do want to suppress all output, this syntax is wrong for the intended purpose. You'll notice that the `> /dev/null` and `2>&1` pieces of the entry are reversed. In its current form, `stderr` output from the job will continue to be mailed to the user.

Other times something like this is attempted:

```
10 5 * * * /run/some/script > /dev/null
```

While this will remove any normal output (output to stdout), it won't redirect error messages that the script might generate, and those will still be e-mailed to the user. Realistically, this is probably the safest syntax to use. It removes all normal output you would see when the script is run interactively, but still sends e-mail alerts when there are errors.

All of these problems seem to stem from a misunderstanding of the types of output that a process can generate. The file descriptors for the usual output streams are 1 for the standard output stream (also known as stdout), 2 for the standard error stream (also known as stderr), and 0 for the standard input stream (also known as stdin). You can think of these as separate communication channels between the script and its environment. For output, there is a channel for messages coming from a program such as echo or grep, or a statement of the script code, which is stdout. There is also a separate channel for messages that are generated from failures of a command, such as when an attempt is made to open a nonexistent file. In this case, the "No such file or directory" error message will be sent to the stderr stream.

When the > or < character is used without a specific file descriptor, stdout or stdin is assumed, respectively. I think of the characters as arrows showing the direction in which the data will travel for further processing. In the common cases, a command is run and its output is pointed toward a destination file via >. When the reverse pointer < is used, the content of the file is being redirected into the initiating command or code sequence through its input stream.

Common Redirection

The following are some of the most commonly used redirection arguments and their meanings. Additional ones and more detailed explanations are specified in the bash and ksh man pages.

expression < *file*: Redirect the contents of *file* into the *expression*. An example of this usage is the command mail -s "/etc/hosts" you@domain.com < /etc/hosts, in which the /etc/hosts file will be used as the body of the mail message being sent.

expression > *file*: Redirect the output of *expression* to the specified *file*. If the file does not exist, it is created. If the file already exists, it is overwritten unless the noclobber option to set is applied. An example is grep 192.168 /etc/hosts > /tmp/outfile, where /tmp/outfile will contain the results of the grep command after the line finishes executing.

expression >| *file*: Redirect the output of *expression* to the specified *file*. This is similar to the previous example, except that it overrides the noclobber option of the shell. When the noclobber option is set, the file won't be overwritten when the > redirector is used. This syntax forces that overwrite.

expression >> *file*: Redirect the output of *expression* to the specified *file* in append mode. If the command in the earlier example (grep 192.168 /etc/hosts > /tmp/outfile) is followed by the command grep 172.16 /etc/hosts >> /tmp/outfile, then the output of this grep command will be appended to the end of the /tmp/outfile file.

expression 2> /dev/null > *file*: Redirect stderr output from the *expression* to /dev/null while redirecting stdout output to the specified *file*.

expression > /dev/null 2> *file*: Redirect stdout from the *expression* to /dev/null while redirecting stderr to the *file*. This is the converse of the preceding example.

expression > *file* 2>&1: Redirect both stdout and stderr output from *expression* to the specified *file*. This syntax specifies that stderr (2) output is assigned to stdout (1) and both are redirected to the specified *file*.

expression &> *file*: Redirect both stdout and stderr output from the *expression* to the *file*. This is a shorthand version of the previous syntax (*expression* > *file* 2>&1). This is a feature of the bash shell.

expression 2> *file*: Redirect stderr output from the *expression* to the *file*. An example of this is find /home -type f -exec grep -l "some_string" {} \; 2> /dev/null. This command will output all the filenames returned by the find command containing the string *some_string*, but redirect any "permission denied" errors to /dev/null.

Redirection can be used not only for simple commands and script invocations, but also with if, for, while, until, and case structures, as well as pipes and batched commands. The following code segments give a few samples of how you might use redirection of complex statements in your scripts:

```
{
  cat file1
  cat file2
  cat file3
} > file.output

cat nodelist | while read line ; do
  echo $node
  rsh $node uptime
done >> uptime.report
```

```
while read line
do
  count=$((count+1))
  echo -n Field 2 of line $count is:
  echo $line | awk '{print $2}'
done < /input/file

count=0
while [ $count -lt 10 ]
do
  echo $count
  count=$((count+1))
done > count.output
```

Multiple redirections can also be used. In the following short example the code takes the contents of the /etc/hosts file as input to the while loop:

```
count=0
while read line
  do
  count=$((count+1))
  echo $count: $line
done < /etc/hosts > lined.hosts
```

The loop adds line numbers to the file and the final output is then redirected to the lined.hosts file.

Access to User-Specified File Handles

In most programming languages, you can open a file descriptor for reading, writing, or both, then read or make modifications to the data and close the file. Shell scripting languages are no exception. Up to now, I have discussed redirection only of output to a given file or to one of the standard input or output file streams. Now I'll discuss the method of opening a file handle for a specific type of operation (read/write/both), but instead of opening the file each time you want to access it, you create a file handle with a user-defined file descriptor that can then be accessed in various modes, using the same syntax as the standard input/output descriptors. You create a handle for a specified file via the exec command. When opening the file, you give it a single-digit file descriptor in the range of 3–9 to avoid conflict with the standard stream descriptors of 0–2.

Any combination of the following exec commands can be used in your code to open a file and assign it a single-digit file descriptor:

exec 3> file_1: Opens file_1 for output in overwrite mode, which would then be accessed with file descriptor 3.

exec 4< file_2: Opens file_2 for input in read mode, which would then be accessed with file descriptor 4.

exec 5>> file_3: Opens file_3 for output in append mode, which would then be accessed with file descriptor 5.

exec 6<> file_4: Opens file_4 for both reading and writing, which would then be accessed with file descriptor 6. Unlike the other examples, where you must access the files in the same way the descriptors were opened, for either reading or writing, this type of descriptor can be accessed in both ways.

Once the file descriptors are open, you can access them with various input or output statements. To access a specific open file descriptor, complete an expression with the syntax >&*fd*, where *fd* denotes the single-digit descriptor.

Here are some examples of reading and writing to open files:

```
echo "The quick brown fox jumped over the lazy dog" >&3
grep 172.16 /etc/hosts >&5
read line <&4
```

I have matched the file-descriptor numerals (relating to input and output) with the exec commands that opened them originally.

Using the exec syntax you can also specify your output at runtime instead of hard-coding it. The following example demonstrates the technique:

```
If [ -n "$DEBUG" ]
then
  exec 5>&1
else
  exec 5> $LOGFILE
fi
echo "Some Text" >&5
```

Based on the value of the DEBUG variable, the code sends output from file descriptor 5 either to stdout or to a log file.

When file access is complete, you should close the open file with the exec command, as shown here:

```
exec 3>&-
```

This keeps your code clean. In both bash and ksh you will receive a "Bad file descriptor" error if you attempt to access a file descriptor that hasn't been opened. There is no trouble with closing a file descriptor that is not already open.

Descriptor Access from the Shell

One other method of reading from and writing to an open file descriptor is to use the shell's built-in print and read commands. Only ksh has the print command, but both ksh and bash have read. Both of these built-in commands take the -u switch, which gives you the ability to specify the file descriptor you want to access. Once the file is open, you can output directly to or read directly from that specific descriptor using these built-in commands.

Two methods can be used with the print command in ksh. The first of the two examples here is the redirection to a specific file descriptor, as already discussed. The second uses the -u switch with a single-digit file descriptor. These are equivalent commands and are available only in ksh.

```
print "all your base are belong to us" >&3
print -u3 "Now is the time"
```

For bash, the available command is very similar. You have access to only the redirection syntax, however, as the -u switch isn't supported. You also need to replace the print command with echo.

```
echo "all your base are belong to us" >&3
```

Like the built-in print command, the read command can be used in two ways. The first of the following two examples specifies redirection to a file descriptor. The second uses the -u switch, like the print command in ksh. The main difference here is that both bash and ksh have this capability.

```
read line <&3
read -u3 line
```

All of these examples assume the file has been opened for reading or writing as appropriate. When you try to access a file descriptor that has not been opened, you will receive an "invalid file descriptor: Bad file descriptor" error in bash and a "bad file unit number [Bad file descriptor]:" error in ksh.

CHAPTER 10

■ ■ ■

Piping Input to read

This chapter deals with a gotcha that I came across while porting a script from ksh to bash. It was a gotcha only because at the time I wasn't aware of a fairly crucial difference in the behavior of the two shells. In both pdksh and bash, the last command of a pipeline is performed in a subshell. This means that a variable assigned within the subshell is not available to the parent shell. In ksh, the last command of a pipeline is executed in the original shell.

This isn't an issue when using the pipe to set a variable, but if the result of a pipe is sent to a loop structure that then populates variables you will use later, that is more of a problem. Once the loop completes, the variables you were going to rely on don't exist.

Included here are a few of examples of code that you might expect to work, but they actually don't. I also include some workarounds that will perform the intended tasks.

The following is the part of the code that had problems when I ported it. It was used to process a file of extended output one line at a time. To perform this task in ksh, I would use the following:

```
cat somefile | while read line
do
  # Process the $line variable in some form.
  if [ "`echo $line | awk '{print $3}'`" = "somevalue" ]
  then
    all="$all $line"
  fi
done
```

If everything within the loop is self-contained and none of the variables in it are accessed outside the loop, this will work fine. However, the bash code parsed each line in the output of the piped command, and populated some variables based on that output. Once the loop completed, I wanted to access those values ($all in this example) for other purposes, and found that they were undefined.

The following code is the first workaround that I found to overcome the problem. Unfortunately it isn't quite as elegant or intuitive as the original code because it uses a temporary file. To keep the code clean I try to avoid using temporary files, but in this case I had no choice.

```
while read line
do
   # Process the $line variable in some form.
   if [ "`echo $line | awk '{print $3}'`" = "somevalue" ]
   then
     all="$all $line"
   fi
done < somefile
```

First the data originally piped to the while read loop is sent to a temporary file. The file is then redirected into the back end of the loop. This functions the same way as the original code, but allows the variables populated within the loop to remain usable once the loop completes. Chapter 8 offers another example of this technique.

The following is a modified form of the previous example:

```
THE_INPUT=`ps -ef`
while read line
do
   # Process the $line variable in some form.
   if [ "`echo $line | awk '{print $3}'`" = "somevalue" ]
   then
     all="$all $line"
   fi
done <<EOF
$THE_INPUT
EOF
```

This slight modification of the earlier example eliminates the need for a temporary file. Instead of redirecting a file into the back of the loop, we start a *here-document* and feed it the data we want to process through the loop. A here-document is where the shell reads input from the current source until it reaches the matching tag alone on a single line, in this case EOF. This solution works in the same way as a real file with both bash and pdksh.

The following sections show four methods for reading input one line at a time. With each method, I explain what variables are available within the code for each of the four shells (bash, ksh, pdksh, and Bourne sh).

Line-by-Line Option 1

The original method of piping input to a read loop looks like this:

```
ps -ef | while read firstvar
do
   echo firstvar within the loop: $firstvar
   secondvar=$firstvar
   echo secondvar within the loop: $secondvar
done
```

```
echo firstvar outside the loop: $firstvar
echo secondvar outside the loop: $secondvar
```

*KornShell (*ksh*):* Both firstvar and secondvar are available within the loop. Only secondvar is available outside the loop. This is useful because even though you can't use the original read variable, you can assign it to some other variable, which is then available when the loop completes.

*Bash (*bash*):* Both firstvar and secondvar are available within the loop. Neither firtvar nor secondvar is available after the loop completes.

*Public Domain Korn Shell (*pdksh*):* Both firstvar and secondvar are available within the loop. Neither firstvar nor secondvar is available after the loop completes.

*Bourne (*sh*):* Both firstvar and secondvar are available within the loop. Neither firstvar nor secondvar is available after the loop completes.

Line-by-Line Option 2

This is the workaround option I discussed originally. The input will be sent to a temporary file and then redirected to the back of the loop.

```
ps -ef > /tmp/testfile
while read firstvar
do
  echo firstvar within the loop: $firstvar
  secondvar=$firstvar
  echo secondvar within the loop: $secondvar
done < /tmp/testfile
echo firstvar outside the loop: $firstvar
echo secondvar outside the loop: $secondvar
```

*KornShell (*ksh*):* Both firstvar and secondvar are available within the loop. Only secondvar is available outside the loop.

*Bash (*bash*):* Both firstvar and secondvar are available within the loop. Only secondvar is available outside the loop. This version now performs in the same manner as the ksh version.

*Public Domain Korn Shell (*pdksh*):* Both firstvar and secondvar are available within the loop. Only secondvar is available outside the loop.

*Bourne (*sh*):* Both firstvar and secondvar are available within the loop. Neither variable is available outside the loop.

Line-by-Line Option 3

This is the here-document workaround option where we remove the need for a temporary file. This functions in the same way as Option 2.

```
the_input=`ps -ef`
while read firstvar
do
  echo firstvar within the loop: $firstvar
  secondvar=$firstvar
  echo secondvar within the loop: $secondvar
done <<EOF
$the_input
EOF
echo firstvar outside the loop: $firstvar
echo secondvar outside the loop: $secondvar
```

KornShell (ksh): Both firstvar and secondvar are available within the loop. Only secondvar is available outside the loop.

Bash (bash): Both firstvar and secondvar are available within the loop. Only secondvar is available outside the loop. This version now performs in the same manner as the ksh version.

Public Domain Korn Shell (pdksh): Both firstvar and secondvar are available within the loop. Only secondvar is available outside the loop.

Bourne (sh): Both firstvar and secondvar are available within the loop. Neither variable is available outside the loop.

Line-by-Line Option 4

This last option removes the pipe (|) from the loop and processes an input file manually. If you have only the Bourne shell at your disposal, this is your only option, and the script will be somewhat slower. With this option, all set variables from both inside and outside the loop will be available following loop completion. This option is valid for all the shells I've mentioned.

```
ps -ef > /tmp/testfile
filecount=`wc -l /tmp/testfile`
count=0
while [ $count -le $filecount ]
```

```
do
  firstvar=`tail +$count /tmp/testfile | head -1`
  echo firstvar within the loop: $firstvar
  secondvar=$firstvar
  echo secondvar within the loop: $secondvar
  count=`echo $count+1 | bc`
done < /tmp/testfile
echo firstvar outside the loop: $firstvar
echo secondvar outside the loop: $secondvar
```

The following tables summarize all of the previously discussed scenarios. Table 10-1 displays the availability of the variable that is initially set in the loop (firstvar). Note that in all shells except the manual loop method used by the Bourne shell, this variable is unavailable for use following the loop's completion.

Table 10-1. *Availability of Variables That Are Initially Set in a Loop, After Loop Completion*

	ksh	bash	pdksh	Bourne
Opt. 1: Pipe to while read	No	No	No	No
Opt. 2: Redirected file to back of loop	No	No	No	No
Opt. 3: Redirected here-document to back of loop	No	No	No	No
Opt. 4: Manual iteration through loop	Yes	Yes	Yes	Yes

Table 10-2 displays availability of variables that are assigned within the loop (secondvar) once the loop has completed. These variables can have values assigned to them from the initial variable (firstvar), since that variable is accessible within the loop or from any other assignment inside the loop.

Table 10-2. *Availability of Variables That Are Set Within a Loop, After Loop Completion*

	ksh	bash	pdksh	Bourne
Opt. 1: Pipe to while read	Yes	No	No	No
Opt. 2: Redirected file to back of loop	Yes	Yes	Yes	No
Opt. 3: Redirected here-document to back of loop	Yes	Yes	Yes	No
Opt. 4: Manual iteration through loop	Yes	Yes	Yes	Yes

Pipe to read Directly

The next example represents a scenario in which the script does not pipe to a loop, but instead pipes input to a read statement. This method works well in ksh. Within both pdksh and bash, once the following command is executed, both foo and bar variables are undefined:

```
echo a b | read foo bar
```

The workaround removes the use of the read command altogether. This modified version has the same functionality, but it uses two separate commands instead of a pipeline of two commands.

```
set `echo a b` ; foo=$1 bar=$2
```

Using set without any options or arguments takes the echo output and assigns each output *word* using a positional parameter. The parameter can then be reused. This works fine in most instances. However, if $1 is a negative value, the set command interprets the - sign as a switch. It then complains about the switch not being valid.

The workaround for this is to use the double-dash switch for set. This will tell set not to process any further arguments that begin with + or -.

```
set -- `echo a b` ; foo=$1 bar=$2
```

One other workaround for this is somewhat of a brute-force tactic but may be necessary depending on the age of the system or shell you're working with. You prepend some arbitrary character (not a - sign) to the beginning of the echo output to protect against switch evaluation. Once the variables are set, you strip off the first character of the first variable using cut so you are left with the original value.

```
set "@"`echo a b` ; foo=$1 bar=$2
foo=`echo $foo | cut -c1-`
```

Process Input Word-by-Word

The last example enables you to parse through each word of some input string, consuming two words at a time. Words are assumed to be separated by spaces. This once again uses the set command to assign positional variables the value of each word. The same code as we used previously is implemented, but the core function is now surrounded by a loop that continues until the first word is null.

```ksh
#!/bin/ksh
set `echo a b c d e`
while [ "$1" != "" ]
do
  foo=$1 bar=$2
  echo $*
  shift
  echo foo $foo
  echo bar $bar
done
```

The loop assigns the first two positional parameters to foo and bar. It then outputs the value of all positional variables. The shift command drops the $1 value and promotes $2 and all other variables by one position. It then outputs the values of foo and bar for each iteration. The $* variable that is echoed holds all of the current positional parameters. Thus, after each iteration through the loop, the output of the line is shortened by one element. Note that this script is written in ksh, but it should work in all previously mentioned shells.

## PART 2

System Interaction and Advanced Techniques

■■■

## CHAPTER 11

Math from the Shell

Mathematical calculations are an important element of writing shell scripts. In the various flavors of UNIX, there are multiple ways to perform just about any task, and mathematical tasks are no exception.

Although there are many types of mathematical computations, I've limited the discussion in this chapter to the basic operations of addition, subtraction, multiplication, and division, plus remainder, exponentiation, and trigonometric functions. The examples make use of the variables a, b, c, and d.

One note on division: some programming languages don't perform integer division like you might expect from using your traditional calculator. There are two parts to the quotient of an integer-division problem, the *whole* (or *integer*) part and the *remainder*. Take the example of 5 divided by 3; the whole part of the quotient is 1 and the remainder upon division is 2. In some of this chapter's methods for doing math in the shell, there are two distinct operators for integer division. The slash (/) operator returns the whole part and the percent (%) operator returns the remainder. Keep this in mind when performing your calculations.

expr

This chapter's first math method is the use of expr. expr is a utility that evaluates various types of expressions, including ones containing string, logical, and mathematical functions. The following are examples of how to use expr to carry out mathematical operations:

Addition: answer=`expr $c + $d`

Subtraction: answer=`expr $c - $d`

Multiplication: answer=`expr $c \* $d`

Division: answer=`expr $c / $d`

Remainder: answer=`expr $c % $d`

There are no explicit trigonometric or exponentiation functions in expr.

There are a couple of items to keep in mind when using expr. As shown in the examples, single spaces are required between the expr call and its arguments, and between the operators and their arguments. Also, when using the asterisk (*) character for multiplication, the shell will interpret it as a wild card and expand it to the elements in your current directory before attempting to evaluate the expression unless you either escape the asterisk via * or turn off globbing[1] (path and file expansion) using set -f.

Internal Shell Math

The shell itself can perform mathematical operations. The advantage of using the internal math functions is that your code doesn't have to call an external program, which reduces the footprint of the code and allows it to run faster. This method is available in bash and ksh. The Bourne shell does not have this functionality. The following are examples of how to employ internal shell math to carry out mathematical operations.

■**Note** The largest integer available for internal shell math is $2^{63}-1$, or 9,223,372,036,854,775,807 (in bash and expr; ksh uses scientific notation for large numbers). This is the maximum 64-bit integer. If you need numbers that are larger than this, you must use the bc or dc calculator.

Addition: answer=$(($c+$d))

Subtraction: answer=$(($c-$d))

Multiplication: answer=$(($c*$d))

Division: answer=$(($c/$d))

Remainder: answer=$(($c%$d))

Exponentiation: The first argument raised to the power of the second; answer=$(($c**$d))

Order of operations: The default order can be modified by using parentheses, as with the other methods of performing shell math; answer=$((($c+$d)*$c)). Without the use of parentheses to order the calculations as you desire, the common order is as follows:

1. Perform any calculations surrounded by parentheses. These are ones that you may not have specified.

---

1. *Globbing* is the term used for the shell's completion of paths and filenames that contain metacharacters.

2. Perform all calculations that are exponents or roots, such as a square or cube root.

3. Working from left to right, perform any multiplication or division.

4. Working from left to right, perform any addition or subtraction.

A math library available in ksh lets us perform more-sophisticated mathematical calculations. These are the functions it provides: abs(), acos(), asin(), atan(), atan2(), cos(), cosh(), exp(), floor(), fmod(), hypot(), int(), log(), pow(), sin(), sinh(), sqrt(), tan(), and tanh(). Table 11-1 gives a basic description of these functions, but their use is beyond the scope of this book. The following variable assignment demonstrates the use of one of these higher level mathematical functions:

```
answer=$((cos($a)))
```

Table 11-1. *Descriptions of Trigonometric Functions Available in* ksh

Trigonometric Function	Description
abs()	Absolute value
acos()	Inverse cosine
asin()	Inverse sine
atan()	Inverse tangent
atan2()	Four-quadrant inverse tangent
cos()	Cosine
cosh()	Hyperbolic cosine
exp()	Exponential
floor()	Round toward negative infinity
fmod()	Floating-point remainder of division
hypot()	Square-root of sum of squares
int()	Integer portion of a real number
log()	Natural logarithm
pow()	Raise base number to an exponential power
sin()	Sine
sinh()	Hyperbolic sine
sqrt()	Square root
tan()	Tangent
tanh()	Hyperbolic tangent

bc

The bc utility is an arbitrary-precision calculator. This means the precision of the answer can be set at runtime through the use of the *scale* operator. Most of the mathematical shell utilities described up to this point focus on operations on whole numbers. The exception is the special library of functions available in ksh. With bc, you can set the *scale* (number of decimal places following the decimal point) so that results will be expressed as floating-point numbers of the precision you specify. The functional use of bc is very similar to the use of expr, as the following list shows:

Addition: answer=`echo "$c+$d" | bc`

Subtraction: answer=`echo "$c-$d" | bc`

Multiplication: answer=`echo "$c*$d" | bc`

Division: answer=`echo "$c/$d" | bc`

Remainder: answer=`echo "$c%$d" | bc`

Exponentiation: answer=`echo "$c^$d" | bc`

Scale: The scale of a floating-point number is the number of digits that follow the decimal point. To set the scale when performing a calculation, you use answer=`echo "scale=5;$c/$d" | bc`.

Trigonometric functions: To use the trigonometric functions, you must enable the math library by invoking bc using the -l switch. When the library is enabled, the default scale is set to 20 decimal places. The following examples set the scale to 5 places:

- Sine in radians: answer=`echo "scale=5;s($a)" | bc -l`

- Cosine in radians: answer=`echo "scale=5;c($a)" | bc -l`

- Arctangent in radians: answer=`echo "scale=5;s($a)" | bc -l`

dc

The dc utility is another arbitrary-precision calculator, and it works much like bc. Its main distinction lies in its use of reverse Polish notation.[2] dc uses a stack to store numbers; evaluating a number pushes it onto the stack, and the operations pop their arguments off the stack and push the result back onto the stack. For shell scripting purposes, I have not used

---

2. More information on reverse Polish notation (RPN) can be found at http://en.wikipedia.org/wiki/Reverse_polish_notation.

the dc calculator. It is a valuable program, but the majority of the calculations I've needed are fairly simple and don't require the advantages it provides. I mention it only for the sake of completeness.

cron

The system scheduler on UNIX and Linux systems is called cron. Its purpose is to run commands, series of commands, or scripts on a predetermined schedule. Normally these tasks are performed on systems that run 24 hours a day, 7 days a week. Writing cron scripts to perform system maintenance, backups, monitors, or any other job that you would want to run on a schedule is a very common task. There are a few subtleties with cron however, that many users and administrators may be unaware of.

crontab Entries

On a UNIX or Linux system, the cron daemon process runs all the time. A daemon is generally a program that runs as a background task and provides some type of service, in this case a scheduler. A run control (rc) script starts the daemon when the system boots. The cron daemon searches for entries in the systemwide or individual user's crontab (short for "cron table") files and loads them into memory. Once each minute, the daemon determines—based on its predetermined schedule—if any of the entries should be run. A scheduled job can run as often as every minute or as infrequently as once a year.

A crontab entry is a specially formatted line in a crontab file that specifies on which minute, hour, day, day of the week, and day of the month a particular task should run. To add a task to the cron table, you run the crontab -e command, which allows an individual user to maintain the entries in his personal crontab file; this launches a session with the editor that is defined by the EDITOR shell environment variable. Each user on a machine may have a crontab file for his own purposes. However, a system administrator can curtail individual users' capabilities according to security policy. The following line is a simple cron entry scheduled to run at 4:15 pm on Tuesdays:

```
15 16 * * 2 /some/path/myscript.sh
```

There are six fields in each entry. The first five fields define the schedule, and the remainder of the line is the job that you want to run on that schedule. The last field is what I want to focus on here. Many users are aware that they can run a job within cron, although they may not be aware that the task can be quite complex and may therefore contain multiple elements. You can source environment files, set variables, debug the code, put logic into your entry, and call scripts and other commands from the crontab file.

This cron entry is a more complex example:

```
* * * * set -x ; cron_count=`ps -ef | grep [c]ron | wc -l`\
 ;[ $cron_count -ne 5 ] && echo "Cron Count $cron_count" | mail -s\
 "Cron Count $cron_count" rbpeters
```

The entry first sets the set -x expansion flag, assigns a variable, performs a test, and then, based on the results, sends an e-mail message. crontab entries can be powerful tools in your scripting arsenal.

Environment Problems

I've worked with many users who have had problems with a script they have coded and debugged for a significant amount of time, only to arrive at the conclusion that "It works from the command line, but not from cron?!" I have run into this problem from time to time myself, but knowing the issues tends to help you find the solution much more quickly.

A script running from cron is not run in the same shell environment as a command typed at the prompt. When you log in to a machine and you are at the shell prompt, many variables need to be set to enable your interactive shell session. cron is not run from an interactive session, however. A cron job runs with only some of the shell environment variables that are set in an interactive shell session. The cron job has only a very rudimentary environment. Most problems with users' cron scripts stem from the assumption that the code runs in an environment with the characteristics of an interactive session, rather than the cron environment.

Here's an example to illustrate the difference. This is one of my user environments, which is displayed when I use the env command:

```
SSH_CLIENT=172.16.5.199 3433 22
USER=rbpeters
MAIL=/var/mail/rbpeters
HOME=/home/rbpeters
SSH_TTY=/dev/ttyp1
PAGER=more
ENV=/home/rbpeters/.shrc
LOGNAME=rbpeters
BLOCKSIZE=K
TERM=xterm
PATH=/sbin:/bin:/usr/sbin:/usr/bin:/usr/games:\
/usr/local/sbin:/usr/local/bin:/usr/X11R6/bin:\
/home/rbpeters/bin
SHELL=/bin/sh
```

```
SSH_CONNECTION=172.16.5.199 3433 172.16.5.2 22
FTP_PASSIVE_MODE=YES
EDITOR=vi
```

I then set up the following cron job to run temporarily for illustrative purposes:

```
* * * * * env > /usr/home/rbpeters/env.out
```

After the job ran and created the env.out file, I found the following lines in it:

```
USER=rbpeters
HOME=/home/rbpeters
LOGNAME=rbpeters
PATH=/usr/bin:/bin
SHELL=/bin/sh
```

Notice that there is a fairly significant difference between the two environments. For instance, the PATH variable in the cron job environment doesn't have nearly as many directories to search, which can easily break a script because of the assumption that the paths available in the interactive shell environment are available for the cron job. The system cron daemon automatically sets the environment variables that make up the minimal environment. It sets SHELL to /bin/sh, and PATH to /usr/bin:/bin. The USER, LOGNAME, and HOME variables are set based on your entry in the passwd file. That's all you get in the default cron environment.

In the following slightly modified version of the example cron job, note the addition of the command to source the .profile file, which sets up some environment parameters prior to running the command. The additional command adds a more useful environment to the cron job:

```
* * * * * . /home/rbpeters/.profile >/dev/null ; env > /usr/home/rbpeters/env.out
```

Here is the new output in the env.out file:

```
USER=rbpeters
HOME=/home/rbpeters
PAGER=morec
ENV=/home/rbpeters/.shrc
LOGNAME=rbpeters
BLOCKSIZE=K
PATH=/sbin:/bin:/usr/sbin:/usr/bin:/usr/games:/usr/local/sbin:\
/usr/local/bin:/usr/X11R6/bin:/home/rbpeters/bin
SHELL=/bin/sh
EDITOR=vi
```

Now you can see several additional items, as well as a more complete PATH variable. Another way of getting similar results is to fully qualify all paths, commands, and other files mentioned in the script called by the cron job. Supplying the full path to any element that may otherwise rely on the variables set in the interactive shell environment is a good idea in general when writing scripts, since it keeps you aware of the external files you are depending on.

Finally, you can replace the env command with the set command and see similar results to those in the preceding example. The output is much more extensive, but the same principle applies.

Output Redirection

When a scheduled cron task is run, it may or may not create output. Since there is no inter-active session attached to the task, the output, if any, is sent to the owner of the crontab file via an e-mail that has the subject set to the cron entry, and the body of the message as the output of the job. This is the e-mail message I received from the example of a complex cron entry shown earlier:

```
++ ps -ef
++ grep '[c]ron'
++ wc -l
+ cron_count=4
+ '[' 4 -ne 5 ']'
+ echo 'Cron Count 4'
+ mail -s 'Cron Count 4' rbpeters
```

Since the cron entry started with set -x, the subsequent commands executed while the jobs run were expanded and printed as they were executed. This is a valuable feature when you have to debug a job. Any output from the job will be mailed in the same way. Even though this is useful output, many cron users redirect all output to /dev/null because once the job is in place they don't want to become desensitized by too many routine e-mail messages that don't indicate a problem. A typical job might look like this:

```
30 * * * * /usr/local/bin/some_script > dev/null 2>&1
```

This entry, which uses a very common pattern, not only redirects normal output (stdout) to /dev/null, but also redirects all errors (stderr) to the same target. This can become a problem. I have seen jobs scheduled like this that have run for years without ever doing anything. They may have environment issues, as described in the previous section. They may have worked at the time of implementation, but at some point a change somewhere else in the system caused the cron script to break. In either case, the output that would have warned the user about emerging problems was dropped in the bit bucket. An issue like this will be an annoyance in that the job simply doesn't run. A more worst-case scenario is that a routine system-maintenance job doesn't run properly and eventually allows bigger problems to crop up. I have seen these types of problems cause downtime on production systems, and for these reasons I would not recommend using this type of output redirection in a cron entry.

Whenever I write a script to be run from cron, my goal is to have the script emit output only if a debug flag has been set. Normal usage would not display any output. This way the crontab entry sends mail only when error messages are generated. Additionally, I would redirect the script's output (stdout) to /dev/null. If any error messages were to be created, they would still be sent to the user for diagnostic purposes.

The following modified form of the unsafe cron job discussed previously would yield the desired result:

```
30 * * * * /usr/local/bin/some_script > dev/null
```

CHAPTER 13

■■■

Self-Linked Scripts

The technique I am about to discuss allows you to have a single script that can be called in several ways by different names. The script itself contains all the code necessary to perform a number of tasks, but you may want to determine the specific task to be performed at runtime by calling the script by a specific name. This lets users invoke an individual task by name without having to learn specialized command-line switches for the options they want.

There are two of ways of specifying the precise behavior of a script. One way is to have the script accept command-line options telling it how to act. This method is covered in Chapter 5, which dealt with the use of getopts. This chapter illustrates the second method: calling a script by giving it multiple names.

Sometimes you want to have multiple scripts perform tasks that are related in some way but have slight differences. An example, albeit a silly one, is a script that monitors disk consumption of the / file system. The script will determine the disk utilization percentage from the output of the df command. The following is a sample of df output:

```
Filesystem 1K-blocks Used Available Use% Mounted on
/dev/hda2 18334940 13019804 4383768 75% /
/dev/hda1 256666 25241 218173 11% /boot
none 257300 0 257300 0% /dev/shm
/dev/hdb1 16577308 11732468 4002760 75% /snapshot
```

For illustrative purposes, our script doesn't do the obvious and use the Use% value from the df output; it instead calculates disk consumption directly from the 1K-blocks and Used values. So now you have a script that can display the percent utilization of the / file system. Let's call this root_check.

```
#!/bin/sh
fs="/"
fs_total=`df -k $fs | tail -n 1 | awk '{print $2}'`
fs_used=`df -k $fs | tail -n 1 | awk '{print $3}'`
percent_used=$((100*$fs_used/$fs_total))
echo "$fs is at ${percent_used}% capacity"
```

Now suppose you want to have a similar script, called boot_check, that will perform the same file-system-capacity check on the /boot partition. First we create a soft link (ln -s) called boot_check that points to the original root_check script. The following shows the modification to the root_check code that will allow the script to determine how it was called:

```
#!/bin/sh
whatami=`basename $0`
```

The basename command strips off a file's leading path elements. In this case, basename returns the positional parameter $0 containing the name used to invoke the script. The script could be called with its fully qualified name or with a relative path; the basename command gives you only the name of the script without those variable items.

Note If the script is being run in Setuid[1] mode, the shell will drop the environment variables for security reasons, and the value of $0 will become the name of the shell that is running the script.

This case structure is what allows multiple command names to work. If the name of the command is root_check, we set the fs variable to the / file system. If it is boot_check, we set the fs variable to /boot, and so on. The following example sets only one value in each case, but it could just as easily change many more elements, depending on your needs:

```
case $whatami in
  root_check)
    fs="/"
  ;;
  boot_check)
    fs="/boot"
  ;;
  snap_check)
    fs="/snapshot"
  ;;
  *)
    echo "Don't know what to do. Exiting"
  ;;
esac
```

Once the fs variable is set, all the rest of the code is the same as before.

```
fs_total=`df -k $fs | tail -n 1 | awk '{print $2}'`
fs_used=`df -k $fs | tail -n 1 | awk '{print $3}'`
percent_used=$((100*$fs_used/$fs_total))
echo "$fs is at ${percent_used}% capacity"
```

---

1. Setuid is a permission setting that allows a program to be run as the *owner* of the program instead of as the user who is running the utility.

One interesting item to note with this example is that the Use% column displayed by the df -k command output is significantly different from this script's output, even though they are both supposedly based on the same numbers. The df command is likely performing its calculations with some rounding involved for a quick view of the percentage used instead of the exact value. The df output tends to report a larger value than does the calculated output. The actual difference in calculation wouldn't be known without consulting the source code for the df command.

CHAPTER 14

■ ■ ■

Throttling Parallel Processes

I have often needed to perform a task across multiple remote systems. A common example is the installation of a software package on each machine in a large environment. With relatively small environments, you could simply write a script that loops through a list of systems and performs the desired task serially on each machine. Another method would be to loop through the list of machines and submit your job to the background so the tasks are performed in parallel. Neither of these methods scales well when you run a large environment, however. Processing the list sequentially is not an efficient use of resources and can take a long time to complete.

With too many background parallel processes, the initiating machine will run out of network sockets and the loop that starts all the background tasks will stop functioning. Additionally, even if you were permitted an unlimited number of socket connections, the installation package may be quite large and you might end up saturating your network. You might also have to deal with so many machines that the installations will take an extremely long time to complete because of network contention. In all of these cases you need to control the number of concurrent sessions you have running at any given time.

The scripts presented in this chapter demonstrate a way of controlling the number of parallel background processes. You can then tune your script based on your particular hardware and bandwidth by timing sample runs, and you can play with the number of parallel processes to control the time it takes to run the background jobs. The general idea of this algorithm is that a background job is spawned whose only task is to feed a large list of items back to the parent process at a rate that is controlled by the parent process.

Since not a lot of us have to manage remote jobs on hundreds to tens of thousands of machines, this chapter uses an example that has broader applicability: a script that validates web-page links. The script takes the URL of a web site as input. It gathers the URLs found on the input page, and then gets all the URLs from each of those pages, up to a specified level of depth. It is usually sufficient to carry the process to two levels to gather from several hundred to a few thousand unique URLs.

Once the script has finished gathering the URLs, it validates each link and writes the validation results to a log file. The script starts URL validation in groups of parallel processes for which the size is based on the number specified when the script was called. Once a group starts, the code waits for all the background tasks to complete before it starts the next group. The script repeats the URL validation process until it has checked all web pages passed to it.

You could easily modify the script to manage any parallel task. If you want to focus on URL validation, you could limit the list of URLs to be validated to those residing within your own domain; you would thereby create a miniature web crawler that validates URLs on your own site.

Parallel Processing with ksh

One feature available within ksh is called a *co-process*. This is a process that is run and sent to the background with syntax that allows the background child process to run asynchronously from the parent that called it. Both processes are able to communicate with each other. The following version of the web crawler uses the co-process method.

You start by defining the log file for the script to use, and then you have to determine whether it already exists. If there is a previous version, you need to remove it.

```
#!/bin/ksh
LOGFILE=/tmp/valid_url.log
if [ -f $LOGFILE ]
then
  rm $LOGFILE
fi
```

The main loop calls the url_feeder function as the background co-process task. The function starts an infinite loop that waits for the message "GO" to be received. Once the function receives the message, it breaks out of the loop and continues executing function code.

```
function url_feeder {
  while read
  do
    [[ $REPLY = "GO" ]] && break
  done
```

The script passes this function a variable containing the list of unique URLs that have been collected. The script collects all links based on the starting web-page URL and the link depth it is permitted to search. This loop iterates through each of the pages and prints the links, although not to a terminal. Later I will discuss in greater detail how this function is called.

```
  for url in $*
  do
    print $url
  done
}
```

The find_urls function finds the list of web pages and validates the URLs.

```
function find_urls {
  url=$1
  urls=`lynx -dump $url | sed -n '/^References/,$p' | \
  egrep -v "ftp://|javascript:|mailto:|news:|https://" | \
  tail -n +3 | awk '{print $2}' | cut -d\? -f1 | sort -u`
```

It takes a single web-site URL (such as www.google.com) as a parameter. This is the function that is called as a background task from the script's main code, and it can be performed in parallel with many other instances of itself.

The urls variable contains the list of links found by the lynx command on the page defined by the url variable. This lynx command lists all URLs found on a given site, in output that is easy to obtain and manipulate in text form. To remove links that do not represent web pages, I piped the output of lynx to egrep and ordered and formatted the links with tail, awk, cut, and sort.

Now you need to determine the number of URLs found on the page that was passed to the function. If no URLs were found, then the script checks whether the second positional parameter $2 was passed. If it was, then the function is acting in URL-validation mode and it should log a message stating the page was not found. If $2 was not passed, then the function is acting in URL-gathering mode and it should echo nothing, meaning it didn't find any links to add to the URL list.

```
  urlcount=`echo $urls | wc -w`
  if [ "$urls" = "" ]
  then
    if [ "$2" != "" ]
    then
      echo $url Link Not Found on Server or Forbidden >> $LOGFILE
    else
      echo ""
    fi
```

If a single URL was found and it matches http://www.com.org/home.php, then we log that the web page has not been found. This is a special-case page that lynx will report; you can ignore it.

```
  elif [ $urlcount -eq 1 -a "$urls" = "http://www.com.org/home.php" ]
  then
    if [ "$2" != "" ]
    then
      echo $url Site Not Found >> $LOGFILE
    else
      echo ""
    fi
```

As in the previous section of code, if $2 is not passed, the function is acting in URL-gathering mode.

The following code applies when the URL was found to be valid:

```
else
  if [ "$2" != "" ]
  then
    echo "$url is valid" >> $LOGFILE
  else
    echo " $urls"
  fi
fi
}
```

If this is the case and $2 was passed to the function, you would log that the web page is valid. If $2 was not passed, the unchanged list of URLs would be passed back to the main loop.

The following is the beginning of the code where the script processes the switches passed by the user. The three possible switches define the levels of depth that the script will check, the URL of the beginning site, and the maximum number of processes permitted to run at the same time.

```
OPTIND=1
while getopts l:u:p: ARGS
do
  case $ARGS in
    l) levels=$OPTARG
    ;;
    u) totalurls=$OPTARG
    ;;
    p) max_parallel=$OPTARG
    ;;
    *) echo "Usage: $0 -l [levels to look] -u [url] -p [parallel checks]"
    ;;
  esac
done
```

If the user passes any other parameters, the script prints a usage statement explaining the acceptable script parameters. You can find more detail on the processing of switches in Chapter 5.

The following code shows a nested loop that gathers a complete URL list, starting with the opening page and progressing through the number of levels to be checked by the script. The outer loop iterates through the levels. The inner loop steps through all previously found URLs to gather the links from each page. All URLs found by the inner loop are appended to the totalurls variable. Each pass through this inner loop generates a line of output noting the number of sites found.

```
while [ $levels -ne 0 ]
do
  (( levels -= 1 ))
  for url in $totalurls
```

```
do
  totalurls="${totalurls}`find_urls $url`"
  url_count=`echo $totalurls | wc -w`
  echo Current total number of urls is: $url_count
done
done
```

Now that the whole list has been gathered, we sort it with the -u option to reduce the list to unique values. In this way we avoid redundant checks. Then we determine and output the final number of sites the script found.

```
totalurls=`for url in $totalurls
do
  echo $url
done | sort -u`
url_count=`echo $totalurls | wc -w`
echo Final unique total number of urls is: $url_count
```

This is where the script becomes interesting. You now call the url_feeder function as a co-process by using the |& syntax; then you pass the total list of URLs to process.

```
url_feeder $totalurls |&
coprocess_pid=$!
```

As pointed out before, this is a capability unique to ksh. A co-process is somewhat like a background task, but a pipe acting as a channel of communication is also opened between it and the parent process. This allows two-way communication, which is sometimes referred to as *IPC*, or *interprocess communication*.

The url_feeder function prints out a list of all URLs it receives, but instead of printing them to standard output, the function prints them to the pipe established between the co-process and the parent process. One characteristic of printing to this newly established pipe is that the print being performed by the child co-process won't complete until the value is read from the initiating parent process at the other end of the pipe. In this case, the value is read from the main loop. This allows us to control the rate at which we read new URLs to be processed, because the co-process can output URLs only as fast as the parent process can read them.

Next we initialize a few variables that are used to keep track of the current number of parallel jobs and processed URLs by setting them to zero and then sending the GO message to the co-process. This tells the url_feeder function that it can start sending URLs to be read by the parent process. The print -p syntax is needed because that is how the parent process communicates to the previously spawned co-process. The -p switch specifies printing to an established pipe.

```
processed_urls=0
parallel_jobs=0
print -p "GO"
while [ $processed_urls -lt $url_count ]
```

```
do
  unset parallel_pids
  while [ $parallel_jobs -lt $max_parallel ]
  do
```

The main loop is permitted to continue executing only while there are URLs remaining in the list. While this is the case, the variable for the list of process IDs currently running in parallel needs to be reinitialized and then the internal loop started. The internal loop is where the maximum number of parallel jobs is initiated based on the value that was passed to the script.

Now we have to determine whether we have exhausted the whole list while in the middle of starting a group of parallel jobs. If we have completed running the whole list, we then have to break out of the loop.

```
    if [ $(($processed_urls+$parallel_jobs)) -ge $url_count ]
    then
      break
    fi
```

For, if the total number of URLs to check were 43 and each grouping of parallel jobs were set to a maximum of 20, the third grouping would need to be stopped after 3 jobs.

The script reads a single URL from the established pipe of the co-process. Note that the read command, like the print command, uses the -p switch. Once we have a URL to validate, we call the find_urls function with the v switch to validate the URL. We also send the function call to the background as one of the parallel jobs. Finally, we add the process ID of the background task to the list and increment the number of currently running parallel tasks.

```
    read -p url
    find_urls $url v &
    parallel_pids="$parallel_pids $!"
    parallel_jobs=$(($parallel_jobs+1))
  done
```

To complete the main loop, we wait for all background jobs to complete, then we add the total of those completed jobs to the total number of processed URLs. After that we output the running tally of validated URLs. We then reset the number of parallel jobs to 0 and run the loop again, repeating until the entire list of web sites is processed.

```
  wait $parallel_pids
  processed_urls=$(($processed_urls+$parallel_jobs))
  echo Processed $processed_urls URLs
  parallel_jobs=0
done
```

Parallel Processing with bash

The bash shell doesn't use co-processes. Named pipes, however, fulfill a similar purpose. The term *named pipe* refers to the fact that these pipes have an actual name since they are a special file type that resides in the file system. A named pipe, also referred to as a *FIFO*, or *first in, first out*, is a special type of file that ensures that data written to the file in a particular sequence comes out of the file in the same sequence.

You can create a pipe file with either the mknod or mkfifo command. The mknod command requires the appropriate system-dependent switches, as it can create other special file types. (Refer to your systems man page for more detail.) You can determine a pipe file by the first character position of a long listing (ls -l), as in this example:

```
$ ls -l dapipe
prw-r--r-- 1 rbpeters users 0 Jul 2 21:52 dapipe
```

The permissions and ownership of a pipe file are identical to the permissions and ownership of a traditional file. When writing to or reading from a pipe, the action will appear to hang until the opposite end of the pipe is connected and the data is allowed to pass through, as in this example:

```
$ cat /etc/hosts > dapipe
```

If you display the output of a file using cat and redirect it to the pipe file, the command would appear to hang until another complementary command is issued from a separate session, as in this example:

```
$ cat dapipe
```

When this command is run, the output is delivered from the pipe and the initiating command cat /etc/hosts completes. These characteristics of pipe files are used in the following script to emulate the co-process technique from ksh. By using a named pipe, we can communicate asynchronously with separate processes from our script.

This bash script doesn't perform any real task. It demonstrates the same technique used in the ksh script, but using named pipes. It drives a bash version of the URL-validation script without duplicating unnecessary code.

First we start the script and assign a text string to the thevar variable with some values that the background process will send. We also define the named pipe file that we will use.

```
#!/bin/bash
thevar="one two three four five six"
pipe=/tmp/dapipe
```

The some_function function is analogous to the url_feeder function in the ksh script. It is called as a background task and loops through all the values passed to it; it then writes them to the pipe file one at a time so the main loop can read and process them.

```
some_function () {
  all=$*
  for i in $all
  do
    set -m
    echo $i > $pipe &
    wait
    set +m
  done
}
```

There are a few interesting items in this function. The first is the echo statement that sends the data to the pipe file. This command is sent to the background, and then the wait command is issued to wait for the most recent background task to finish executing. The echo command requires these steps to send the data to the pipe file and force it to "hang" until the parent process has read the data from the other end of the pipe. This is somewhat counterintuitive, but this technique is required for the script to work.

The second group of items is the set -m and set +m lines. These lines, taken together, allow the pipe file to act like a co-process by sending only one data element at a time. When working with pipe files from the command line as demonstrated previously, this isn't necessary, but it is required when running a script. The set -m directive turns on the *monitor* mode, which enables job control. Monitor mode is not set by default for background tasks. Job control allows suspension and resumption of specified tasks. This is the key ingredient to make this script work.

The script calls the function as a background task. It starts the loop that will read the background function output through the pipe file. The loop simply assigns the variable to the value it receives from the pipe file. After every read statement, the backgrounded some_function completes and loops to its next echo output, which is then written to the pipe.

```
some_function $thevar &
for i in 1 2 3 4 5 6
do
  read read_var < $pipe
  echo The read_var is $read_var
  sleep .005s
done
```

The sleep command issued here adds a slight delay to the main loop. When we have two asynchronous loops running at the same time, it is often, but not always, the case that the main loop iterates faster than the background task can send the next value. The delay is then needed to align the two loops, although your mileage may vary and you may need to tune the loops since their speeds are, ultimately, system-dependent.

CHAPTER 15

■■■

Command-Line Editing and History

When working from the command line, you will at some point enter a command multiple times, possibly with minor modifications. In those cases the ability to recall and modify previous commands quickly and efficiently is beneficial. In the old DOS days, a utility called *doskey* would keep your history in a buffer. You could go back or forth through the command history one command at a time by using the up and down arrow keys. Individual commands could be edited by using the cursor and Delete or Backspace keys to make replacements. This basic form of recall and modification of recently typed commands is also available in bash.

Modern shell versions (ksh and bash) also provide more-advanced command-line capabilities. You can set your shell session to act as though you were in a vi editing session. The vi editor has two modes of operation, *insert* and *command*. When typing commands at the prompt, you are working in the shell's equivalent of vi's insert mode. You type a command, use the Backspace key to fix any typing mistakes, and then press Enter to input the command.

When using the shell's vi editing mode, you can press Escape to change to command mode. This allows you to move around on the command line as in vi: you use the H key to move left, the L key to move right, the B key to move one word left, the W key to move one word right, and so on. Once you have positioned the cursor where the modification is to be made, you can press the I key to go back into insert mode and start typing. Many vi commands besides cursor motion are available, such as using the X key to delete a character, pressing D+W to delete a word, pressing Shift+A to append text to the end of the line, and many others that, once you are familiar with the vi editor, will be second nature. In case you're not familiar with vi, there are many online references and tutorials.

In addition to the editing commands, command mode gives you the ability to move through your command history. If you press the Escape key at the command prompt to change to command mode, the J and K keys will move you down and up through the command history list.

Think of your command history as a list in a simple flat file, where the earliest commands in your history are at the top of the list and the most recent ones are at the bottom.

When you enter command mode you start at the bottom of your history and press the K key to move back up through the list. Pressing the J key moves you forward (down) through the history list. Once you have found the desired command, you can make any appropriate modifications and press Enter to run the command.

One last command-history function that has been extremely valuable to me is the ability to search for previous commands that match a pattern. You do this search in the same way as a search in a vi session. First you press Escape to change to command mode and then you press the forward slash (/). This gives you an opportunity to type in a substring to search for within the commands in the history stack. If the first match displayed isn't the correct one, you can press N to see further matches, as you would in vi, until you find the command you're looking for.

I have been using this method to work at the prompt for a long time, and my fingers are accustomed to moving to the correct keys. This has improved my speed and agility immensely when working at the command line. If you're not comfortable with the vi editor, I recommend practicing; vi is the default text editor on UNIX/Linux systems, and you'll certainly have to use it at some point. Although learning the vi editor is not the easiest thing to do, once you are comfortable with it you will be amazed at how powerful it is.

There is also an emacs editing mode available. I recommend the vi mode if you have no previous experience, mainly because it is a more standard tool and is available on all systems. If you're a fan of emacs and comfortable with that editor, then by all means use the emacs mode. The goal here is to become quicker and more efficient.

Setting Up vi Editing

You can configure vi editing for either ksh or bash systemwide or for individual users. You can also configure it right at the command prompt if you like.

bash

With bash there are a few ways to enable the vi editing mode. The first is to modify the inputrc file. There is a systemwide /etc/inputrc file that all users use who have bash set as their shell. There is also an individual .bashrc file that is usually kept in the user's home directory. Adding the following line to one of those two files will enable vi mode:

```
set editing-mode vi
```

Another way to enable vi mode in bash is to modify either the systemwide /etc/profile or the .bash_profile in an individual user's home directory to include the following line:

```
set -o vi
```

ksh

In ksh configuring vi editing mode can once again be set either systemwide or for an individual user. Modifying the systemwide /etc/profile file enables this editing mode for all users, and modifying the .profile file in a user's home directory enables it at an individual level. The line to add to either of these two files is the same as for bash:

```
set -o vi
```

Command and File Completion

One additional option, available in both shells, that increases your efficiency at the command line is command and file completion. With this feature, you can start to type a path or command, and once you've typed a sufficient number of characters for the path or command to be uniquely determined, pressing a special key or key sequence will complete the command. For bash you simply press the Tab key. In ksh, you press either the Tab key or Escape and then a backslash (\)—whichever is your preference. The Escape+\ sequence works only when vi editing mode is set.

Command completion can be explained with a simple example. My shell on the system I'm working on is bash and my home directory is /home/rbpeters. If I wanted to cd to that directory using command completion, I could type the following key sequence:

```
cd /h<TAB>rb<TAB><ENTER>
```

The first TAB would complete the /h to make it /home/ because no other subdirectories of the root directory begin with *h*. The second TAB would complete the /home/rb entry to /home/rbpeters. Pressing Enter then executes the command.

CHAPTER 16

■ ■ ■

Scripting from the Command Line

One of the advantages of working at the shell command line is that you're working in a shell. That sounds sort of obvious and dumb, but please bear with me; pretty much anything you can do in a shell script, you can also do from the command line. I've coded many ad hoc scripts right at the command line. I wouldn't recommend writing anything significant that way, but for quickies it's just the ticket.

If you start a loop or conditional, such as a `while`, `for`, or `if/then` statement, while working at the shell prompt, the command line is extended until you have finished the steps in the code block. In a traditional script, such code would customarily span several lines in a file. Here is a typical interaction with the shell when entering code directly from the command line:

```
$ while : ; do
> clear
> ls -lrt
> sleep 3
> done
```

Note that after the first line is entered and the Enter key is pressed, the command line returns a > prompt to continue the code block. You can then keep adding lines until the loop completes. Once the last line has been entered, in this case the `done` line, the code will begin to run. In our case, it is an infinite loop, which can be stopped by a `<ctrl>-c`.

The following examples are formatted using more traditional indentation for the sake of readability. If you were to enter these from the command line, you would see results similar to those shown above. None of the examples are particularly complex; they are just representative of what can be done from the command line.

A Few Examples

This `while` loop does nothing more than create a long listing of specific files over and over while sleeping for three seconds between iterations. It is part of a set of scripts I use for concurrent package installation on a large number of remote systems. Each concurrent installation produces its own log file that documents its progress and any issues it encounters. All log files are stored in a single directory.

While watching the output of the installation loop, I can tell by the size of the log file when an installation of a specific node is complete. This saves me from having to review each log individually. Successful installations all have log files that end up being of a particular size. Files of a different size stand out and show me that I need to review that log.

Also, watching the growth rate of the files can convey information about how the install is progressing. A typical installation goes something like this: the install package is pushed out to the remote nodes; then the package is uncompressed on each of the remote systems, where the install script is run until it completes. By watching the file size of all log files increase, I can review the status of all installations at once and generally know at which point they have arrived, as well as note any problems, without actually viewing the contents of the log files themselves.

This is a representative example of the miniscript I use for this task:

```
$ while : ; do
>   clear
>   ls -lrt install_log.*
>   sleep 3
> done
```

Note that I use the -lrt switch with ls. This sorts the output by modification time, with the newest files being listed last.

The following miniscript is nothing more than a series of nested for loops:

```
$ for i in 1 2 3 4 5 6 7 8 9
> do
>   for j in 1 2 3 4 5 6 7 8 9
>   do
>     for k in 1 2 3 4 5 6 7 8 9
>     do
>       touch $i$j$k
>     done
>   done
> done
```

I've used this type of script to create large numbers of empty files in a directory. It is the result of an effort to test a monitor script that is supposed to send notifications in case the number of files in a directory exceeds a certain threshold. Another use for it would be to perform a task a specific number of times. In this case there are 729 files created by the 3 nested loops of 9 individual digits. In the example, I could have replaced the touch command with something that didn't reference any of the counter variables ($i, $j, or $k). It could have easily been an echo statement repeating 729 times, but that's just boring.

The last example is something I do fairly regularly. I often want to gather information from each system named in a list of machines. This example shows how to get the list of node names by using a command call within back-ticks (` `). A command string enclosed within back-ticks denotes not the given string, but the string obtained by evaluating the command string and replacing it with what is returned.

```
$ for node in `cat some_nodelist_file`
> do
>    if [ "$node" = "cheese" ]
>    then
>       continue
>    else
>       ssh $node uname -a
>       ssh $node uptime
>    fi
> done
```

In this case, `cat some_nodelist_file` would be replaced with an actual list of nodes originally contained in that file. The file is assumed to contain the list of nodes that are space-delimited or that appear individually on each line of the file, or a combination of both. This loop does not iterate through the file line-by-line.[1] The for loop iterates through each of the nodes. I've also included an if/then statement that will skip any node named "cheese" to provide an example that includes a conditional.

A final trick for using these kinds of scripts efficiently is command-line recall, which is discussed in Chapter 15. If you make a mistake while typing (not unlikely when you're working with many lines at once), you can return to the previous (mistyped) command in your history and then edit the command sequence using vi-style command-line editing. You can also recall a previously entered miniscript for easy modification and reuse.

---

1. To read a file line-by-line where the lines contain more than a single "word," refer to Chapter 10.

## CHAPTER 17

Automating User Input with expect

The expect utility's name suggests precisely what it does: "expect" some output from an interactive program, and send the program some input in response. expect has much more functionality than I cover in this chapter, but this chapter provides a good example of how it can be used. To find more complete information, you can consult the expect manual page.

You may find that when you try to automate a task, the utilities or tools you are using don't lend themselves well to scripting. In the past, use of the format or fdisk command (along with many others) was difficult to automate. Today we have versions of these utilities, such as sfdisk, that are much easier to use within a script. A more modern use of expect might include logging into specialized hardware to gather information or to customize settings, as is required when administering network routers, switches, and firewalls.

This chapter presents a pair of scripts for automating the control of a serial terminal server. This is a type of network-accessible hardware that looks very much like a network hub or a switch with multiple RJ45 ports. Each physical port can be connected to serial devices, such as serial consoles. Once consoles are attached to the terminal server, you can telnet to a specific network port on the terminal server and establish a connection with the attached console.

The first example in this chapter is a shell script that processes user-provided command-line switches that specify what commands to send to the terminal server. The second script, which is called by the first, is an expect script that performs all the manual labor. expect is an extension of the Tcl scripting language. expect was designed to communicate with an interactive program, and it works well with ssh, telnet, ftp, and other interactive utilities.

A Shell Script to Customize Parameters for an expect Script

The first script obtains the user input necessary to connect to the desired terminal server(s) and perform the intended tasks. It displays usage instructions and allows the user to specify a specific terminal server or to provide a file containing node names if there are multiple terminal servers with which the user wants to communicate in the same way and at the same time. First we need to define a few variables:

```
#!/bin/sh
NODE=""
CMDS=""
NODEFILE=""
AUTO=""
USAGE="There is a problem with the command, type $0 -h for syntax"
```

The variables are initialized to null strings, except for the USAGE variable, which contains a message that is displayed whenever the script finds a problem with the command-line call the user provided.

The script gets the information it needs from the user on the command line, so we check that switches have been passed.

```
if [ $# -eq 0 ]
then
  echo $USAGE
  exit 1
fi
```

If no switches are passed to the script, the script displays the usage statement and quits with a nonzero return code (here, 1).

The next section is where the command-line switches are handled.

```
while getopts idhlc:f:n: opt
do
  case $opt in
    i) CMDS="$CMDS \"sho ip\""
    ;;
```

The code uses the getopts construct, which is explained in greater detail in Chapter 5. The -i switch indicates that the terminal server's IP settings should be displayed. It causes the command sho ip to be appended to the CMDS variable, which holds the commands that will be sent to the terminal server.

Next we account for customized commands.

```
    c) CUSTOM_CMD=$OPTARG
       CMDS="$CMDS \"$CUSTOM_CMD\""
    ;;
```

The -c switch is for user-provided terminal-server commands that aren't hard-coded in the script. The user can provide as many such commands as desired when invoking the shell script, as long as a -c option precedes each command and the command itself is double-quoted; most commands interpreted by the terminal server contain multiple words that are space-delimited and so need to be tied together with quotes when the shell script is called.

The OPTARG variable used in handling the -c switch is part of the getopts construct. Note that this switch is followed by a colon in the getopts specification. When a colon follows a switch in the getopts command, getopts will expect some type of argument to follow that switch whenever it is used. OPTARG is the variable that receives the additional argument to the switch. For example, if you had a script that takes a command-line parameter to specify an optional input file, the invocation might look something like this: sample_script -f input_file. The corresponding getopts line would look like this: while getopts f:<other switches> opt, and OPTARG would be set to the string "input_file".

The -h switch causes the script to display its usage information.

```
    h) cat << EOT
Usage:
$0 [-idhl] [-c "custom command"] [-f node_file] [-n node]
where:
-i Sends the "sho ip" command to the Xyplex terminal server
-d Logs in and drops you to the command prompt
-h Displays this information
-l Logs out ports 1-15
-c Takes a custom command and sends it to the terminal server.
   Double quotes are required. You can have as many of these as you like.
-f Defines a file with a list of terminal servers to apply the commands to.
-n Defines a specific node to apply the command to.
EOT
    exit 0
    ;;
```

Note that the cat command is used here to format the output, instead of multiple echo commands. Chapter 28 contains more discussion of free-format output using cat.

The -d switch in the following code indicates that the terminal-server session is not automated, and that the user simply wants to be left at a prompt after logging in:

```
    d) AUTO="no"
    ;;
```

The presence of this switch causes the AUTO variable to be set to no. The expect script examines this variable, and if it is set to no, the expect script leaves the user at the command prompt of the terminal server's shell after logging in, and performs any commands specified via the other options before logging out automatically. (See the following section, "An expect Script to Automate telnet.") If the AUTO variable is left undefined, the script will perform any specified tasks in an automated fashion without any user interaction.

The -l switch adds a command to tell the terminal server to log out all of its serial ports.

```
l) CMDS="$CMDS \"logout por 1-15\""
;;
```

On occasion, a terminal server will have a hung and unresponsive serial port. A command to log it out resets the port and it becomes usable again. The preceding CMDS variable assignment is an example of a command that performs an action on managed hardware. This command is specific to the hardware involved.

The -f switch specifies a file containing a node list (that is, a list of terminal servers).

```
f) NODEFILE=$OPTARG
;;
```

The script loops through the list of terminal servers and performs the specified command(s) against each one.

The -n switch indicates that a specific terminal-server node is the target, rather than those in a list of nodes, as specified using the previous switch.

```
n) NODE=$OPTARG
;;
```

The following are two alternatives for robustness:

```
?) echo $USAGE
   exit 1
;;
*) echo $USAGE
   exit 1
;;
  esac
done
```

If anything besides the anticipated options were provided in the invocation of the script, the script should echo the contents of the USAGE variable to the screen, and exit.

Finally, after processing the switches and building the command list, the script calls the expect script to contact the terminal server. If a NODEFILE was specified using the -f switch, it validates the file and then iterates through it, calling the expect script once for each terminal server with the parameters the user supplied. If a NODEFILE was not specified by the user via the -f switch, the script validates that an individual terminal server was specified with the -n switch and that the NODE variable is not null. If the NODE variable is null, the expect script is called with the appropriate parameters; otherwise it displays the usage string.

```
if [ "$NODEFILE" != "" ]
then
```

```
  if [ -s $NODEFILE ]
  then
    for node in `cat $NODEFILE | grep -v '^#'`
    do
      eval ./xyp_connect $NODE $AUTO $LOGNAME $CMDS
    done
  else
    echo There is a problem with $NODEFILE
  fi
else
  if [ "$NODE" != "" ]
  then
    eval ./xyp_connect $NODE $AUTO $LOGNAME $CMDS
  else
    echo $USAGE
  fi
fi
```

The eval command is used here to evaluate the variables on that line of code once before the code is executed. This is because the CMDS variable may contain terminal-server commands that are, as a result of the processing of the switches, surrounded by backslash-escaped double quotes; these escaped characters must be replaced with unmodified quotes or else the multiple commands will be read incorrectly as one long command. This is also where the call to the xyp_connect expect script that performs the interactive functions takes place.

An expect Script to Automate telnet

The xyp_connect script, an expect script, performs the communication with the interactive program used to connect to the terminal server, in this case telnet. The script starts out by initializing some variables to hold the parameters that the shell script passed to it. These parameters are accessed by their positions in the argument vector, argv[], of the expect script's process. The -f switch in the first line of the following code is used so the script will accept additional command-line options.

```
#!/usr/bin/expect -f
set TERMSERV [lindex $argv 0]
set AUTO [lindex $argv 1]
set USER [lindex $argv 2]
```

The first parameter is the terminal server to which the expect script will attach. The second parameter defines if this will be an automated session in which the expect script performs the work, or an interactive one in which the script simply logs you in and leaves you at the terminal-server shell prompt. The third parameter is the user who is to be logged in.

The next line of the expect script initiates an interactive telnet session with the terminal server.

```
catch {spawn -noecho telnet $TERMSERV 2000}
```

The spawn command starts by trying to establish a telnet connection at the specified port (2000). Port 2000 is being used because of the way this vendor has designed its equipment. Other manufacturers will likely be configured differently. The noecho switch tells expect to avoid echoing on the user's console the command that is being spawned. Finally, a catch command surrounds the whole spawn command. It *catches* the output that is generated by the spawned telnet so that the script can use it later when determining how the telnet command responded.

Once the telnet connection has begun, a timeout should be set to check that the command completes within a reasonable amount of time.

```
set timeout 10
expect {
   timeout { send_user "Telnet timed out waiting for $TERMSERV\n" ; exit }
   "onnection refused" { send_user "Connection was refused to $TERMSERV\n" ; exit }
   "nknown host" { send_user "System $TERMSERV is unknown\n" ; exit}
   "Escape character is '^]'."
}
send "\r"
```

Here we set the timeout period to 10 seconds; following the setting of the timeout is the first true expect command. A single expect command can handle multiple events, performing the appropriate task based on which one is detected. In this case, a number of responses may be received from an attempted telnet connection. A timeout, connection refused, or actual connection are three possibilities. For each type, the code needs to determine the appropriate response to make.

This first expect command handles the three error events that may arise from the telnet attempt. The first event is the timeout. Once 10 seconds have passed with no response, the script displays an error message and exits. The next two events are represented by patterns matching the error messages that may be caught from the telnet invocation in case of failure: "Connection refused" and "Unknown host," respectively. Because the error message may or may not be initial-capped, depending on the telnet server, and we want to handle both possibilities, the first character is not included in the pattern used to match against the caught output. In each event, we use a send_user command to echo the appropriate error output to the user and exit the expect script.

If none of these error conditions occur, then we have successfully begun a telnet session with the terminal server. The previous expect command then has no effect, and the script falls through to the next statement, send "\r". But the terminal server does not yet know this. Once we are attached to the terminal server, there is no further reply from it until it receives a single carriage return from us. This send command delivers that carriage return, at which point both parties know that we have arrived via telnet at the point just prior to login. Now comes the interaction for the actual login to the terminal server.

If expect succeeds in establishing a telnet connection, the caught output consists of the success string, which for our terminal server is the pound or hash sign, #. When the script detects this response, it proceeds with expect commands, implementing the login dialogue.

Our particular terminal-server hardware will by default take anything for the initial username and not require a password. The expect script here assumes these factory defaults. You may need to change this dialogue to match your environment. (For example, it would be fairly simple to add another switch to the shell script allowing the password to be given from the command line, so that the login/password would not be hard-coded in an unencrypted text file.)

```
expect "#" { send "access\r" }
expect "username>" { send "$USER\r" }
expect ">" { send "set priv\r" }
expect "Password>" { send "system\r" }
expect ">>"
```

In our case, the basic login is complete when the > character is received in reply for the username; however, to perform administrative tasks on the terminal server, we must upgrade privileges via a set priv command. As shown in the preceding code, the default password for this level of access is system, and once you're logged in at the privileged level, you receive a >> prompt.

Next we check whether the AUTO variable is set to no. Recall that the value of this variable was passed to the expect script as a parameter, and allows the script to determine whether the user wants to perform a command or a set of commands on the terminal server, or simply wants to be left logged in to perform her own administration.

```
if { "$AUTO" == "no" } {
  send_user "Script ended: You have been dropped to the command line\n"
  send "\r"
  interact
  exit
}
```

If AUTO is set to no, a message is sent to the user that the script has completed its run and control of the terminal server session will now be handed over to the user. The next-to-last interact command in this part of the script carries out this handover before exiting.

If the script reaches this point, then AUTO has not been set to no, and there may be terminal-server commands that were intended for the expect script that were included in the shell script's command line as described earlier. Next we determine the number of these parameters and assign that value to argc.

```
set argc [llength $argv]
for {set i 3} {$i<$argc} {incr i} {
  send "[lindex $argv $i]\r"
  expect ">>"
}
```

This code lets us know when to stop looking in the expect script's argument vector argv for terminal-server commands. Each time through the for loop, a terminal-server command is sent; after the command finishes running, a >> prompt should be received before the next command is issued. (The loop starts at 3 because the first few parameters, at index positions 0, 1, and 2, are those that were used earlier by the expect script: AUTO, TERMSERV, and USER.)

When the list of commands has been processed and all commands have been sent, we perform the telnet logout dialog.

```
send "^]"
expect "telnet>"
send "quit\r"
send_user "\n"
```

The first send command in this code segment contains a single special character—not a caret followed by a right square bracket, but rather a Ctrl+] character. To enter the special character in vi's insert mode, you would press Ctrl+v and then Ctrl+]. The Ctrl+v command tells vi to insert the following key sequence as a Ctrl character sequence, without attempting to interpret it. (Another example of this type of vi editing maneuver might be to replace Ctrl+] with Enter, which would specify a carriage return sequence and be displayed as ^M.)

Sending the ^] special character causes the script to break out of the active telnet connection and drops you to the telnet's interactive prompt. At this point the script sends a quit command to the terminal server and the telnet session closes. After the telnet port connection closes with the quit command, expect sends the user a final carriage return, \n, to ensure that when the script finishes cleanly, the user will be back at her usual shell prompt.

## CHAPTER 18

User Input Timeout

Sometimes you want a program that accepts user input to run automatically. If the user does not type anything within a specified amount of time, the program should continue running and use a default value for input.

A boot loader is a good example of this type of application. It would give the user a prompt where they will be able to choose the OS or kernel to be booted, but if the user lets the timeout expire, the boot loader uses a previously defined default operating system to boot the system.

An automated system-build script is another example. I wrote one to perform an automated system build while running from a bootable CD. This script would allow the user to choose how to build the system. If there were no response within a predetermined amount of time, the script would continue, using the default build option.

There are several ways to write a script that will time out while waiting for user input, yet continue to run. The first method in this chapter is a brute-force method I devised. It is simple and demonstrates what you can do with multiple processes. The second and third methods are a bit more elegant.

Manual Timeout Method

The code in the following set of three scripts doesn't perform any real action, but it does demonstrate a general framework that can be used to perform timeout-enabled input. The first script was originally a main shell program that prompted the user to decide whether to perform or to skip a specific type of disk partitioning. The main script called two other scripts. The first subsidiary script prompts the user to enter a choice and the second subsidiary script kills the process running the first subsidiary script after a timeout has elapsed, thereby allowing the main script to continue even if no user response is received.

This set of scripts operates as follows: First, the main script invokes the subsidiary `killit` script to run in the background, where it waits for a set amount of time. After that time period has passed, the `killit` script wakes up and checks to see if a second process spawned by the main script to read the user's input (`readit`) is still running. If the `readit` process is still running, the `killit` process terminates it. If the `readit` process does not exist, the killit process exits quietly. In either case, the main script continues with other tasks after the readit process has terminated.

The following code is a template for the initiating script, called buildit. It calls the two helper scripts (killit and readit), and its purpose is to determine and display the return code from the readit script. In a genuine application (as opposed to our template), the main script would be able to establish its next course of action based on that return code.

```
#!/bin/sh
HOMEDIR=$HOME/scripts
$HOMEDIR/killit &
$HOMEDIR/readit
ans=$?
echo The return code is: $ans
```

Next, is a template for a readit script. This template displays the chosen timeout value and asks for input from the user. It requires only a simple yes or no answer, but it could just as easily accept a more complex question with more than two possible answers. Once the user has given a response, the script exits with the appropriate return code.

```
#!/bin/sh
echo Timeout in 3 seconds...
echo -e "Do you want to skip or not? (y and n are valid):"
read ans
ans=`echo $ans | tr "[A-Z]" "[a-z]"`
if [ "$ans" = "y" ]
then
  exit 1
else
  exit 2
fi
```

Finally, the following is an example of a killit script. It puts itself to sleep for the predetermined timeout period (three seconds) and then checks the process table for a running readit script. If the readit script is found, the killit script assumes after awakening that the user hasn't answered the question from the readit script yet and that the readit script has waited long enough. The killit script then kills the readit process, thereby allowing the calling script, buildit, to continue.

```
#!/bin/sh
sleep 3
readit_pid=`ps -ef | grep readit | grep -v grep | awk '{print $2}'`
if [ "$readit_pid" != "" ]
then
  kill $readit_pid
fi
```

There are a couple items to note when using this method of timing out while waiting for user input. First, the return code returned by the buildit script may be a value other than what is defined in the readit code, and probably won't be obvious. When the readit script terminates normally, after the user enters an appropriate value, the return code displayed by the buildit script will be either 1 or 2. However, if the killit script kills the readit script, the readit script does not generate a return code. The shell recognizes that a process has been terminated and it assigns to that process a return value that is the sum of a specified value and the kill signal that was used to kill it. The specified value returned by the buildit script depends on the shell. The specified value of a process terminated in bash is 128 plus the terminating signal value, whereas in ksh it is 256. Assuming bash for our example, one of the most common signals for terminating a process would be 15 (or SIGTERM) and the return code would be 143 (the sum of 128 and 15). If the "kill it no matter what" signal of 9 (SIGKILL) were used, the return code would be 137. There are many different terminating signals; these are just two of the most common.

Second, when the readit process is killed, it generates a message that is sent to the stderr (standard error) I/O stream of the main buildit script, stating that the process was killed. If you don't want to see that message, you will have to deal with that output, for example by redirecting the stderr of the buildit script to a file or to /dev/null.

Timeout Using stty

The second method of handling a user timeout is based on some cool features of stty. It is also more elegant, as you don't need to write several scripts or spawn jobs that run in the background. The stty command lets you list and modify line settings of your terminal. It can be used to define various keystrokes such as ^+C or Backspace. We will use the stty command's min and time settings. Both must be used with the -icanon switch, which disables canonical-mode input processing. In this mode, normal input that usually is read as a whole line is disabled and input bytes are then controlled by the min and time settings.

```
#!/bin/sh
/usr/bin/echo -n "Input a letter or wait 3 seconds: "
stty -icanon min 0 time 30
```

The min value is the minimum number of characters for a complete read of user-requested input. We set the value to 0 so the read will always be complete, even if there is no input from the user. The time value is the timeout measured in tenths of a second. This is much more fine-grained than the earlier example code that used full seconds to measure time using the sleep command.

Once you've set the stty values, the script uses the dd command as shown in the following code to receive input from the user and to save that input (if the input is received within the timeout period) in the ANSWER variable:

```
ANSWER=`dd bs=1 count=1 2>/dev/null`
stty icanon
echo ; echo Answer: $ANSWER
```

In this case, only a single character will be received. If user input is to exceed one character, you would need to increase the `min` value of `stty` and modify the `count` value of the `dd` command to match the required input.

Here the `stty` settings are reset to normal and the answer is displayed. However, in a "real" application script, the presence or absence of an answer from the user would have to be tested and handled by subsequent code.

In current versions of both the `ksh` and `bash` shells, the built-in `read` command has a timeout option (`-t seconds`). This takes all the difficulty out of user input.

General Timeout Utility

The final utility[1] in this chapter is much like the design of the manual method discussed previously, but is much simpler and is self-contained. Instead of requiring three separate scripts, this single function handles all the work. It is also not specific to user-input applications. It can be used for any type of command to which you may want a timeout value applied. Since this is a self-contained utility, it is a good candidate for addition to a shell library discussed in Chapter 2.

I recently used this method for setting a timeout value within a system monitor that attempts an `ssh` to a remote machine. In some cases a system will seem to be alive based on a `ping` result, but an attempted connection to the machine will hang forever. This is where the timeout ability is required.

The first half of the function sets the timeout value and the command that is received from the function call. It then runs the command in the background and determines the process ID of that backgrounded task.

```
timeout()
{
  waitfor=5
  command=$*
  $command &
  commandpid=$!
```

The second half is where the cleverness lies. First the function sends a combination of two commands to the background. The first command is a `sleep` that delays for the specified amount of time. The second command kills the original process after the `sleep` completes.

```
(sleep $waitfor ; kill -9 $commandpid >/dev/null 2>&1) &
watchdogpid=$!
sleeppid=`ps $ppid $watchdogpid | awk '{print $1}'`
```

---

1. This script is based on an idea by Heiner Stevens. You can find the original implementation at http://shelldorado.com/scripts/cmds/timeout.txt/.

```
  wait $commandpid
  kill $sleeppid >/dev/null 2>&1
}
```

Once this combination of commands is backgrounded, the background process ID is determined. The function then waits for the original backgrounded process to complete, whether it was killed or not. If the original backgrounded process completes normally and doesn't need to be killed, the function kills the backgrounded watchdog process.

■ ■ ■

## CHAPTER 19

Instant Keyboard Response

There are times you may want to enter some input or perform an action without having to use the Enter key. A while back, I encountered this problem when I needed to view the numerical output of ballistic equations. I wanted to be able to increment or decrement an input value and recalculate the results by pressing just one key. I came up with a script that would do this, and display both the changed input value and the new results calculated from it. The example script here, while interesting, is just a simple demonstration of how to process instant response.

My script accomplished its task quite well. The following script is a simplified version that calculates and displays the values for a projectile's trajectory. The user can set the launch angle and the firing velocity in the manner described. The script will then display the projectile's distance, maximum height, and duration of flight.

First we initialize some variables and, because we will alter the terminal settings, we save the current settings so that we can restore them later.

```
#!/bin/sh
old_stty_settings=$(stty -g) # Save original settings.
stty -icanon
theta=0
velocity=0
distance=
height=
time=
```

To do the keystroke processing, we have to first set up the terminal using stty. We then obtain keystrokes using the head (or dd) command, as described later in this chapter. Here, setting stty with the -icanon switch disables canonical mode for terminal manipulation. This changes input data from being read as a whole line to a more fine-grained byte-based input. The first two attributes of the –icanon switch (erase and kill) enable the special characters that will erase the last character typed and erase the current line, respectively. The last two attributes (werase and rprnt) aren't very common. The werase attribute enables the special character that will erase the last word typed, whereas rprnt enables the special character that redraws the current line on the screen. For more information, review the stty man page.

The script consists of a loop that repeatedly computes trajectory values based on the current inputs and then updates the input values based on the user's keystrokes.

The following code section is where the calculations are performed for the values we seek. Every iteration of the loop recalculates the projectile's distance, height, and duration.[1]

```
while :
do
    # convert the angle from degrees to radians
    angle=`echo "scale=5;$theta/57.29578" | bc -l`
    # gravity is 9.8m/s^2
    distance=`echo "scale=5;(($velocity^2)*2*(s($angle))*(c($angle)))/9.8" | bc -l`
    height=`echo "scale=5;(($velocity*s($angle))^2/(2*9.8))" | bc -l`
    time=`echo "scale=5;(2*($velocity*s($angle))/(9.8))" | bc -l`
```

The value of the angle variable is the radian equivalent of the theta value, which is expressed in degrees. The bc utility performs trigonometric functions in radians, so this conversion must be performed before angles can be used. The -l switch used with bc is required to load the standard math library that allows bc to evaluate trigonometric functions, such as the cosine of the angle. The scale value that is passed to bc sets the number of decimal places that follow the decimal point. More information on shell math functions can be found in Chapter 11.

Next the script outputs usage instructions that inform the user how to vary the launch angle and velocity and how to quit the program, plus displays the values just calculated from the current values of launch angle and velocity.

```
clear
echo "j to decrease launch angle --- k to increase launch angle"
echo "h to decrease launch velocity --- l to increase launch velocity"
echo
echo "x or q to exit."
echo
echo "Launch angle deg.=$theta Velocity M/s=$velocity"
echo
echo "Distance: $distance meters"
echo "Maximum height: $height meters"
echo "Flight Time: $time seconds"
```

The next command is the central one for handling the input of the script.[2] Here each character the user enters is assigned to the Keypress variable.

```
Keypress=$(head -c1)
# Keypress=$(dd bs=1 count=1 2> /dev/null)
```

---

1. Trajectory calculations can be found at http://hyperphysics.phy-astr.gsu.edu/hbase/traj.html.
2. Thanks to Stephane Chazelas, who supplied the keypress-detection code found on http://tldp.org/LDP/abs/html/system.html.

Note that two commands could be used. The head command on many UNIX systems normally displays only the first few lines of a file. The GNU version of the head command, however, has a -c option, as shown here. The -c switch specifies how many bytes or characters of data to display. The line of code that has been commented out uses the dd command to do the same thing; this command, with the bs (block size) set to 1 byte and a count of 1, is functionally the same as the head -c1 command. You will need only one of these lines. I've shown both here because not all UNIX systems have the GNU version of head that has the -c switch, and I wanted to include an alternative command that can be used on both GNU and non-GNU systems.

Once the Keypress variable has been assigned, you have to decide how to process it.

```
case $Keypress in
  j|J)
    if [ $theta -ne 0 ]
    then
      theta=$(($theta-1))
    else
      theta=90
    fi
  ;;
  k|K)
    if [ $theta -ne 90 ]
    then
      theta=$(($theta+1))
    else
      theta=0
    fi
  ;;
```

For each of the valid value-updating keystrokes, the new values are validated. In the case of the launch angle, the valid values lie between 0 and 90 degrees. If the angle is going to become greater than 90 or less than 0, we roll the variable to the opposite end of the valid range. If the current angle theta were 90 degrees and you wanted to add another degree, the value of theta would be reset to zero. The converse happens when decrementing an angle of 0 degrees.

The launch velocity should, of course, have only a positive value. If the value for some reason goes below 0, we reset it to 0. There is no upper bound on this value, so you can increase the initial velocity as much as you like.

```
  h|H)
    if [ $velocity -ne 0 ]
    then
      velocity=$(($velocity-1))
    else
      velocity=0
    fi
```

```
    ;;
    l|L)
      velocity=$(($velocity+1))
    ;;
```

Note that the keys used to increment and decrement the input values were chosen to match the keys used for cursor movement within vi, where J is down, K is up, H is left, and L is right.

If one of the keys to quit is pressed, we break out of the loop. Otherwise the next iteration of the loop displays the recalculated trajectory values and waits for more input.

```
    q|Q|x|X)
      break
    ;;
  esac
done
```

Finally, the script resets the terminal settings to the original values and exits cleanly.

```
stty "$old_stty_settings"
exit 0
```

CHAPTER 20

■ ■ ■

Directory Copying

Copying files from one place to another seems a trivial task hardly worth mentioning in an advanced shell-scripting book. However, copying groups of files with the typical cp command doesn't result in a true copy. You might expect an exact duplicate of the source files, but there may be soft links, hard links, subdirectories, pipes, dot files, and regular files, among others, and the cp command doesn't work as you might expect with all of them. You need to make a few tweaks to get a copy command that performs well for all file and link types. For testing purposes, I created a directory that contains some of each of these file types that can be used to check whether the copy has been performed correctly.

Using cp

The following is the cp command that comes the closest to duplicating the test directory:

```
cp -Rp * /dest/dir
```

The -R option tells cp to recurse through the directory structure it is copying; the -p option preserves permissions, ownership, and access and modification times of the original files. The copy is based on the access rights of the user performing the copy.

However, the actual functionality of the cp command falls short of expectations. Symbolic links in the destination directory are created with the modification time noting when the copy was performed, not when the original files were created, although this shouldn't be a significant issue since the actual files that are linked keep their original modification time. The main issue with the cp command is that hard links are not maintained. Hard links are copied as individual files; they are not treated as links to the same file. This may result in a significant storage issue if you have many hard links whose copies no longer conserve disk space as duplicate files.

Newer versions of the cp command have an -a switch. This option preserves as many source-file attributes as possible, including hard links.

```
cp -a * /dest/dir
```

In its application memory, the cp command keeps track of files that contain a link count greater than one. This works fine for relatively small copies, but has the potential downside that during execution the process could run out of memory and fail because of an excessive number of hard links that need caching.

Using tar

One possible alternative to the cp command is tar. tar was originally intended for backup tape archives, but it has the ability to send its output to stdout and to receive stdin as input.

```
tar cvf - * | (cd /dest/dir && tar xvfp -)
```

Thus, you can create a tar archive with the c option (create; often used with v for verbose and f for file) and use the - switch to send output to stdout through a pipe. On the other end of the pipe you have to attach a succession of commands: first a cd to take you to the intended destination directory, and second an extracting tar command that receives the data stream via stdin and then saves the files to the intended target. This tar command is combined with the first tar command prior to the pipe by using the short-circuit && operator to make its execution dependent on the success of the cd.

With this method the files are copied correctly, and hard links and their modification times are preserved. Soft links still have the date of archive extraction as the creation date, instead of the creation date of the original link that was being copied. The main problem with this command is that the wild card * does not capture all files hiding in the source directory. It will miss dot (or hidden) files. I have seen examples where regular expressions are used to gather all files, but there is another way.

Using find

Replacing the wild card that gathers all the files in the source directory with a find command is a simple way of retrieving all files and directories.

```
find . -depth | xargs tar cvf - | (cd ../tar_cp/ && tar xvfp -)
```

The -depth option minimizes permission problems with directories that are not writable or not searchable; you can deal with the latter by processing a directory's contents before the directory itself. The list of files found by recursively searching the source directory is then passed to the tar command via xargs. The rest of the command is the same as in the previous example.

This command pipeline will not only copy directories from one location on an individual machine to another, but also copy files across the network using ssh. Simply add the ssh command to the pipeline, and the files will arrive at the correct place.

```
find . -depth | xargs tar cvf - | \
  ssh machine_name 'cd /dest ; mkdir dir ; cd dir ; tar xvfp -'
```

Note In the example I create the destination directory prior to extracting the archive. This can also be performed using rsh instead of ssh, but I wouldn't recommend it because rsh is not an encrypted protocol and is therefore vulnerable to interception.

If you are more familiar with cpio than with tar, you may want to use the following command, which is the equivalent of the combination of find and tar:

```
find . -depth | cpio -dampv {/dest/dir}
```

The modification times of destination soft links and directories are still set to the time when the command was run. The options to cpio used here are as follows: -d creates directories as needed, -a resets the access time of the original files, -m preserves the modification time of the new files, and -v lists the files being processed to keep you apprised of the command's progress. The most important option here is -p. This switch puts cpio into a "copy pass-through" mode, which acts like a copying operation as opposed to an archive creation. This is somewhat like the *tar create piped to tar extract*—tar cvf - * | (cd /dest/dir && tar xvfp -)—command example presented earlier, but it achieves its goal with only one command.

As with tar, you can combine cpio with ssh and copy files across a network connection to another machine.

```
find . -depth | ssh machine_name 'cpio -dampv /dest/dir'
```

The main concern is to ensure that the destination directory exists. You could add directory-creation commands to the ssh command line as shown earlier in this chapter, so that you won't have the archive files incorrectly dumped in the destination's parent directory.

Using rsync

One final option for copying a directory is rsync, which was originally intended to be an expanded version of rcp. The rsync utility has an archive switch -a that allows it to perform a copy of a directory that includes dot files while maintaining all permissions, ownership, and modification times. The -v switch is used for verbose mode. Once again, the destination soft links have the modification time of when the copy was performed, but that shouldn't matter much. This is a very slick way of copying files.

When using the following command, there is a very subtle syntax difference that you may use but will have quite different results:

```
rsync -av /src/dir/ /dest/dir
```

The directory will be copied well enough, but the destination location may not be what you expected. If you use the preceding command, the contents of /src/dir will be copied to /dest/dir. If you remove the trailing / from the /src/dir/ string, as in /src/dir, the directory itself will be copied into /dest/dir. In that case you'll end up with /dest/dir/dir.

rsync has the added benefit for which it was originally intended of performing copies to remote machines across the network, as well as many other options that are beyond the scope of this discussion. Remote copies can also be performed with ssh (using the -e switch to specify the remote shell to use) for increased security. In the following example, the source directory is located on a remote machine but the remote machine could either be the source or destination:

```
rsync -av -e ssh user@remotehost:/src/dir/ /local/dest/dir/
```

This last rsync command adds the -z switch:

```
rsync -avz -e ssh user@remotehost:/src/dir/ /local/dest/dir/
```

This performs the remote copy in the same way as before but also includes compression in the remote transfer to reduce network traffic.

Most of these options and syntax variations are rather cumbersome to remember; so I wouldn't have to remember the code, I wrote a small script that copies directories.

```
#!/bin/sh
if [ $# -ne 2 ]
then
  echo Usage: $0 {Source Directory} {Destination Directory}
exit 1
fi
```

This script is used much like a standard cp command, except that the source and destinations aren't files but rather directories. It first validates the number of parameters passed to it and outputs a usage statement if the count is incorrect.

Then you need to set the source and destination variables.

```
SRC=$1
DST=$2
if [ ! -d $DST ]
then
  mkdir -p $DST
fi
```

This isn't a required step, but variables like SRC and DST are more readable to humans than 1 and 2. You also need to determine whether the destination directory exists. If the directory does not exist, it will be created. Some additional code to validate the existence of the source directory might be useful here.

Finally, you can now perform the directory copy via the command line that uses find and tar. You could easily replace the find/xargs/tar combination with whatever copy method you want to use, such as cpio or rsync.

```
find $SRC -depth | xargs tar cvf - | (cd $DST && tar xvfp -)
```

■ ■ ■

## CHAPTER 21

A Brief Tour of the X Display Environment

This chapter is not an exhaustive discussion of the X Window System architecture; there are many books devoted to this topic. I will, however, explain how to send windows to remote displays. In short, an X-enabled application (xterm, xclock, xeyes, etc.) can be run from one system and the display (that is, the window) can be viewed on a totally separate system.

The variants of the Microsoft Windows operating system cannot export the display of an individual application to be viewed on a separate machine. If an application runs on one of those systems, the user can see the display only on that system if he is logged in directly to the console. A separate application, called a *remote desktop manager*, makes it possible to view a whole desktop as opposed to an individual application remotely across the network. X-enabled programs are different in that they have the ability to set display details at the individual application level. The X Window System (or *X*) allows a user to run individual programs on multiple remote systems while viewing them all locally on a single display. I will demonstrate this functionality in Chapter 22 when discussing the X Navigation Window.

Now, how is this related to shell scripting? Part of scripting consists of understanding system capabilities that you can exploit in your scripts. This chapter explains some of the basic settings and utilities for displaying X client applications that a shell script can exploit.

The Display

X applications consist of a client and a server. In X, however, the relationship between clients and servers is confusing because it is quite different from what you might assume. The X client is an application program, such as xclock or xterm, and the location of the viewable display is called the server (or display server), since it is *serving* the application's graphical display functions.

Some common X servers are XFree86 and X.org on Linux and other UNIX-related operating systems, and Exceed and Cygwin/X on Windows. There are many more.

Once you have one of these X servers running on your system, you can send to it the display data of an X-enabled application's user interface. Let's assume you're running an X server on a laptop and the X application (i.e., client) that you want to run is located on a remote system. You can arrange to have the application output display on the laptop. The following paragraphs will shed more light on this scenario.

First you need to understand the DISPLAY variable. The -display option is critical to all X applications because it denotes the network location to which the display output will be sent. A display consists of nothing more than a system name or IP address followed by a colon and a number. An example is ron.mydomain.com:0, which is display 0 on the system with the domain name ron.mydomain.com. If you are working on the console of a system that has an X server running and you start an X application on that system, it is not necessary to specify the local system name, as it is the default value. Thus the display for a local system where the X server and client are both running is commonly called simply :0. An X server can be configured to have multiple displays, each of which is identified by a number; zero is the most commonly used as the primary display.

Here is what an invocation of xclock, specifying the display on the command line, would look like:

```
/usr/bin/xclock -display ron.mydomain.com:0 &
```

Another way to set your display is with an environment variable. The environment variable checked by all X applications when they run to determine the display server is DISPLAY. If DISPLAY is set correctly prior to running the application, the -display switch is not required. Setting the value is simple but depends on the shell you're running:

```
export DISPLAY=ron.mydomain.com:0
```

Any X applications started after the DISPLAY variable is set will use that value and the application window will show up on that X server. Of course, I could set my display variable to rons_friend.mydomain.com:0 and send the application display to that system instead of to my own. Technically, this is perfectly reasonable. However, while there can be valid reasons for this action, you can see how it could present you with potential security problems.

This brings us to the xhost utility, which gives you the ability to allow or to restrict X applications from displaying on your X server. This power is traditionally called *access control*. The xhost command to limit access has the form xhost [+|-]nodename|username, where the plus sign allows access and the minus sign disallows access. This gives you fine-grained control of what systems and users have access to your X server. Using the xhost + command disables all access control, and any users or systems will be able to send displays to your X server, although normally this is not what you would want. By default, the security denies access to those not specifically allowed.

X Traffic Through ssh

One of the downsides of X network traffic is that it isn't secure. A malicious third party able to view X network traffic can listen in on your sessions and log keystrokes, view the windows you are viewing, or even hijack the session. This isn't a good thing. One good way to tighten up the security of X traffic across the network is to use ssh, the secure shell.

You can use the ssh utility to tunnel pretty much any network protocol across an encrypted connection, including X traffic. In this case, the insecure X protocol is being packaged and carried within the secure encrypted ssh protocol. As long as the ssh server and client are configured correctly, X traffic is tunneled securely but otherwise acts exactly the same as if there were no encrypted connection. There is a little overhead, however, since all traffic has to be encrypted before being sent.

You must configure a few settings on the sshd server and the ssh client to implement X protocol tunneling. The option for X11Forwarding in the sshd_config file should be set to yes. Then the sshd process should be restarted to enable the new configuration. There is also an option on the ssh client side to enable X forwarding or tunneling. To enable it from the command line, you add -X (when using OpenSSH) to the ssh command. However, on Linux and Solaris systems X forwarding is enabled without using the switch; the Cygwin ssh client requires the -X switch.

There are many ssh clients, each of which has a number of settings to enable X forwarding. One popular client is PuTTY, which is a free implementation of telnet and ssh for Windows and UNIX platforms. Once you have created a session, you enable X forwarding by clicking Connection ➤ SSH ➤ X11. There is a check box on this screen to 'Enable X11 Forwarding'.

Once the ssh session is configured, you can start your X server then open your ssh session to the remote system and log in. At that point, you can start an X application using the ssh session, and the application window will come up on your local X server.

Caution When enabling tunneling under X, there is a file called .Xauthority in the user's home directory on the remote system. It contains the authorization information for connecting to the X server. This file should be readable only by its owner. If another user on the remote system has the ability to read that file, that user will have access to your display through the forwarded connection. The user may then be able to monitor keystrokes processed by your X server.

X Applications Through a Third-Party System

As just mentioned, the .Xauthority configuration file contains the authorization for a specific user to attach to and use a specific display. Suppose you have an environment comprising various systems that you want to access via the Internet, and you want to use X applications from those systems. However, for security reasons you have ssh access only through a single portal system, and thus you don't have direct access to all of the machines in your environment. What do you do?

If your Internet-facing system has its ssh daemon set as described, then once you open your initial ssh session you will have a secure connection through which to send X traffic. Enabling all other systems in the environment to use this secure link is just a matter of giving them the appropriate authority to link up to the original session.

To make this simple, the following example consists of a three-system environment. Machine A is the machine you're working on, and it has an X display server running. The Internet-facing remote ssh server B is the machine with which you open an ssh session; this is where you will create a secure tunnel through which to pass X traffic destined for the X server on A. Machine C is the box behind the ssh server; the ssh server portal machine can access it, but that machine is not directly accessible from the Internet. Assume that system C does not have ssh enabled, although there is an X application there that you need to access.

First, we open an X-enabled ssh session between systems A and B. Then we obtain the X authority information for that session. You can view this information by running the command xauth list on system B; it shows you all sessions and displays contained in your .Xauthority file. Here are a few sample lines from the output on my system:

```
casper:17  MIT-MAGIC-COOKIE-1  47c872e9b9e62080749e3f6cb601e173
casper:16  MIT-MAGIC-COOKIE-1  d778834a45880121769f333b41a119d1
casper:15  MIT-MAGIC-COOKIE-1  427868f7541d8f1a84538841fd362a3f
casper:14  MIT-MAGIC-COOKIE-1  95bacf26a4e6ab10c6a5bf95ac228ad8
```

Each record of this xauth output represents a specific display, shown in the first field of each line. The second field shows the protocol used for creating the token to allow access to that display. The last field is the 128-bit hex token that is presented to the X server by the client that authorizes the application to be displayed.

To extract the authority information for the current display in a usable form and send it to a file called xauth-cookie_file, run the following command:

```
xauth nextract - $DISPLAY > xauth_cookie_file
```

The DISPLAY variable is set automatically when the ssh session is opened, so this should work. Note the DISPLAY value, though. The output from this xauth command consists of a long list of characters that represents the token for the current session. The xauth_cookie_file can then be moved to the remote system (Machine C) and merged into the .Xauthority file on that system. This is done by running the following command on Machine C after copying the file there:

```
xauth nmerge - < xauth_cookie_file
```

To validate the entry that has been added, run the 'xauth list' command again, but this time on Machine C. Now that authorization for Machine C to connect to the display on Machine A is in place, the last task is to set the DISPLAY variable for the X client on

Machine C to use. For this example, we'll take the last line from the xauth list sample output shown previously to be our current DISPLAY.

Notice that the display number is 14, instead of 0 as it was earlier.

```
export DISPLAY=casper:14
```

Since the ssh server can have many tunneled X sessions attached at the same time, the display number increases with the number of sessions attached to the ssh server. Also, when you set the DISPLAY variable, you may need to fully qualify the name of the display system (Machine B) in order for Machine C to know which system should be attached. You may recognize a small oddity in that the DISPLAY variable is set to Machine B instead of Machine A, where the X server is running. This is because you are attaching to one end of the ssh tunnel. The other end of the tunnel is on Machine A, which is where the application is actually displayed.

The authority and display are now set on Machine C. You should be able to run an X application on Machine C, and its display will be sent to the X session that is being tunneled through Machine B via ssh. The display information will travel through the tunnel and show up on Machine A.

Caution The X traffic traveling between Machine C and Machine B is *not* encrypted, and the usual security concerns for unencrypted X traffic should be noted for this connection. Our model assumes that Machines B and C are part of a single trusted environment, and that the security boundary is between them and Machine A.

User-Profile Entry

One way to make this procedure a lot simpler is to include commands in the system or personal profile (i.e., in the /etc/profile or ~/.profile file that runs on login) that create a file containing the current authorization cookie and the current value of the DISPLAY variable. Additional code then checks for that file, merges the authorization cookie into the remote system's .Xauthority file (using xauth -nmerge), and sets the DISPLAY variable. This makes the X experience seamless. Keep in mind that security issues relating to remote file access still apply.

If your home directory is NFS-mounted to a central location, the process is even easier. All that is required is to add these entries to your personal .profile or .bash_profile. All the systems in the environment will then have access to the same ssh tunnel session.

You would use the following code in your personal .profile or .bash_profile file in an environment where home directories are NFS-mounted. The main idea of the code is that you would create the configuration files that contain the .Xauthority information and the DISPLAY value when you initially log into the machine used to set up the encrypted tunnel via ssh. After that, when you log into any other system in the environment, you then simply gather these settings from the configuration files that were created, using them to import the saved authority value into the .Xauthority file and to set the DISPLAY variable.

This first if statement in the following code applies when you log into the node in your environment where the ssh server used to tunnel X is located. (The code assumes you are using an ssh client with X forwarding enabled.)

```
if [ "`uname -n`" = "casper" ] && [ "$REMOTEHOST" != "casper" ] \
  && [ "$DISPLAY" != "" ]
```

An X session is created on only a single system. If the three conditions in this test are fulfilled, then we are on that single machine and the files containing the display and authority information should be created. The first condition checks if the node logged into is named casper This is the name of my ssh server; you'll want to modify this as appropriate for your server.

The second condition checks whether the value of the REMOTEHOST variable is casper. The check is needed for the window.sh script that is called in the body of the if statement. (This is an X utility called the X Navigation Window and is explained in Chapter 22.) It is also needed because you don't want to re-create the configuration files if you ssh to the local system (casper in this case).

The final condition determines if the DISPLAY variable is set. The DISPLAY variable will be set when sshing into a system with a session that has X forwarding enabled. If you don't have X forwarding enabled in your ssh client, no DISPLAY variable will be defined, and thus there will be no need to create your X-environment files.

If all these checks turn out to be true, you can create the files that hold the X-environment settings for this session.

```
then
  xauth nextract - $DISPLAY > $HOME/.xauth.$LOGNAME
  chmod 600 $HOME/.xauth.$LOGNAME
  echo $DISPLAY > $HOME/.xdisp.$LOGNAME
  chmod 600 $HOME/.xdisp.$LOGNAME
  ~/scripts/window.sh
```

If you then log into some other system that has your home directory mounted, you'll have access to the .Xauthority and DISPLAY information that you need in order to set both correctly on that system and allow X-based clients running there to attach to your X server.

The action creates two files based on your current X-server settings: .xauth.$LOGNAME and .xdisp.$LOGNAME. It also changes the permissions on the files so that they are accessible only by the files' owner. The security issue mentioned earlier in regard to protecting the .Xauthority file holds true, because your files exist on an NFS server and its administrators have access to your files.

The last command calls up a script that opens the X Navigation Window application that I mentioned previously. You can read about it in Chapter 22.

If the three conditions of the `if` statement are not satisfied, you are on a machine other than the one where the X tunneling takes place, and you need to determine whether `.xauth.$LOGNAME` exists.

```
else
  if [ -f $HOME/.xauth.$LOGNAME ]
  then
    cat $HOME/.xauth.$LOGNAME | xauth nmerge -
    DISPLAY=`cat $HOME/.xdisp.$LOGNAME`
    export DISPLAY
  fi
fi
```

The hope is that it does, but you shouldn't count on this. If the file does exist, you have to import the authority information into the local `.Xauthority` file and set the `DISPLAY` variable appropriately. The assumption here is that if one of the files exists, they both do. To be prudent, you would want to implement another check for the existence of the display file. Once you've done that, all X clients you run from this remote node will be able to access the `ssh` session where X is being tunneled.

Similar code could be added to the system `/etc/profile` on each of the nodes in your environment so that it will be effective for all users instead of just one. This may be a tedious task if you have many systems and operating-system types, each with its own configuration details; you will have to address these issues if you pursue this option.

Root-Profile Entry

If you intend to add similar code to the system `/etc/profile`, you may be interested in also entering the following code to the root user's personal profile to handle the scenario in which an administrator logged into a system as himself and became the root user via the `su -` command. The code determines which user became root. Then it imports the original user's X-environment settings. Thus, the administrator can run X client applications and have them display with his personal settings.

First the code determines which `xauth` utility to use; it also needs the parent and grandparent process IDs of the running shell (`MYPPID` and `MYPPPID`).

```
XAUTH=`which xauth`
MYPPID=`ps -fp $$ | tail -n 1 | awk '{print $3}'`
MYPPPID=`ps -fp $MYPPID | tail -n 1 | awk '{print $3}'`
MYID=`ps -fp $MYPPID | tail -n 1 | awk '{print $1}'`
MYOID=`ps -fp $MYPPPID | tail -n 1 | awk '{print $1}'`
```

Once the code has found the values, the script determines the owners of those processes (`MYID` and `MYOID`). The reason for determining the owner of both the parent and grandparent process IDs is that the parent ID (which represents the `su` command) is sometimes owned by root, and sometimes owned by the user that is becoming root depending on the system you're on. We have to check for both.

```
if [ "$MYID" != "root" ] || [ "$MYOID" != "root" ]
then
  for user in $MYID $MYOID
  do
    if [ "$user" != "root" ]
    then
      MYID=$user
    fi
  done
```

If either of those two variables (MYID and MYOID) is not root, you have to assume that someone has become root using su -. The for loop then determines which variable is not root and sets MYID to that user.

Now that MYID is set to the appropriate user, the script needs to find that user's home directory.

```
  MYHOME=`grep "^$MYID:" /etc/passwd | cut -d: -f6`
  if [ -f $MYHOME/.xauth.$MYID ]
  then
    cat $MYHOME/.xauth.$MYID | $XAUTH nmerge -
    DISPLAY=`cat $MYHOME/.xdisp.$MYID`
    export DISPLAY
  fi
fi
```

In a Network Information Service (NIS) environment, you'll want to change the MYHOME command to get the value from the appropriate NIS map. Once the home directory is known, we can determine whether the .xauth.$MYID file exists. If it exists, we import .Xauthority and DISPLAY information into the current shell environment. Once again, you may want to check for the existence of the display file instead of assuming it exists. The root user should now be able to start X client applications and have them display on the user's X server.

Throw a Temporary Root Window

Sometimes application owners may need root access on a system, such as when applications that are owned and managed by someone other than the administrator need to run as root because of their design (or need to be modified by the root user). There are obvious security implications when root access permissions are given to ordinary users, so you have to be very selective about extending root access.

The following script sets this up in a reasonable fashion by restricting access with a timeout value that will kill the root window after a preset amount of time. The code assumes a user who has the profile code described earlier set up, so that .xauth and .xdisp files are created.

First the code checks the number of parameters passed to the script. If the count is not one, some information about the script and its usage is echoed out.

```
#!/bin/sh
if [ $# -ne 1 ]
then
  echo "This script will send a root window to a user's display who is using"
  echo "ssh to access the environment"
  echo
  echo "Usage: $0 {username}"
  exit 1
fi
```

Next the user variable is set to the username and the corresponding home directory is found by searching the /etc/passwd file. Once again, if you are in an NIS environment, you will need to modify this command appropriately.

```
user=$1
userhome=`grep "^$user:" /etc/passwd | cut -d: -f6`
```

If the .xdisp file for this user exists, the script imports her X display and authority information into the current shell environment. If not, it echoes an error message and exits.

```
if [ -f $userhome/.xdisp.$user ]
then
  cat $userhome/.xauth.$user | /usr/openwin/bin/xauth nmerge -
  DISPLAY=`cat $userhome/.xdisp.$user`
  export DISPLAY
else
  echo "SSH Display information not available for $user. Is $user using it?"
  exit 1
fi
```

Now that the X environment has been set up, we set a variable holding a message that will be sent in the title bar of the xterm window, notifying the user of the window's expiration date.

```
RIP="This root@`uname -n` xterm window expires in 1 hr from `date '+%H:%M'`"
```

An xterm window can be launched with a switch that allows you to specify what is displayed in the title bar of the resulting window, as shown here:

```
nohup /usr/bin/xterm -ls -sb -T "$RIP" &
PID=$!
echo "kill $PID" | at -m now + 1 hour
```

You start the xterm via the -ls and -T switches. The -ls switch qualifies the shell within the window as a login shell and thus gives the full root user environment. The -T switch changes the title bar to the value following the switch. Then the PID variable is set to the xterm's process ID. Finally, the script sets up an at job, which is a scheduled task (somewhat different from a cron job, as seen in Chapter 12) that will kill the PID after one hour. The at command specifies a job to run once at the specified time. The time can be specific such as in the form of HH:MM or relative as in now + 1 hour. See the at man page for more specifics on its use.

CHAPTER 22

■ ■ ■

X Navigation Window

The scripts we are about to analyze are for an X-based application that gives you a way of easily accessing systems based on their system names or IP addresses. When managing environments with a machine count in the hundreds or more, saving every bit of time is vital. The navigation window has grown and matured over many years and now we have a cleaned-up version that's running on both Linux- and Solaris-based X displays as well as on X servers that run on Windows-based systems.

The navigation window also provides a simple method for users to access these systems. Having users set up their own environment is sometimes problematic because of varying skill levels. Providing a utility that is easy to use and is owned and used by the administrators can help eliminate some issues.

When using the navigation window, you see a small xterm window on your desktop, with a Node: prompt. The usage is simple enough: just type in the node name or IP address of a remote machine, and an xterm window will connect you to that system. Depending on your method of connecting to the remote machine, you may still need to provide a password. Other logic in the script makes the user interface and connection type (ssh, telnet, etc.) configurable.

Note that this chapter does not provide an explanation of X or display values. The preceding chapter provided an overview of X-display usage.

Navigation Window Usage

When you run the window script, you will see a window much like the one in Figure 22-1. To use the program, simply type in a node name or IP address, and the script will do the rest to bring up an xterm with a remote connection to the desired machine.

Figure 22-1. *X navigation window*

To specify the connection type to the remote machine and override the preconfigured value, enter the node name or IP address followed by a space and one of the following switches:

- s, which specifies an ssh connection

- r, which specifies an rlogin connection

- t, which specifies a telnet connection

If you don't add a switch indicating a connection type, the script will default to the any connection option, which attempts to establish a connection to the remote machine by trying ssh first, then rlogin, and finally telnet.

Navigation Setup

The code consists of two scripts. The first one (window) sets up the configuration environment and then opens a small window in which it starts the where script. The second script (where) is run within the window. It performs all the logic for the new connection. It determines the connection type, opens the connection, and configures the colors and appearance of the new window connected to the remote system.

First we set up some default variables for the where window initialization. We also set up variables for the location of the configuration file for the initial window's title, and the foreground and background colors.

```
#!/bin/sh
CONFIG_FILE=$HOME/.whererc.$LOGNAME
RLOGIN_TITLE="Where..."
RLOGIN_FG=red
RLOGIN_BG=ivory
```

Now the script has to check for a preexisting configuration file.

```
if [ -f $HOME/.whererc ]
then
  . $CONFIG_FILE
else
  cat > $CONFIG_FILE <<EOF
# These are the environment settings for the where... window
#
# These are the foreground and background
# color settings for systems on production subnets
FONT=fixed
PROD_FG=yellow3
PROD_BG=black
```

```
# systems on non-production subnets
NON_PROD_FG=lightblue
NON_PROD_BG=black
# These are the foreground and background color settings for
# systems on all other subnets
OTHER_FG=DarkSeaGreen2
OTHER_BG=black
```

This file contains color and font information, as well as a few other items. If the configuration file is found, it is sourced to put its contents into effect in the current shell environment. If the configuration file does not exist, the script creates it using the here-document technique and populates a new configuration file using default values. Then the script has to source the newly created file. The configuration file is located in the user's home directory so that each user can make his own customizations.

The CONNECTION_TYPE variable in the following code snippet specifies the type of connection the user would like to have as the preferred method of attaching to a remote system. The connection types include ssh, rlogin, and telnet, among others.

```
# This is the default connection type to use.
# Options are rlogin, telnet, ssh and any. Any will
# try ssh first, then rlogin, then telnet as a last
# resort.
CONNECTION_TYPE=any
# These are the foreground, background and other
# settings for the where window itself
RLOGIN_TITLE="Where..."
RLOGIN_FG=red
RLOGIN_BG=white
WHERE_WIN_GEOM="20x1+1200+0"
XTERM=`which xterm`
EOF
   . $CONFIG_FILE
```

During the evolution of this script the capability to automatically switch to an alternate connection type if the initial attempt is unsuccessful was added. This came about because some users wanted to connect with a specified default protocol instead of the original default of rlogin. For instance, some devices have only a telnet daemon to which remote machines are able to attach; the users of those machines would want telnet as their default connection method.

When nmap became available, it was then possible to determine what ports were available on the remote machine. nmap is an open source utility for network exploration and auditing. In our script, nmap is used to determine if a specified port on a remote machine is open; the code will then choose the appropriate connection method. If the value of the CONNECTION_TYPE variable is set to any, the code will try ssh first, then rlogin, and then telnet instead of simply using a single specified connection method. The script will then attach to the remote machine using the first available protocol. Note that for security reasons, you may not want to make nmap available to the general user population.

Some other connection types that could be added here are rdesktop to attach to Microsoft Windows systems, ftp or sftp to send and receive files, or some other connection type based on local needs. Customizations can be quite varied, but I'm going to limit this demonstration to simpler uses.

If the configuration file didn't exist and one was just created, we use the following code to let the user know how to modify their interaction with the remote machine and adjust the interface colors and settings. This window comes up only when the user logs in with this script for the first time.

```
xmessage -fn 12x24 "Note: If you don't like the \
colors of the windows, modify this file: $CONFIG_FILE." &
fi
```

The navigation window evolved over quite a long period of time. There were many instances where the script was being run by multiple users at the same time that changes were being made to the code. To keep existing users up-to-date with the current configuration values, the expanding list of configuration options needed to be checked against each user's personal configuration file. Options not present in the user's file had to be added using the default entries.

The following code starts a for loop that iterates through the possible configuration entries, some of which may need to be added to the user's configuration file:

```
changes=0
for conf_val in NON_PROD_FG.lightblue NON_PROD_BG.black \
  CONNECTION_TYPE.any WHERE_WIN_GEOM."20x1+1200+0" \
  XTERM.`which xterm`
do
  var=`echo $conf_val | awk -F. '{print $1}'`
  val=`echo $conf_val | awk -F. '{print $2}'`
  is_there=`grep $var $CONFIG_FILE | grep -v "^#"`
  if [ "$is_there" = "" ]
  then
    echo "${var}=${val}" >> $CONFIG_FILE
    changes=1
  fi
done
```

In this example, the for loop contains five configuration values that need to be checked. Notice that each entry is a two-part value, where each part is separated by a dot. The first part is the configuration-variable name and the second part is the default value for that variable. For each of these entries, the code then splits the VARIABLE.default_value pair apart into the variable and value pieces. Next it determines if this particular variable is already in the user's configuration file. If it isn't, it appends the new variable and its default value to the user's configuration file and sets the value of the changes variable to 1 to note that a modification was performed.

Then we check the changes variable and re-source the configuration file to make sure the environment has been updated.

```
if [ -f $CONFIG_FILE -a $changes -eq 1 ]
then
  . $CONFIG_FILE
fi
```

Now that the environment is set up completely, the code will start up the navigation window itself on the local X display and call the where.sh script in that window.

```
nohup $XTERM -cr $RLOGIN_FG -fg $RLOGIN_FG -bg \
  $RLOGIN_BG -fn 12x24 -rw -geom $WHERE_WIN_GEOM -T \
  "$RLOGIN_TITLE" -ls -e \
  /usr/local/bin/where.sh >/dev/null &
```

The where script makes the actual connections to the remote machines. The nohup command that calls the *where* xterm window lets us avoid interrupting any of the child windows when the parent window is closed. This completes the first script in the pair.

Navigation Window

The where.sh script is run within the original small window appearing on the user's X display. The only output this small window gives is a Node: prompt for user input. The script determines the type of connection and the output color of the new window that contains the remote system connection. First the script defines a few variables.

The stty commands set up the Backspace and Ctrl+C (interrupt) key sequences for use in the small where window.

```
#!/bin/sh
CONFIG_FILE=$HOME/.whererc.$LOGNAME
LOG_FILE=$HOME/.whererc.${LOGNAME}.log
stty intr '^C'
stty erase '^?'
```

The text ^C and ^? are each considered single control characters. To insert these correctly in the script on your system while using vi, start by typing Ctrl+v and then the desired key sequence. The Ctrl+v sequence tells vi to ignore the actual usage of the next key sequence typed (Ctrl+c, Backspace, Enter, etc.) and insert it as a control character instead. The Ctrl+v sequence thus works somewhat like an escape character. For example, to input the ^? character for a backspace, in vi you would be in insert mode, press Ctrl+v, and then press the Backspace key.

Now the script starts an endless loop that accepts the user's input specifying remote system names or IP addresses.

```
while true
do
  if [ -f /usr/ucb/echo ]
  then
    /usr/ucb/echo -n "Node: "
  elif [ -f /bin/echo ]
  then
    /bin/echo -n "Node: "
  else
    /usr/bin/echo "Node: "
  fi
```

To make the code more portable in heterogeneous environments, we first check for the echo command in various places. The script then reads in the nodename and the connection type if one is specified. Earlier I discussed how the script chooses from different connection types, and that if a switch is given following the nodename entered, the script will open a connection using that connection type.

If the nodename variable is null, the script should just continue to the next iteration of the infinite loop. This step may seem superfluous, but it keeps the script from hanging.

```
read nodename conn
if [ "$nodename" = "" ]
then
  continue
fi
```

Once again, we have to source the configuration file.

```
nodename=`echo $nodename | tr "[A-Z]" "[a-z]"`
if [ -f $CONFIG_FILE ]
then
  . $CONFIG_FILE
fi
```

This allows any configuration updates to appear when the next window is started. That way changes to the available configuration options can be made without having to restart the script. The script also makes sure the nodename variable is always translated to lowercase to qualify the user input.

If the preferred connection type is *any*, the script uses nmap to check for open ports to determine the type of connection to be opened.

```
if [ "$CONNECTION_TYPE" = "any" ]
then
  S=`nmap -p 22 --max_rtt_timeout 100 $nodename | grep open`
  R=`nmap -p 513 --max_rtt_timeout 100 $nodename | grep open`
  if [ "$S" != "" ]
```

```
  then
    CONNECTION_TYPE=ssh
  elif [ "$R" != "" ]
  then
    CONNECTION_TYPE=rlogin
  else
    CONNECTION_TYPE=telnet
  fi
fi
```

nmap listens for a port for100ms before timing out; the script then moves on to the next connection type. It currently checks for ssh and then rlogin (login), and if those attempts fail, telnet is used. This is the place in the code where you could add other connection types.

By adding a space and one of the characters r, s, or t after inputting the node name, the user can specify the type of connection to use for this specific remote session.

```
if [ "$conn" != "" ]
then
  case $conn in
    r) # Use rlogin
      CONNECTION_TYPE=rlogin
    ;;
    s) # Use ssh
      CONNECTION_TYPE=ssh
    ;;
    t) # Use telnet
      CONNECTION_TYPE=telnet
    ;;
    *) # make no change and use the default.
      echo
    ;;
  esac
fi
```

This allows the user to override the defaults and attach to a specific system with a specific type of connection. This can be useful for remote systems to which one can connect in multiple ways.

We're now ready to open the connection to the remote system.

```
echo `date` $nodename $CONNECTION_TYPE $conn >> $LOG_FILE
third_ip=`grep -w $nodename /etc/hosts | grep -v '^#' | tail -1 | awk '{print $1}' |
cut -d\. -f3`
if [ "$third_ip" = "" ]
then
  third_ip=`echo $nodename | awk -F. '{print $3}'`
```

```
  if [ "$third_ip" = "" ]
  then
    nohup $XTERM -fn $FONT -bg $OTHER_BG -fg \
      $OTHER_FG -sb -sl 500 -T "$nodename" -e \
      "$CONNECTION_TYPE" -l $USER $nodename \
      >/dev/null &
    continue
  fi
fi
```

First we create an entry in the user's log file for tracking and debugging purposes. Next the script tries to determine the subnet that the node is a part of. This is because systems that are critical to the environment may be segregated by subnet, and you may want the window foreground and background colors to distinguish the critical systems from less important ones. The subnet can be determined in various ways. You could look in the /etc/hosts file or see if the node name is actually an IP address. You could also add an nslookup or dig query, or possibly an NIS lookup of the hosts map. If the subnet can't be determined, we open the connection with foreground and background colors of OTHER_FG and OTHER_BG as defined in the user's configuration file.

If the script can determine the subnet, the connection should be opened with the appropriate foreground and background colors. Many color groupings are possible, but I show you only a few combinations here. Using windows with meaningful color settings can help reduce the risk of typing the wrong command in the wrong window.

This part of the code is where the new xterm windows are launched:

```
if [ $third_ip -ge 1 -a $third_ip -le 10 ]
then
  nohup $XTERM -fn $FONT -bg $PROD_BG -fg \
    $PROD_FG -sb -sl 500 -T "$nodename" \
    -e "$CONNECTION_TYPE" -l $USER $nodename >/dev/null &
elif [ $third_ip -ge 11 -a $third_ip -le 20 ]
then
  nohup $XTERM -fn $FONT -bg $NON_PROD_BG \
    -fg $NON_PROD_FG -sb -sl 500 -T "$nodename" \
    -e "$CONNECTION_TYPE" -l $USER $nodename \
    >/dev/null &
else
  nohup $XTERM -fn $FONT -bg $OTHER_BG -fg \
  $OTHER_FG -sb -sl 500 -T "$nodename" \
  -e "$CONNECTION_TYPE" -l $USER $nodename \
  >/dev/null &
fi
done
```

The main difference between the three xterm launch lines is the colors used for the foreground and background. The if statements determine whether the remote machine is in a specific IP address range. If it is, we start the xterm with the appropriate color combination. The switches passed to xterm are for the font, color combination, scroll-back configuration, and title-bar definition. All of these can be specified in the user's configuration file. The -e switch to xterm defines what you want to have executed within the xterm window. In our case, it will be either an ssh, rlogin, or telnet connection to the remote machine.

■ ■ ■

Command-Line E-mail Attachments

I often send e-mail to myself containing information gathered from a running system. Most of the information comes as flat text obtained from various files, or output from system commands. From time to time the file that I would like to send is a binary of some type. Sometimes I want a file to show up as an attachment regardless of whether it is a binary.

I wrote a few scripts that can perform such a task. They encode the binary file as flat text for transmission and then e-mail the file. The file can then be decoded at the receiving end manually or, more conveniently, by the e-mail client receiving the file. Each script takes as input the binary file and the destination e-mail address.

uuencode

The first method uses uuencode to convert the binary file to flat text. This method works, but some e-mail clients, for instance my web-based SquirrelMail client, will not recognize the encoded file. If that is the case, you can simply save the text and decode it yourself with uudecode to obtain the original binary file.

First we define a variable specifying the temporary file that will contain the encoded message as well as a variable that holds the script-usage string.

```
#!/bin/sh
tmpfile=/tmp/uu_output.$$
usage="Usage: $0 {filename} {email_address}"
```

Now we validate the input by determining whether the positional parameter holding the binary file is defined.

```
if [ ! -z $1 ]
then
  file=$1
```

```
if [ ! -f $file ]
then
   echo $usage
   exit 1
```

If it is, we assign the `file` variable to its value. This is the file that will be encoded later in the script. If the parameter is not defined, we output the script usage and exit. Please note that the `exit` command is used with a value that will be the return code of the script. In this case it is nonzero (1), indicating that there was an issue encountered during execution.

Next you have to validate the positional parameter for the e-mail address that is passed to the script. This is done in the same way as for the file argument.

```
else
   if [ ! -z $2 ]
   then
      address=$2
   else
      echo $usage
      exit 1
   fi
fi
```

Finally, if no parameters were passed to the script, we display the script usage and exit with the nonzero return code as before.

```
else
   echo $usage
   exit 1
fi
```

Next is the heart of the script; it is the part that encodes the file and then sends the file to its destination.

```
basefile=`basename $file`
echo "A uuencoded file is attached called: $basefile" > $tmpfile
echo >> $tmpfile
uuencode $file $file >> $tmpfile
mail -s "$basefile attached from $from" $address < $tmpfile
rm $tmpfile
```

First a `tmpfile` is created with the `echo` command containing a summary of what is attached for the reader of the message. A blank line is added using the `echo` command between the text of the e-mail and the text of the encoded binary file. The file is encoded with the `uuencode` utility and appended to the `tmpfile` following the text of the message. The `uuencode` and `uudecode` commands were originally designed for this very purpose, to transmit a binary file via a transmission method that supports only text. After the file has been encoded, we send the `tmpfile` to the destination e-mail address with the `mail` command; the `tmpfile` is then removed.

Tip If the `uuencode` and `uudecode` commands are not installed on your system, you can find the appropriate installation package of the UNIX `sharutils` utilities, where both commands are included. A version of `sharutils` should be available for most current platforms.

MIME Encoding

The next script performs roughly the same task as the first, but it uses MIME encoding. This type of encoding is more current than the `uuencode` method; it is also standard for e-mail clients that have to be able to process a message with an attachment.

The code here is very similar to the code used in the previous example except that it doesn't create an encoded file that is e-mailed; instead the script creates a specially formatted file constituting an e-mail message that contains the appropriate headers for e-mail clients to process and recognize as an attachment.

Once again we first define the temporary file that contains our message and the usage statement.

```
#!/bin/sh
tmpfile=/tmp/mime_output.$$
from="$USER@`cat /etc/dnsdomainname`"
usage="Usage: $0 {filename} {email address}"
```

The difference here is that we need to identify the message sender and add the sender's identity to the mail message manually.

Validation of the parameters passed to the script is the same as in the `uuencode` script.

```
if [ ! -z $1 ]
then
  file=$1
  if [ ! -f $file ]
  then
    echo $usage
    exit 1
  else
    if [ ! -z $2 ]
    then
      address=$2
    else
      echo $usage
      exit 1
```

```
      fi
   fi
else
   echo $usage
   exit 1
fi
```

Next the e-mail message is created, which includes a simple text message specifying which file is attached.

```
basefile=`basename $file`
cat > $tmpfile << EOT
From: $from
To: $address
Subject: $file attached from $from
MIME-Version: 1.0
Content-Type: multipart/mixed;boundary="mime-attachment-boundary"
--mime-attachment-boundary
Content-Type: text/plain; charset="iso-8859-1"
Content-Transfer-Encoding: 8bit
A MIME encoded file is attached called: $basefile
--mime-attachment-boundary
Content-Type: application/octet-stream; name="$basefile"
Content-Transfer-Encoding: base64
Content-Disposition: attachment; filename="$basefile"
EOT
```

In determining how to create the headers, I used my e-mail client to attach a binary file to a basic text message, and then sent it to myself. When I received it, I copied the headers into the test message. I have preserved the line spacing of the copied message.

Notice the line in the preceding code that defines a *boundary* string (--mime-attachment-boundary). This bounds the beginning and end of the text as well as the MIME-encoded portions of the message.

Once we've created the headers, we encode the binary file using the mimencode utility and then append the encoded file, which includes another boundary statement, to the temporary file to complete the message.

```
mimencode $file >> $tmpfile
echo --mime-attachment-boundary-- >> $tmpfile
```

Now that the temporary file containing the message is ready, we send it with the sendmail program using the -t option.

```
/usr/lib/sendmail -t < $tmpfile
rm $tmpfile
```

This option tells sendmail to look in the input for the To: header instead of specifying the destination address manually. Finally we remove the temporary file for cleanup.

■**Tip** If the `mimencode` utility is not installed on your system, find it by installing the `metamail` package, which includes this utility.

One modification that could upgrade either of these two scripts would be to reverse the order of the input parameters so that the destination e-mail address comes first. That way you could accept multiple files and attach them all to a single message. With the `uuencode` version, it would simply be a matter of adding whitespace between the text segment for each encoded file. The `mimencode` version would be a bit more complex. You would need to separate the encoded sections with the appropriate boundary strings to signify the beginning and end of each attachment. To see exactly how this is done, send yourself a test message containing a couple of small attachments, and open the message with a text viewer instead of an e-mail client. This will allow you to see how the mail-message syntax is constructed for both the message headers as well as the embedded attachments.

CHAPTER 24

∎ ∎ ∎

Text-Processing One-Liners

Even though this book is about using the shell's command language, I use a fair number of calls to other utilities for text processing. Sed, awk, and grep are the primary UNIX text-processing utilities, although I have used others. This chapter gives you a collection of short and useful one-liners that illustrate quite a few methods for gathering specific information from various textual sources.

Very often when writing a script, you need to know source data locations before you start pruning the data for further processing. For instance, you can find the load average of a running Linux system from the first line of the output of the top utility, the output of the uptime command, the output of the w command, and in the /proc/loadavg file. There are almost always multiple ways to gather and process information, and the tools introduced in this chapter should give you an excellent start on knowing what you will need to do in many situations.

For more information about any of these utilities, consult Appendix C of this book or the man pages of individual utilities. This chapter is not intended to cover these utilities exhaustively; several of these utilities have had complete books written about them.

An extremely common use of the utilities discussed in this chapter is to modify or filter a string that is obtained from any one of a number of sources, such as from an environment variable or from output of a system command. For consistency in these examples, the following common variable is echoed and piped to the utility to illustrate the mode of use:

```
VAR="The quick brown fox jumped over the lazy dog."
```

Displaying Specific Fields

The following example is a simple awk statement to extract data fields from a string containing a record with multiple fields, assuming that whitespace characters separate the fields. The awk field variables start at $1 and increment up through the end of the string. In our example string, there are nine fields separated by whitespace. The awk positional variable $0 is special in that it holds the value of the whole string. Quite often, the print statement will target only a single field, but this example shows how to extract and reorder several of the input fields:

```
echo $VAR | awk '{print $1, $8, $4, $5, $6, $7, $3, $9}'
```

This produces the following output:

```
The lazy fox jumped over the brown dog.
```

Specifying the Field Separator

Here is another simple use of awk, where the field separator is specified using the -F command-line switch. Using this option causes the source string to be split up based on something other than whitespace. In this case it is the letter o.

```
echo $VAR | awk -Fo '{print $4}'
```

This produces the following output:

```
ver the lazy d
```

Simple Pattern-Matching

Matching specific fields of the input is very useful in finding data quickly. A grep command can easily return lines that match a given string, but awk can return lines that match a specific value in a specific field. The following example finds and displays all lines whose second field is equal to the string casper in /etc/hosts. The test used for the second field could be changed from equal (==) to not equal (!=) to find the lines in the file that do *not* contain the string casper in the second field, and more complicated conditions can be constructed in the usual way.

```
awk '$2 == "casper" {print $0}' /etc/hosts
```

This produces the following output:

```
172.16.5.4 casper casper.mydomain.com
```

Matching Fields Against Several Values

Another pattern-matching technique, which is similar to the previous one, is to look for one of several alternatives in a specific field. The example here extends the previous one a bit by looking for lines in my /etc/hosts file whose IP addresses (in field 1) start with either 127 or 172. Note that each alternative between the slashes (/) is separated by the pipe (|) character; this is awk notation for the regular expression specifying the pattern "starting with 127 or starting with 172." The pattern-matching operator ~ could also be replaced with the negated operator !~ to return the lines in the file that don't match the expression.

```
awk '$1 ~ /^127|^172/ {print $0}' /etc/hosts
```

This produces the following output:

```
127.0.0.1 localhost
172.16.5.2 phred phred.mydomain.com
172.16.5.4 casper casper.mydomain.com
```

Determining the Number of Fields

This one-liner illustrates the use of a special awk internal variable NF whose value is the number of fields in the current line of input. You may want to try changing the field separator as shown in the earlier example and note the difference in the result.

```
echo $VAR | awk '{print NF}'
```

This produces the following output:

```
9
```

Determining the Last Field

This is a slightly modified version of the previous example; it adds a dollar sign ($) in front of the NF variable. This will print out the value of the last field instead of the number of fields.

```
echo $VAR | awk '{print $NF}'
```

The following output results:

```
dog.
```

Determining the Second-to-Last Field

We can use NF to get the second-to-last field of the string, as in the next example. This could be easily modified to reference other positions in the input relative to the last field. The previous three examples all relate directly to the standard numeric awk field variables. From our example string, $NF would be equal to $9. This variable is one layer more abstract than directly referencing a positional variable. It allows you to reference any particular field of an arbitrary string length through logic.

```
echo $VAR | awk '{print $(NF-1)}'
```

You get the following output:

```
lazy
```

Passing Variables to awk

In some cases you may not know until the command is run which field you want. You can deal with this by passing a value to awk when it is invoked. The following example shows how you can pass the value of the shell variable TheCount to an awk command. The -v switch to awk specifies that you are going to set a variable. Following the -v switch is the variable being assigned within awk.

```
TheCount=3
echo $VAR | awk -v counter=$TheCount '{print $counter}'
```

This produces the following output:

```
brown
```

The -v switch is a relatively new option for assigning a variable, and it may not be ideal when you're shooting for portability. In that case, this usage should do the trick:

```
TheCount=3
echo $VAR | awk '{print $counter}' counter=$TheCount
```

It produces the following output:

```
brown
```

Using a Variable Passed to awk in a Condition

Here is another use of shell variables with the awk command. The NODE=$node assignment sets the internal awk variable NODE to the value of the shell variable $node. The awk command then checks whether each line of the input file for $2 is equal to the value of NODE. If a line is equal, then $3 is output. In this example, the /etc/hosts file was used. The code works like that in the "Simple Pattern-Matching" example shown earlier, except that the value to compare against can be specified independently of the field that is output.

```
awk -v NODE=$node '$2 == NODE {print $3}' /etc/hosts
```

The output depends on the contents of your /etc/hosts file, but the intended effect is to display the domain name corresponding to the specified node name. Try setting the node variable to the name of your system before running this command. My system is named casper and this is its hosts file entry:

```
172.16.5.4 casper casper.mydomain.com
```

Thus, if on some line in the /etc/hosts file, the system name stored in the node variable is in field 2, then the third field of that line will be displayed. When I run this command after setting the shell variable $node to casper, the output is the third field of the /etc/hosts entry for casper: casper.mydomain.com.

Displaying a Range of Fields (Main Method)

Usually, printing a range of fields from an input line cannot be expressed using simple syntax. Unless the range is fixed, you generally need to have awk loop through a previously specified list of fields, printing each one in turn. In this example, the for loop starts with a fixed field number (here, 3) and ends with the value of the NF variable. You can modify this easily to permit any range. The printf (formatted print) command in the body of the loop prints the current field, followed by a space. The last print statement outside the loop adds a final carriage return at the end of the output.

```
echo $VAR | awk '{for(i=3; i<=NF; i++) {printf "%s ",$i}; print ""}'
```

Here is the output:

```
brown fox jumped over the lazy dog.
```

Displaying a Range of Fields (Alternate Method)

One last use of external variables being passed to awk is related to potential problems with awk versions. In some cases, the versions of awk, nawk, or gawk handle the -v switch differently. There are also issues when passing variables that have spaces included in literal strings. Most awk commands from the command line are contained within single quotes: '. When passing external shell variables to awk, in the space within the awk command where the variable containing spaces would normally be applied you should embed the shell variable directly into the command by surrounding it with more single quotes. In the following example, the awk command starts with a single quote and then begins a for loop. The counter variable i is set to the initial value of 3 and will continue to loop while i is less than or equal to $end. $end is a shell variable that is embedded between two single quotes. The first of these quotes ends the initial awk statement and the shell is then used to expand the value of the $end variable. The second single quote that follows the $end variable reopens the awk command, which includes the loop increment value as well as the print statements. The final single quote ends the whole awk statement.

This example is very simple and nearly the same as the range-printing solution. It illustrates the use of a shell variable within an awk command. The differences are that the ending variable ($end) is passed from the shell environment and it is not contained within the single quotes of the awk command. The shell variable $end is set to the value 6.

```
echo $VAR | awk '{for(i=3; i<='$end'; i++) {printf "%s ",$i}; print ""}'
```

Here is the output:

```
brown fox jumped over
```

Determining the Length of a String Using awk

The length value in awk is another internal variable that contains the number of characters in the current line.

```
echo $VAR | awk '{print length}'
```

Here's the output:

```
45
```

Determining the Length of a String Using expr

Another solution for this task uses the internal length function of expr.

```
(expr length "$VAR")
```

The following output results:

```
45
```

Displaying a Substring with awk

Substring extraction can be performed using a built-in function of awk. The function has the following form:

```
substr(string,position of first character of substring,substring character count)
```

The following example extracts a substring of three characters from the third field of the VAR variable, starting from the second character in the field.

```
echo $VAR | awk '{print substr($3,2,3)}'
```

You get the following output:

```
row
```

Displaying a Substring with expr

Here is a method of extracting a substring using expr. It uses the substr() function of expr. As before, the first argument is the string, the second is the position of the desired substring's starting character, and the last is the number of characters in the substring. The example gets 4 characters from the string stored in VAR, starting at character number 12.

```
(expr substr "$VAR" 12 4)
```

The following output results:

```
rown
```

Conducting Simple Search and Replace with sed

The following example searches for space characters within each line of input and replaces them with the string %20. The search-and-replace syntax follows the pattern s/*search string*/*replacement string*/. The g at the end of the expression is optional; it stands for *global* and indicates that you want to replace all instances of the search term found in the line. Without the g, the command replaces only the first instance of the search term.

```
echo $VAR | sed -e "s/ /%20/g"
```

The following output results:

```
The%20quick%20brown%20fox%20jumped%20over%20the%20lazy%20dog.
```

Disregarding Blank and Commented Lines from a File

This example is a little more involved. First it uses a sed command to filter all lines that have been commented out in a specified file (here, /etc/ntp.conf). The output is then piped to awk, which is used to print only non-null lines (i.e., lines whose length is not 0). The sed command checks whether each line starts with a pound sign (#) and is followed by a string that matches the pattern .*, which denotes "any number of any characters." If a line matches this overall pattern, sed produces no output; otherwise it echoes the line.

The effect of this is to echo the original contents of the file, minus any commented lines (those beginning with #). The sed output is piped into an awk one-liner that filters out lines of length 0. The resulting sequence is a quick way to remove all blank and commented entries of a file.

```
sed -e "s/#.*//g" /etc/ntp.conf | awk '{if(length !=0) print $0}'
```

The output will, of course, be specific to the file used as input.

Conducting Dual Search and Replace with sed

A more advanced search and replace first checks the input for a string other than the one that is going to be replaced, and performs the search-and-replace operation only if this string is found. For instance, you might have a file in which each line contains a name and address, and you want to change "Portland" to "Gresham" on the lines containing the name Ron Peters.

This can be accomplished using sed by including a pattern before the search expression. Continuing with our "quick brown fox" example, the following code first searches for the word "quick" in the input and then replaces all instances (g) of the string he with the replacement string she on the line if the word was found.

```
echo $VAR | sed -e "/quick/s/he/she/g"
```

Here's the output:

```
Tshe quick brown fox jumped over tshe lazy dog.
```

Filtering Lines with sed

Sometimes filtering out certain lines is desirable. For instance, when parsing ps output, you might not want the header line displayed. The following sed example removes the first line from the stdout of a call to ps. This is similar to the head command, but it has the opposite effect: while a head command grabs the specified number of leading lines and drops the rest, our example removes the specified number of initial lines from the output of ps (here, 1) and displays the rest. (You could use the tail command, but you would need to know the total number of lines.) Removing more than the first line is as simple as changing the specified line to a range of lines; to remove the first three lines, you would change 1d to 1,3d.

```
ps -ef | sed -e '1d'
```

This produces the following output (the italicized line is the header that was removed):

```
UID    PID  PPID  C   STIME  TTY     TIME CMD
root    1    0    0   22:32   ?   00:00:05 init [5]
root    2    1    0   22:32   ?   00:00:01 [keventd]
root    3    1    0   22:32   ?   00:00:00 [kapmd]
...
```

Searching for Multiple Strings with egrep

egrep is a utility that works in much the same way as the traditional grep command. Handily, it will search for more than one string at a time. In this example, I search for any one of three alternative search strings within the /etc/passwd file.

```
egrep "desktop|mysql|ntp" /etc/passwd
```

It produces the following output:

```
ntp:x:38:38::/etc/ntp:/sbin/nologin
desktop:x:80:80:desktop:/var/lib/menu/kde:/sbin/nologin
mysql:x:27:27:MySQL Server:/var/lib/mysql:/bin/bash
```

A Clean Method of Searching the Process Table

Traditionally a command to find a specific process in the process table would look something like this:

```
ps -ef | grep some_string
```

When this command is run, the output includes not only the process data you were looking for, but also the data for the grep process itself since the search string is also contained in the invocation of grep. To clean up the output, you can add an additional pipe to remove the additional grep process entry with the –v switch to grep, like this:

```
ps -ef | grep some_string | grep -v grep
```

There is a little trick for performing this task without the additional pipe:

```
ps -ef | grep "[s]ome_string"
```

This turns the original search string into a regular expression. The new grep command has the same effect as the previous one because the regular expression evaluates to the same string as in the original grep command (some_string). The entry for the grep process, however, shows the command as it was issued, prior to the evaluation of the regular expression ([s]ome_string). The entry for the grep process itself thus fails to match when the grep command is run and is not included in the output.

Summing Columns Using awk

On occasion I've run across the need to add up the values in a column of output. Most of the time this is from a simple directory listing, but it could be any custom data. The following file listing is the input for the awk command. This input specifies only the *gz files (although this is arbitrary and could have been any directory listing) and is then piped to awk, where the fifth field of each line is summed together to output a total. The following is the directory listing that will be used as input to the awk command:

```
$ ls -l *gz
-rwxr--r-- 1 rpeters rpeters    3337 Jul  9 2007   mysqlstatus.tar.gz
-rw-r--r-- 1 rpeters rpeters    1367 Sep 21 2007   countdown.tgz
-rwxr--r-- 1 rpeters rpeters 1214743 Mar 12 12:35  dokuwiki.tgz
-rw-r--r-- 1 root    root       6724 Sep 21 2007   lvm.tar.gz
-rwxr--r-- 1 rpeters rpeters 1043064 Jul 25 2007   rrdtool.tar.gz
-rwxr--r-- 1 rpeters rpeters 5271568 Aug 17 2007   PerlAPI.tar.gz
```

The awk portion of the one-liner is itself a simple two-part script. The awk utility takes input one line at a time and performs any necessary processing over and over as long as there are lines of input. In this case, the processing takes field number 5 ($5 is the file size) and adds the value of that variable to the total variable.

```
$ ls -l *gz | awk '{total+=$5} END {print total/1024/1024}'
7.19147
```

There are two special rules in awk: BEGIN and END. These allow customized processing to happen *outside* the main input loop either before or after its processing. In this case we're using the END rule to signify that the main processing of the sum total is complete and awk should move on to postprocessing. Following END, the final element converts the total variable to megabytes and displays the result.

Generating Random Numbers Using awk

I don't use random-number generators very often. However, I have sometimes needed one when writing simple games and when starting multiple tasks at random intervals so that they wouldn't conflict with each other.

The following command generates a random number between 0 and 100. The rand() function of awk generates a number between 0 and 1. The srand() function initializes the random-number generator using the seed value passed to it as an argument. If the seed expression is left out (as in the example here), the time of day is the default value used for the seed. For testing purposes, you may want to remove the srand() function from the code so the "random" number returned won't be random, but rather predictable.

```
echo | awk '{srand(); print int(100 * rand())}'
```

Generating Random Numbers from the Shell

Both bash and ksh have the ability to generate random numbers. There is a built-in shell variable called RANDOM that you can use for this purpose. This variable will generate a random integer between 0 and 32767 every time it is accessed.

```
echo $RANDOM
```

Displaying Character-Based Fields with sed

awk is very good at displaying fields separated by whitespace or by specific delimiters. It is more challenging to extract a specific character or range of characters from a string whose length you don't know. You could find the length of the string with awk and then use the cut command to grab specific characters, but that requires more than one command. The same result can be achieved more simply by using sed.

You can use sed to split strings based on character patterns rather than fields. A pattern describes the elements into which the string will be split. These elements are represented by parentheses containing one or more dots (.), which stand for single characters. Each element in the pattern corresponds to a field in the input string when it is split.

The possible elements are shown here:

(.): One character

(.*): An arbitrary number of characters

(...): Here, three consecutive characters; in general, as many consecutive characters as there are dots

The split instruction consists of two parts separated by forward slashes (/) before and after. The first part is the pattern and the second specifies the field or fields from the string that should be displayed. When sed is invoked, the entire split instruction, including the pattern, is quoted and the parentheses in the pattern are escaped with backslashes (\).

The following examples clarify this technique. In the first example, the first element in the pattern specifies an arbitrary number of characters leading up to the second, final element. The second element consists of a single character. The dollar sign ($) used here signifies the end of line or, in this case, the end of the input string. The output is the second field of the input string. Thus this command prints the last two characters in the input string. In our case, this is the last character of the phrase and the period at the end of the sentence.

```
echo $VAR | sed 's/\(.*\)\(..\)$/\2/'
```

Here's the output:

g.

The second example has three elements in the pattern. The first consists of the first four characters in the string. The second consists of all characters apart from the first four, leading up to the final element. The third element consists of the last three characters in the string. The first and third elements are then printed. Note that the fourth character in the output is a space.

```
echo $VAR | sed 's/\(....\)\(.*\)\(...\)$/\1\3/'`
```

Here's the output:

```
The og.
```

Escaping Special Characters

You have seen several occasions in which special characters had to be escaped because they were not to be evaluated using their normal meanings. This occurs frequently in sed operations, particularly replacements. These replacements can be somewhat tricky because of all the backslashes and forward slashes.

The next few examples show the code for several replacement operations. The code works within a script, but because of the way the shell evaluates escape characters, the code will not work from the command line in case you want to test the code manually. There are two possibilities for most of these examples. The first uses escapes to search for and replace the special characters. The second uses square brackets ([and]) to specify the character in the search.

Note This option doesn't always work, such as when searching for a square bracket or an escape character itself. See Chapter 25 for another method of escaping special characters.

You have to escape all characters that have a special meaning, such as !, @, #, %, ^, ., *, and so on. This example shows how to escape a period:

```
some_var=`echo $some_var | sed -e s/\\\./\\\\\\\./g`
some_var=`echo $some_var | sed -e s/[.]/\\\\\\\./g`
```

To escape the dollar sign, use the following code:

```
some_var=`echo $some_var | sed -e s/\\\\\$/\\\\\\\\$/g`
some_var=`echo $some_var | sed -e s/[$]/\\\\\\\\$/g`
```

The following lets you escape the ampersand or parenthesis:

```
some_var=`echo $some_var | sed -e s/\&/\\\\\\\\\&/g`
```

To escape forward slashes you use the following code:

```
some_var=`echo $some_var | sed -e s/\\\\//\\\\\\\\\\\\//g`
some_var=`echo $some_var | sed -e s/[/]/\\\\\\\\\\\\//g`
```

The longest and ugliest of all is escaping backslashes, because you're trying to escape the escape character. The syntax with the square brackets doesn't work in this case and you're left with seven consecutive backslashes as the search string.

```
some_var=`echo $some_var | sed -e s/\\\\\\\/\\\\\\\\\\\\\\\\/g`
```

Returning Trailing Lines from a Pattern Match Using grep

It's easy to grab certain lines from a file or output identified by running grep with a regular expression. What isn't quite so simple is getting lines that follow the lines matching the grep search expression. Consider a log file in which a particular entry precedes the record of a certain type of sequence of events, and you want to grab both the initial entry and the sequence that follows from the log.

The following awk command performs the task by searching for a line containing the STRING that identifies the initial entry. The getline command can then be used to get the next line of the input. Several getline statements with a print statement between each could be used to retrieve more than one line. You can print each retrieved line, or any field or range of fields within it. This example shows a print statement applying to only the first field of the two lines following the initial line that contains the STRING:

```
some_command_output | awk ' $1 ~ /^STRING/ \
{ getline;print $1;getline;print $1}'
```

If you want to omit printing selected lines, you would perform several getline commands in a row without a print in between.

Note that STRING is preceded by a caret, ^. This forms a regular expression specifying that STRING occurs at the beginning of the string being matched, $1 in this case. This match works if you want to find text that starts with STRING, possibly followed by additional text. If you want to match STRING exactly, you can add $ to the end of the regular expression to specify the end-of-line character, like so: /^STRING$/. To match STRING anywhere in the line, remove both the ^ and the $.

The current GNU grep utility has the ability to return an arbitrary number of lines following a matching search already built in. This feature is accessed using the -A switch.

Returning Preceding Lines to a Pattern Match Using grep

This technique is a bit more involved, as you need to cache previous lines and print them out when necessary. I outline three examples here, each more complex than the previous one.

The first command searches through the file for the pattern string. As it processes each line of the file, it saves the line prior to the match, and its record number, in the variables pO and pNR, respectively. (The awk internal variable NR represents the number of records in the current line of input.) When a line containing the pattern string is found, the record number of the previous line (pNR) and the previous line itself (pO) are displayed. Here the record number is simply used to display the number of the line that is being output.

```
awk '/pattern/{print pNR, pO}{pNR=NR;pO=$0}' /some/file
```

The next example works in almost the same way except that it saves and prints the two lines preceding each line that matches the pattern string.

```
awk '/pattern/{print ppNR, ppO,"\n", pNR, pO}\
{ppNR=pNR;pNR=NR;ppO=pO;pO=$0}' /some/file
```

The last example pushes the limits of what I would consider a reasonable one-liner. It grabs and retains previous lines as in the first two examples, but in a more general fashion. Instead of using distinct variables as in the second example, it saves the data in an array that it populates with a loop.

The first part of the command is a for loop that iterates through an array containing the previous lines of input. The loop moves the second through the last elements to the bottom of the array and then saves the current line ($0) in the highest element of the array. This loop is executed once for each line in the file.

Once it finds the pattern string, it prints an entry delimiter *Entry*. (This isn't required, but the final output can easily get confusing without some type of demarcation between groupings of lines.) Then another loop iterates through and prints out the lines stored in the array.

To configure this command for your own purposes, change the upper value of the j loop to the number of previous lines you want to return, plus 1. If you want the 3 previous lines for each of the pattern entries, set this value to 4. Also change the array assignment to set the highest element $0 to 4.

Next modify the upper value in the k loop to the number of previous lines you want printed. If you want 3 as before, use 3. If you would like to include the pattern line as well as the previous lines, make the upper limit of the k loop the same as that of the j loop. In this case it would be 4.

Since this is a somewhat complex command sequence, a generic example and a more specific one are presented here. It is worth some experimentation time to get a feel for how this works.

Here's the generic example:

```
awk '{for(j=0;j<='prevlines+1';j++){a[j]=a[j+1];a['prevlines+1']=$0}}\
  /some pattern/{{print "Entry"}\
  {for(k=0;k<'prevlines or prevlines+1';k++)\
  {print a[k]}}}' /some/file
```

And here's the more specific example:

```
awk '{for(j=0;j<=4;j++){a[j]=a[j+1];a[4]=$0}}\
  /some pattern/{{print "Entry"}{for(k=0;k<3;k++)\
  {print a[k]}}}' /some/file
```

Note The current GNU version of the grep utility has the ability to return an arbitrary number of lines found immediately prior to the actual matched lines found. You can access this feature via the -B switch.

CHAPTER 25

■ ■ ■

Editing Files in Place

Sometimes you want to modify a file as part of the tasks run from a shell script. Although the use of sed to modify files on the fly is common, the use of ed is less familiar to many. ed is a line-oriented editor that works much like any other text editor. It opens a file, makes modifications, saves the changes, and exits. The advantage of using ed to script these interactive sessions is that the modification is performed directly on the file itself and the results are neither redirected to another file nor used to overwrite the file itself.

For example, you might want to process a large list of files, applying a single modification to all of the files. In most of these cases, the modification may not be more than a simple search-and-replace operation. You could pipe the file through sed and then redirect the sed output to another file; once the output has been validated, you could move the modified file back into place and either overwrite the original or, more conservatively, back up the original file to another location before replacing it with the modified version.

The alternate method discussed here carries a little more risk because the original file itself is modified. There is a chance that the system will crash during the editing process for reasons not related to editing. Disk failures do occur on occasion, and it is also possible that another user might be modifying the file at the same time that you make changes of your own, or simply that your modification is incorrect and isn't validated. The upside is that editing files with ed works well and there isn't any need to create temporary files while modifications are in progress, although you may want to back up the original files for safety.

The procedure in this chapter uses the ed utility to modify files in place. ed is not a full-screen interactive editor, and any modification you want to perform on a file needs to be specified by an ed command. These commands include moving to specific locations in a file, searching and replacing, inserting and deleting data, and so on. When you script the use of ed, you first create a file containing all the modification commands you want to apply to the target file. Once that command file is created, you then apply all the commands at once to the target file.

This discussion will focus mainly on performing search-and-replace commands, plus a couple of other types of edits. The ed editor can do much more than what I'm going to suggest here, but this chapter will give you a good start on this style of editing.

Simple Search and Replace with ed

The following code is the simplest example. It shows the contents of a file named ed.script that contains an ed script consisting of a single search-and-replace command:

```
g/search/s/search/replace/g
w
q
```

The script saves the newly modified file and quits. A more advanced script would contain many more commands, but the final two write (w) and quit (q) lines would remain the same. The script can then be applied to a target file.

The ed command file is redirected into ed, which is then run against the target file. The -s switch suppresses diagnostic information.

```
ed -s /target/file < ed.script
```

The following is a slightly different method of creating ed input without the need for a separate script file:

```
ed -s /target/file <<EOF
g/search/s/search/replace/g
w
q
EOF
```

Note that the script's text is redirected into the ed command in the form of a here-document for input; in this case the delimiter is EOF. You then give the commands you desire, and complete the here-document with an ending delimiter. This is very similar to the discussion of free-formatted output using cat found in Chapter 28.

Now that the mechanics of how to create the command file and use it are set, let me explain some of the commands in more detail.

Search and Replace Using ed, Dissected

Now I want to explain, using the search-and-replace command from the preceding ed.script, what parts make up the search-and-replace instruction and what they do. This command is composed of six elements delimited by forward slashes (/).

g/*search*/**s**/*search*/*replace*/**g**

The first element, g for "global," instructs ed to perform the search-and-replace task throughout the entire target file. This element is optional. Without it, ed would default to editing only the *first* line that matches the search.

The second element describes what you are searching for in the target file.

The third element, the s, is fairly simple as well: it tells ed to search for the fourth element. At first this doesn't make sense, as the second element already provided the search string. Read on to see why it's necessary.

The fourth element is a secondary search term. It qualifies the search specified by the first search term (the second element of the command). For example, say you had a file containing names and addresses in which the first field of each line was either Name or Address, indicating what information follows. If you wanted to modify a particular street name and did a simple search and replace, you might end up inadvertently modifying some personal names as well as the desired street names. With the technique shown here, you could search for all lines starting with Address, and then (using the secondary search term) search for and modify a specific street name within these lines. This gives you more control over how the term that is to be modified is matched.

The fifth element specifies what will replace the fourth element.

The final element is another g, once more representing a global replacement. Again, this element is optional. This g tells ed to make the replacement for *all* instances of the secondary search term on lines that match the primary search string. If the second g is not present, the replacement will be performed on only the first match of the secondary search string. Any subsequent matches of the secondary string on that line will be ignored.

Examples of ed Commands

The following code represents the target file for each of the examples of ed search-and-replace commands provided in this section. As you can see, it is part of a hosts file. I have left the final w and q entries out of the displayed ed scripts. In practice you wouldn't want to forget these, as the changes then wouldn't be saved when ed completes. After the entry or entries that would be in the ed script file, I explain what the code will do, and finally I show you the modifications.

```
172.16.5.1 node1 node1.somedomain.com alias1.somedomain.com
172.16.5.2 node2 node2.somedomain.com alias2.somedomain.com
172.16.5.4 node3 node3.somedomain.com alias3.somedomain.com
```

The following command searches for occurrences of somedomain in the lines of the file and, on each line where this string is found, replaces all entries of somedomain with newdomain.

ed Command

```
g/somedomain/s/somedomain/newdomain/g
```

Modified File

```
172.16.5.1 node1 node1.newdomain.com alias1.newdomain.com
172.16.5.2 node2 node2.newdomain.com alias2.newdomain.com
172.16.5.4 node3 node3.newdomain.com alias3.newdomain.com
```

The next example replaces all occurrences of somedomain with newdomain on the first line where the somedomain string is found:

ed Command

```
/somedomain/s/somedomain/newdomain/g
```

Modified File

```
172.16.5.1 node1 node1.newdomain.com alias1.newdomain.com
172.16.5.2 node2 node2.somedomain.com alias2.somedomain.com
172.16.5.4 node3 node3.somedomain.com alias3.somedomain.com
```

The following command replaces the first instance of somedomain with newdomain on the first line where the somedomain string is found:

ed Command

```
/somedomain/s/somedomain/newdomain/
```

Modified File

```
172.16.5.1 node1 node1.newdomain.com alias1.somedomain.com
172.16.5.2 node2 node2.somedomain.com alias2.somedomain.com
172.16.5.4 node3 node3.somedomain.com alias3.somedomain.com
```

Here we replace all instances of the somedomain string with newdomain on all the lines where the IP address 172.16.5.2 is found:

ed Command

```
g/172.16.5.2/s/somedomain/newdomain/g
```

Modified File

```
172.16.5.1 node1 node1.somedomain.com alias1.somedomain.com
172.16.5.2 node2 node2.newdomain.com alias2.newdomain.com
172.16.5.4 node3 node3.somedomain.com alias3.somedomain.com
```

The next command lets us replace all instances of somedomain with newdomain in the file whenever an entry for the 172.16.5 subnet is found:[1]

ed Command

```
g/^172.16.5/s/somedomain/newdomain/g
```

Modified File

```
172.16.5.1 node1 node1.newdomain.com alias1.newdomain.com
172.16.5.2 node2 node2.newdomain.com alias2.newdomain.com
172.16.5.4 node3 node3.newdomain.com alias3.newdomain.com
```

In the next example, we search for node2 and insert a new entry prior to the line that is found. There are three commands:

1. The search for the term where you want to insert the new text.

2. The i for inserting the new text. This command switches the editor into insert mode instead of command mode, similar to the vi editor. Now comes the text of the line you want to insert.

3. The final command is the single period (.). This returns the editor to command mode.

ed Commands

```
/node2
i
172.16.5.14 node14 node14.newdomain.com alias14.newdomain.com
.
```

Modified File

```
172.16.5.1 node1 node1.somedomain.com alias1.somedomain.com
172.16.5.14 node14 node14.newdomain.com alias14.newdomain.com
172.16.5.2 node2 node2.somedomain.com alias2.somedomain.com
172.16.5.4 node3 node3.somedomain.com alias3.somedomain.com
```

In the next example, we search for node2 and insert another entry following the line that is found. This command sequence is nearly identical to the previous example, with only a slight modification so the new text follows the line that was found in the search. The i command to insert the new text has been replaced with the a to append the new text. The text and the closing period remain unchanged.

---

1. Note the leading carat (^) in the subnet that specifies lines beginning with that subnet. Without this character, IP addresses that simply contain 172.16.5 also would be replaced.

ed Commands

```
/node2
a
172.16.5.14 node14 node14.newdomain.com alias14.newdomain.com
.
```

Modified File

```
172.16.5.1 node1 node1.somedomain.com alias1.somedomain.com
172.16.5.2 node2 node2.somedomain.com alias2.somedomain.com
172.16.5.14 node14 node14.newdomain.com alias14.newdomain.com
172.16.5.4 node3 node3.somedomain.com alias3.somedomain.com
```

This last example shows how to delete a line entirely. We search for a line containing the string node2 and delete it. This command deletes only the first line that is found in the file. A leading g on the command would implement the deletion for all lines found in the file.

ed Command

```
/node2/d
```

Modified File

```
172.16.5.1 node1 node1.newdomain.com alias1.newdomain.com
172.16.5.4 node3 node3.newdomain.com alias3.newdomain.com
```

You should now be able to start using ed effectively. Take note again that the ed input can contain multiple entries to perform several tasks on a single file. Often the desired search strings or their replacements become known just before the target file is manipulated. For example, your ed command input may depend on accessing variables that were set prior to creating the ed script. For more examples of this technique in action, take a look at the scripts in Chapters 36 and 37.

Escaping Special Characters in a File

The following is a short script to escape all the special characters in a file that is specified from the command line. The script is meant to be a baseline that can escape any character, though you will likely tailor it to your own needs. The script performs its task using here-document syntax. The here-document notation can be found in the shell manual page.

The script starts simply enough. The usage is defined and then the input is validated to make sure a file is specified and that it exists.

```
#!/bin/sh
usage="$0 {target file containing any special characters to be escaped}"
if [ $# -eq 0 ]
  then
  echo $usage
  exit 1
fi
if [ ! -f $1 ]
then
  echo File $1 does not exist
  echo $usage
  exit 1
else
  file=$1
fi
```

If these requirements aren't met, the script displays the usage information and exits. The following code starts the here-document for input to the ed command:

```
ed -s $file <<EOF
g/[\]/s/[\]/\\\\\\\/g
```

The first search and replace is for the escape character itself. This replacement must be first or it will replace the backslash of characters that have already been escaped.

These replacements are the most simple of the bunch:

```
g/ /s/ /\\\ /g
g/!/s/!/\\\!/g
g/@/s/@/\\\@/g
g/#/s/#/\\\#/g
g/,/s/,/\\\,/g
g/%/s/%/\\\%/g
```

This grouping of replacements could have been written with the search character being surrounded by square brackets instead of the double escape. There isn't any difference in the length of the lines and it can be written either way.

```
g/\\$/s/\\$/\\\\$/g
g/\\&/s/\\&/\\\\&/g
g/\\*/s/\\*/\\\\*/g
```

The following set of replacement characters doesn't work with the search character surrounded by square brackets. They must be escaped so they aren't interpreted by the shell.

```
g/\\;/s/\\;/\\\;/g
g/\\:/s/\\:/\\\:/g
g/\\[/s/\\[/\\\[/g
g/\\]/s/\\]/\\\]/g
g/\\^/s/\\^/\\\\^/g
g/\\\`/s/\\\`/\\\\\`/g
```

This large section of replacements demonstrates the search character being specified by containing it within the square brackets. The replacement is still an escaped value.

```
g/[/]/s/[/]/\\\//g
g/[(]/s/[(]/\\\(/g
g/[)]/s/[)]/\\\)/g
g/[+]/s/[+]/\\\+/g
g/[=]/s/[=]/\\\=/g
g/[{]/s/[{]/\\\{/g
g/[}]/s/[}]/\\\}/g
g/[|]/s/[|]/\\\|/g
g/[']/s/[']/\\\'/g
g/["]/s/["]/\\\"/g
g/[<]/s/[<]/\\\</g
g/[>]/s/[>]/\\\>/g
g/[?]/s/[?]/\\\?/g
g/[~]/s/[~]/\\\~/g
g/[-]/s/[-]/\\\-/g
g/[_]/s/[_]/\\\_/g
```

The script finally completes by closing the here-document. This finishes the input to the ed command, and the modifications are then made to the input file.

```
w
q
EOF
```

■ ■ ■

## CHAPTER 26

Evaluating Variables
in a Flat File

One common scripting technique is to create a flat file that is one of a potential number of canned messages for users to receive—messages such as notifications of downtimes, changes in the environment, or use of system quota. (I consider a flat file simply a file that contains text.) Based on the logic in the script, the proper message will be sent to the user or users. A more advanced implementation of this technique provides a template that refers to environment variables and contains customizable elements so the message can be tailored specifically to the recipient.

In Chapter 36, I present a script that checks every morning for user passwords that are aging and therefore should be changed. In that script, when a password has reached the predetermined cut-off age, the script sends an e-mail to the account owner to state that the account will be locked if the owner doesn't update her password. The script annoys the user every day for a couple of weeks, after which the account is locked. After that, if the user wants to use the account she would have to call and explain why she didn't heed the friendly e-mail warnings.

The canned template file looks like this:

```
$ENVIRONMENT account password for \\"$USERID\\" expires in $REMAINING day\\(s\\)
================================================================
++ ACTION NEEDS TO BE TAKEN OR YOUR ACCOUNT WILL BE LOCKED ++
++ IN $REMAINING day\\(s\\) ++
================================================================
If the password isnt changed within $REMAINING day\\(s\\), account will be locked.

Instructions for changing passwords are located at:
\\<a href=\\"http://server.company.com/chg_passwd.html\\"\\>
http://server.company.com/chg_passwd.html\\</a\\>

If you are unable to change your password, please call the Help Desk.
```

If you no longer need this account, please let us know so we can remove it.
System Administration

Note in particular the shell variables (ENVIRONMENT, USERID, and REMAINING) and their escape sequences. When the script executes, the account expiration date for each possible USERID is checked, and the script determines how many days REMAINING there are before the account is frozen. The ENVIRONMENT variable specifies the environment from which the message is being sent. The occurrences of these variables must be replaced with their values before the script is run and the message is sent. Likewise, each escape sequence \\ evaluates to a single backslash that causes the following special character to be escaped so that it is treated as plain text when the script executes.

For each user with a soon-to-expire password, the template file is evaluated at runtime to replace the included variables with their contents. The code to perform the replacements in each case is fairly simple. It consists of one small loop that looks at each line in the flat file and replaces any variables with their assigned values. You can easily modify the code for other purposes—for example, to display the modified file.

```
cat $flat_file | while read a_line
do
  place_holder=`eval echo $a_line`
  echo $place_holder
done | $MAIL -s "$ENVIRONMENT UNIX Account Notification" $RECIPIENT
```

The loop processes each line of the file using the eval statement, which causes the variables to be replaced with their string values. The expanded line is assigned to the variable place_holder so that it can be echoed to standard output. Once all lines have been processed, the complete output is sent via e-mail to the specified RECIPIENT by the e-mail command in the final element of the command pipeline. The specific e-mail command is up to you; a couple of common ones are mailx and mail, depending on your operating system.

This technique has many potential uses. The example script here is much like a traditional mail merge where you customize the message based on specific users. You could also use this technique for creating and maintaining configuration for an application, or custom files for individual users patterned after a default file.

CHAPTER 27

■ ■ ■

Read Piped Input

Many programs available to the UNIX or Linux operating systems have the ability to process input from standard input through a pipe, Similarly, the following short script demonstrates how to perform this task using a shell script. The script also demonstrates a number of interesting techniques that are covered in more depth elsewhere in this book.

The purpose of the script is to take its input, whether from a file or stdin, and print the data to stdout in reverse order. The script provides two ways to perform this task. The first method works by calling the script with an argument that is the name of the file to be reversed. Alternatively, you can pipe output from some other command into the script, and it will then perform the reversal on its standard input.

First we initialize a counter variable that will track the lines of input the script receives.

```
#!/bin/sh
counter=0
```

Next we define the populate() function.

```
populate () {
  counter=$(($counter+1))
  eval COUNT${counter}='$LINE'
}
```

This function creates a new variable by calling the eval command. The eval command performs variable and metacharacter expansion in what follows before passing the result to the shell to evaluate; it is used here to construct a line of code (an assignment statement) out of the contents of preexisting variables. This is a fairly powerful method for creating command lines at runtime and is explained in more detail in Chapter 7.

The populate() function first increments the counter variable and then creates a variable called COUNTnn where nn is the value of the counter that in this case refers to the specific line of input to be reversed. The collection of these variables behaves analogously to an array, except that the limit on the number of elements is based on the amount of memory the shell makes available rather than the preset limit for the shell's array construct.[1]

---

1. The maximum number of elements in an array in ksh88 is 1024. In ksh93, it is increased to 4096. bash has no range limit.

Now we check to see whether a filename has been passed to the script.

```
if [ "$1" != "" ]
then
  if [ -f $1 ]
  then
    while read LINE
    do
      populate
    done < $1
  else
    echo "$1 Does not exist, please try again"
  fi
```

If it has, the script tests whether the file exists. If the file is validated, the script redirects it into the back end of the while loop. This loop calls the populate function for each line of the file. If the file named in the command line doesn't exist, we just output a simple error message.

You may think performing a cat of the file and piping the result into the front of the while loop would work, but this can have unforeseen results. It works in ksh without a hitch, but not in pdksh or in bash. (For more information about piping data into a while loop, see Chapter 10.) Redirecting the file into the back end of the while loop always works.

If no filename was passed to the script from the command line, we assume the data is being piped into the script.

```
else
  while read LINE
  do
    populate
  done
fi
```

Each line is read in sequence, and the populate function is called to expand the variables to their values.

Once the script has finished processing all the data, the counter variable contains the number of the last line of data that was processed.

```
while [ $counter -gt 0 ]
do
  eval echo '$COUNT'$counter
  counter=$(($counter-1))
done
```

This while loop then counts down from the counter value, decrementing by one each time, outputting the contents of each of the newly created variables. Thus we reverse the order of the lines from the input.

CHAPTER 28

■ ■ ■

Free-Format Output Using cat

There are many ways to send script output to the screen or to a file. The technique demonstrated in this chapter for creating preformatted output is simple to code. Many times I have coded scripts that write entries to a log, create a configuration file, or generate formatted usage output one line at a time by redirecting the output of echo statements. This works perfectly well, but the code looks a bit ugly and becomes tedious; it is also laborious to make changes because each echo statement has to be formatted individually.

The original version of the gold Linux build script in Chapter 38 was written in that way. It created a temporary file used to partition a hard disk by outputting each partition table entry individually. The script has since been updated to use the technique in this chapter. Here are some sample lines of the original code:

```
echo "# partition table of /dev/hda" > $PARTTAB
echo "unit: sectors" >> $PARTTAB
echo >> $PARTTAB
echo "/dev/hda3 : start=0,size=0,Id=0" >> $PARTTAB
echo "/dev/hda4 : start=0,size=0,Id=0" >> $PARTTAB
```

Note that if the partition file already exists, the first command overwrites the file using a single greater-than symbol (>), and if the file does not exist, the file is simply created. All subsequent echo statements append their output to the file. With this method, there is the danger of using the incorrect redirect (overwrite > or append >>). As an example, if the last line in the four lines of the code here had a single redirect > instead of a double redirect >>, the output of all the lines previous to the error would be eliminated. Troubleshooting this error is somewhat difficult since both versions work, are very similar in appearance, and differ by only a single character.

In contrast, the technique described in this chapter uses the cat utility in a form that is not necessarily intuitive. Instead of echoing lines one at a time, you create the formatted text all at once and then output it to the screen directly using a here-document. Alternatively, you can redirect it to an output file either in append or overwrite mode.

This method uses double input-redirect characters (<<), followed by a unique delimiter, in this case SOMETAG, but it could be anything and does not matter if it is all uppercase. The delimiter immediately precedes the preformatted text to mark its start. On the line following the last line of the text, a matching end delimiter is issued to close the here-document. With this technique, you can create free-format output of as many lines as you like in the exact format you want. Once the here-document is closed, the output stream is terminated and the command completes.

This code is functionally the same as the first code segment in this chapter, except that the code has been modified to use cat instead of echo:

```
cat > $PARTTAB <<SOMETAG
# partition table of /dev/hda
unit: sectors
/dev/hda3 : start=0,size=0,Id=0
/dev/hda4 : start=0,size=0,Id=0
SOMETAG
```

This example is much cleaner and easier to read, since nearly all the echo statements, quotes, and redirection syntax have been removed. Also, commented (#), blank, and quoted lines can be entered without further issues arising, as they won't be evaluated by the shell.

Some characters may need to be escaped if you want them to be included in your output. The dollar sign ($) and the back-tick or back-quote (`) need to be escaped with a backslash (\) because otherwise the shell will evaluate them and attempt to use them with their normal meanings.

This slight modification of the here-document adds the hyphen (-) following the initial redirection:

```
cat > $PARTTAB <<-SOMETAG
        # partition table of /dev/hda
        unit: sectors
        /dev/hda3 : start=0,size=0,Id=0
        /dev/hda4 : start=0,size=0,Id=0
SOMETAG
```

This strips any leading tab characters from the preformatted text, allowing the indentation of the code to look more readable and be viewed in more of a code block.

You can see a few examples of this technique at work in this book. You can find the here-document technique in Chapter 22, where a default user-configuration file is created if one doesn't already exist. Additionally, as I already mentioned, Chapter 38 details the partition layout file to build a Linux gold system.

The method of opening a file handle for arbitrary input as a replacement for a file can be used for more than just output using cat. Any utility that you might redirect a file into can use this technique. Some examples can be found in Chapters 10 and 25, where the need for a temporary file is removed.

CHAPTER 29

■■■

Automating Interactive Processes

Automating commands that are normally used interactively is something I've done many times. The simplest and most common script of this sort that I've used automates an ftp session to copy files from system to system. I'll concede that for security reasons, ftp is not a good method for moving files around, especially when the session requires login/password authentication as a user other than "anonymous." Usernames and passwords are then sent across the network unencrypted. Even in a controlled environment, this has its risks, which should be considered carefully. Using this method out in the wild means asking for trouble.

In any case, the point of this section is not to weigh the pros and cons of using ftp, but to demonstrate how to script an interactive session, using file copying as an example. This scripting construct is called a here-document. In this case it is gathering the latest black-list from the SquidGuard[1] project to update your Squid web proxy automatically from less-than-desirable Internet locations.

The script presented here is just a simple ftp session to get a file. Note the tags for the beginning and the end of the interactive session. In this case EOF is used, but it could just as well have been FLOOBY or CaMeLCaSe (or anything that doesn't appear at the start of a line within the session itself). Also, the closing tag needs to be present at the beginning of the line that follows the final command of the ftp session, because the shell recognizes it in that position as the closing delimiter. I would prefer to align the closing tag with the last line of the ftp session to make the indentation match up, but if I did this the end of the session wouldn't be recognized and any following lines of code would be considered part of the session.

First we set up the variables to be used for the ftp session, such as the source and destination file locations and the Squid server name.

```
#!/bin/sh
SGCONFDIR=/opt/apps/squidguard/conf
```

---

1. SquidGuard is a plug-in for the Squid proxy server acting as a filter, redirector, and access controller. More information can be found at http://www.squidguard.org.

```
SERVER=ftp.teledanmark.no
FILE=blacklists.tar.gz
DIR=/pub/www/proxy/squidGuard/contrib
```

Next the script outputs some text about what it is doing and then starts the ftp session.

```
echo "FTPing current squidguard blacklist"
ftp -n $SERVER << EOF
```

The -n switch for ftp is used to disable the auto-login feature. You need to add the -n switch so that you can pass the username and password from the script.

The first line of the ftp session passes credentials to the ftp server.

```
user anonymous you@yourdomain.com
```

It is generally considered poor security practice to include a username and password in a script. In this case, it isn't really a problem since it is an anonymous session. Later in this chapter I will explain how you can remove the credentials from the script itself and store them in a separate file for ftp to use.

These lines are the ftp commands that make up the session:

```
cd $DIR
hash
lcd $SGCONFDIR
get $FILE
bye
EOF
```

In this case, the commands change to the appropriate remote and local directories, then they fetch the file and close the session.

If you would like to avoid having the username and password inside the script, there are a few changes to make. First you should add an entry to the $HOME/.netrc file of the user who is running this script. The .netrc file contains credentials to use for sessions with specific ftp servers by the owner of the file; it looks something like this:

```
machine ftpserver.your.domain.com login johndoe password Vu1n3rab13
machine ftpserver login johndoe password Vu1n3rab13
machine ftp.teledanmark.no login anonymous password you@yourdomain.com
```

The new .netrc entry corresponds to the ftp server that is being used. After modifying the .netrc file, you have to remove the -n switch that was used in the ftp command at the beginning of the script.

You can set up ftp sessions to as many sites as you like in the .netrc file. Remember the security concerns; you'll want to make sure the file is readable by only the owner. One potential gotcha is that ftp will look for the server name used in the script (or command-line) invocation of ftp verbatim. In other words, if you ftp to the fully qualified domain name (FQDN), that FQDN must be in the .netrc entry. If you use the short name without the domain in the ftp invocation, then the short name must have an entry in the .netrc file. One can't be substituted for the other. Both types are shown in the preceding example (in the entries for the server with the FQDN `ftpserver.your.domain.com`). The last entry in the preceding .`netrc` example file is one of the sites where you can obtain a blacklist file for SquidGuard.

This is a very quick and simple example of a scripted session with an interactive program. It would, however, be more secure to use `sftp` (secure `ftp`), which uses an encrypted connection; unlike `ftp`, it doesn't transfer your username and password across the network in plain text.

The here-document technique used in this chapter for an automated `ftp` session can be expanded into a nested structure for multiple layers of interactive automation, as you may have more-complex needs.

```
su - oracle <<-EOF
        sqlplus "/ as sysdba" <<-SQL
                shutdown immediate;
                exit;
        SQL
        lsnrctl stop
EOF
```

In the case of the preceding code, the root account is required to run multiple commands to stop a database as the oracle user account. The oracle user is required to run the interactive `sqlplus` command.

The first here-document is specified by the `EOF` tag where root becomes the user oracle. All of the commands in this element are run as oracle. The next here-document nested within the first is specified by the `SQL` tag. This contains the commands to cleanly shut down the database, which is normally run interactively. Note that the double less-than characters (`<<`) are followed by a hyphen. This syntax strips any leading tab characters from the beginning of lines within the here-document. This provides the ability to indent your code properly for easier reading.

If you prefer, you could use the `expect` utility for scripting interactive programs. `expect` implements a whole language designed for this purpose, with many more capabilities. More information on using `expect` can be found in Chapter 17.

CHAPTER 30

■ ■ ■

Automating E-mail with procmail

An autonomous mail processor, procmail allows you to process your e-mail based on rules. This is much like setting up rules in your e-mail client for the handling of messages based on, for example, the sender's e-mail address or on specified strings in the subject line. One of procmail's advantages, compared to traditional e-mail clients, is that the rules can be defined in such a way that when specific criteria are met, a script is called to perform a task.

Whatever you can do in a shell script, you can do with procmail. Once you have mastered the art of writing procmail scripts, it is a very powerful skill to have in your arsenal. I have used procmail for quite a few tasks. One processed customer feedback surveys and generated reports for use in managing a technical support group. Another received e-mail messages that contained system-setup parameters for numerous remote systems, such as the patch level or the names of installed applications. Procmail would process these messages based on their subject lines and categorize the received information for later review. It was a very convenient way of tracking system-configuration information.

The example I will demonstrate here is a simplified version of a procmail script I set up to deal with the lack of direct access to my home system from work, and the lack of convenient access to my work system from home. My home system periodically dialed my ISP to gather e-mail. From time to time I would want to get a file from my home system or find out a system setting on my work system while I was at home. I set up procmail to receive specially formatted mail messages specifying files to retrieve or commands to be run on the remote machine, and to have the results returned to me through e-mail.

To make this work I sent all my e-mail to procmail. The method depends on your e-mail system. My systems used sendmail and my explanations in this chapter assume this, but the concepts should apply to other mail systems as well.

I first created a .forward file in my home directory that would pipe all my mail to procmail. This is the content of that file:

```
| /usr/bin/procmail
```

Not much to it, except that the path may vary on your machine. Sendmail has to be configured to recognize and use the $HOME/.forward files, but that is a common configuration.

193

On some systems, sendmail is configured to recognize the use of procmail by looking for the existence of a .procmailrc file; this is the file that contains all of your procmail rules. In this case sendmail then sends the mail to procmail automatically, without the need for a .forward file.

The .procmailrc File

Now that we have arranged for mail to be sent to procmail, the mail-handling rules need to be configured. The .procmailrc file lives in the user's home directory and contains their mail rules. The rules are applied in the order they appear in the file; if none of the rules apply to a mail message or if the .procmailrc file is empty, the message will drop out of procmail processing and end up in your inbox as usual.

This is the .procmailrc I used:

```
PATH=/bin:/usr/bin:/usr/local/bin
MAILDIR=$HOME/Mail
LOGFILE=$MAILDIR/procmail.log
VERBOSE=yes
LOGABSTRACT=yes
SUBJECT=`formail -xSubject:`
FROM=`formail -rt -xTo:`
#
# Grab mail messages and feed the body of the message to the pipe
#
:0 getthisfile.lock
  * ^Subject:.*getthisfile
{
  :0 b
  | /usr/local/bin/getthisfile
}
```

Here is a more detailed explanation of the elements that make up this file. The first few lines set up some path and mail-logging variables.

```
PATH=/bin:/usr/bin:/usr/local/bin
MAILDIR=$HOME/Mail
LOGFILE=$MAILDIR/procmail.log
```

The next two lines configure the amount of logging information that your log files will receive:

```
VERBOSE=yes
LOGABSTRACT=yes
```

These values are useful to get logging set up and to ensure that the script is working, but normally you'll want to set these to no so that the log file doesn't grow to take over your hard disk.

The last two lines in the first section are crucial, as they extract the subject and sender lines from the incoming message and save them in environment variables:

```
SUBJECT=`formail -xSubject:`
FROM=`formail -xFrom:`
```

The variables can then be accessed from within the script. The values are pulled out of the message headers using the `formail` utility, which is a filter designed especially for e-mail.

Now we finally come to the body of the rules file.

```
:0 getthisfile.lock
```

This is the main rule for processing special-purpose mail messages. It is the beginning of the rule, and it creates a lock file that exists while the message is being processed. The lock file prevents the next applicable message in the mail queue from being processed until the processing of the current message is complete. If our system receives lots of mail and the script to process mail messages takes a while to finish, there could arise several instances running simultaneously on different messages, all trying to access the same temporary files at once. The presence of the lock file indicates that an instance of the script is already running and another should not start.

The next line of the rule checks the `Subject:` header line for an occurrence of the string `getthisfile`.

```
* ^Subject:.*getthisfile
```

If the string is matched, then the body of the rule will be applied. The body of the rule follows the condition, in this case the subject matching `getthisfile`, and is enclosed in braces. I'm not going to talk in detail about the syntax of the `procmail` rules, because the `procmail` man page is very good; there is also a man page for `procmailex` that is dedicated to examples of rules for the .`procmailrc` file.

Assuming that the subject line of the message contains `getthisfile`, the message itself is sent to the script.

```
{
  :0 b
  | /usr/local/bin/getthisfile
}
```

The single b character in this expression stands for the body of the message. The message body is piped to the `getthisfile` script, which does the actual mail processing. This is the way you would generally send to the script the information contained in the mail message. In our case, most of the header and the body of the mail don't contain anything of value, so the subject line is really all the information we need. If the body of the message were required, the script would need to be ready to receive standard input from the pipe. This would probably be done through a `read` loop. An example of this type of processing can be found in Chapter 27.

The e-mail account is now set up to receive and process the special messages. Any mail sent to this account with a subject line of the following form will be processed by the getthisfile script:

```
Subject: getthisfile {binary|command|help} {path/file|command}
```

Now let's look at what the script really does. The following section shows the script's usage.

Usage Examples

Here are a few examples of subject lines and the actions they would cause to be performed:

Subject: getthisfile help: Sends getthisfile usage information back to the sender.

Subject: getthisfile /etc/resolv.conf: Mails the /etc/resolv.conf file back to the sender.

Subject: getthisfile command ls -l /tmp: Sends the output of ls -l /tmp back to the sender.

Subject: getthisfile binary /usr/bin/diff: uuencodes the binary file /usr/bin/diff and mails the text back to the sender for later decoding. uuencode is a utility that encodes a binary file (executable, data, etc.) into simple ASCII. This way the file can be easily sent through e-mail and decoded on the receiving side.

The Code

The getthisfile script first sets up some variables containing information such as the system name, the log file to write to, and the e-mail address where warnings should be sent if somebody tries to use this tool without authorization. It then adds a couple of entries to the log, such as the date and the mail subject.

```
#!/bin/sh
warn_mail=my_email@mydomain.com
me=`uname -n`
LOG=/home/username/scripts/filetoget.log
echo `date` >> $LOG
echo Subject: $SUBJECT >> $LOG
```

Next it starts parsing the subject line to find out what is being requested.

```
filetoget=`echo $SUBJECT | awk '{print $3}'`
echo filetoget: $filetoget >> $LOG
whattodo=`echo $SUBJECT | awk '{print $2}'`
echo whattodo: $whattodo >> $LOG
command=`echo $SUBJECT | cut -d\ -f3-`
echo Command: $command >> $LOG
```

The variables should be self-explanatory. It is possible that some of them won't be defined at this point, but will be defined later. The values of these variables are also entered into the log.

This next part of the script is important if you don't want just anyone having access to your system.

```
if [ "$FROM" != " user1@good_domain.com" -a \
  "$FROM" != " user2@good_domain.com" ]
then
  echo "Invalid user $FROM trying to get procmail info: \
    $SUBJECT" >> $LOG
  tail -10 $LOG | mail -s \
    "$FROM attempting to get procmail info" $warn_mail
  exit 0
fi
```

The script checks the address of the requester, where the requested information is to be sent. If the requester is not one of the approved addresses, a warning is sent to the e-mail address stored in the warn_mail variable to notify the script's owner of the potential intruder. The script then exits.

There is still potential for a breach, however, so don't be lulled into a false sense of security. If someone knew that this utility existed, they could craft a message that works as a spoof pretending to be sent from one of the allowed addresses. The message would contain a subject line that would cause the getthisfile script to be replaced with a file of the intruder's choosing. The output of the intruder's commands would be sent back to the real allowed e-mail addresses, but by the time they were noticed, it would likely be too late and the intruder would have access (although only to the account that has the procmail setup, which hopefully is not root). Careful setting of permissions and ownership of this script and of the .procmailrc files would make intrusion a lot more difficult, but still not impossible.

Caution Although this isn't the most secure method of transferring files or information, it does demonstrate the use of procmail, which is the goal here.

■**Note** In this section of the code the `if` statement's condition contains a leading space in the e-mail address. This is the way the e-mail address is received from `procmail`. The leading space could be handled in a few ways, but just adding the space in the `if`/`then` conditional works sufficiently well.

Next we examine the parsed subject line and determine what action to perform. Each action adds an entry to the log file.

```
if [ "$whattodo" = "binary" ]
then
  echo "binary filetoget: $filetoget" >> $LOG
  echo "sending it to: $FROM" >> $LOG
  cd /tmp
  filename=`echo $filetoget | awk -F/ '{print $NF}'`
  uuencode $filetoget $filename > /tmp/$filename.uue
  echo "cat /tmp/$filename.uue | \
    mail -s \"uuencoded $filetoget from $me\" $FROM" >> $LOG
  cat /tmp/$filename.uue | \
    mail -s "uuencoded $filetoget from $me" $FROM >> $LOG
  rm /tmp/$filename.uue
```

If the `procmail` script receives a command to send a binary file, the process moves to the /tmp directory and then uuencodes the requested binary file. The script then e-mails the encoded output back to the requester for later decoding.

Another way of performing this task would be an excellent upgrade to this script: craft an e-mail message that, when received, attaches the binary file to the message. This can be done through manipulation of the e-mail headers and proper encoding of the binary file. See Chapter 23 for a script that can perform this task.

If the script determines that the requester wants to run a command, it performs the command and then e-mails the output back to the requester.

```
elif [ "$whattodo" = "command" ]
then
  echo Running command $command >> $LOG
  echo "$command | mail -s \"Output of $command on $me\" $FROM" >> $LOG
  $command | mail -s "Output of $command on $me" $FROM >> $LOG
```

If the requester needs help in formatting his e-mail subject line correctly, and inserts the proper subject line to get help, the script will send back usage information. However, the requester does have to know a little about how it works before he can ask for help.

```
elif [ "$whattodo" = "help" ]
then
  echo "Sending usage to $FROM" >> $LOG
  echo "Subject: getthisfile {binary|command|help} \
    {path/file|command}" | mail -s "Usage" $FROM
```

The final part of the script is the most basic. If the file to get and the command to run are the same, the script sees that there is no command to run.

```
else
  filetoget=$whattodo
  echo "filetoget: $filetoget" >> $LOG
  echo "sending it to: $FROM" >> $LOG
  echo "cat $filetoget | mail -s \"$filetoget from $me\" $FROM" >> $LOG
  cat $filetoget | mail -s "$filetoget from $me" $FROM >> $LOG
fi
```

In this case the user just wants to receive a simple flat file, which will be mailed back to the requester. Another improvement to this script would be to use the file command to first check the type of file that is being requested to make sure it is being processed correctly.

■ ■ ■

## CHAPTER 31

Process-Management Monitor

System process monitors can be a vital tool in determining the health of a running machine. Ensuring that the required processes are running and that the total number of each type of running process is appropriate is a good way to maintain system stability. The downside of these types of monitors is that they let you know only which processes are running and how many there are. They don't give you an indication of the health of each individual process.

This script dives a little deeper into the condition of processes. By using the ps command with a customized format, we'll be able to monitor the age, proportion of CPU usage, virtual-memory consumption, and amount of CPU time consumed by a particular process. If you are monitoring multiple instances of any given process, each instance will be held up to the standard being monitored.

One other feature of this process monitor is that it can be configured not only to warn you of impending peril from processes whose operational values are out of bounds, but also to take action in the form of killing the aberrant process when necessary. The monitor could be modified easily to perform other actions besides killing a process.

Using historical data, you can sometimes predict when a specific application will start to consume too many resources. It was one such application I was working with that prompted me to write this monitor. The monitor helped in characterizing exactly when the application ran out of control and in finding the cause of the behavior. Both were very helpful in fixing the problem.

The syntax for monitor configuration is fairly straightforward, with five colon-separated fields as shown in the following example. The fields are as follows: the process command, the indicator to track, a lower threshold, an upper threshold, and the kill option. You can configure multiple processes by including several records in the configuration string.

```
kill_plist="dhcpd:pcpu:15:30:1 sshd:pcpu:15:30:1"
```

The first field is the process command itself. This will be slightly different, and hopefully simpler, than the traditional ps -ef output. The ps -ef default output (-e for all processes, -f for formatted output) includes the commands that are running, as well as any arguments they were passed. The ps -eo comm output is formatted to include only the commands that are running on a system without any path or argument information.

With this switch combination (-eo) you can also format your output in many ways to show many other options, such as memory size, process age, process CPU time, and so on. (On some UNIX systems, you may need to define the UNIX95 variable within the script for the ps -eo command to function properly. The UNIX95 variable can be set to anything you'd like; it just needs to not be undefined.) When specifying the process for our script to monitor, you'll want to use only the command name, as this is what the script will be looking for.

The second field contains the indicator you want to track. The options are cputime, which measures the number of minutes the cpu has allocated to the process; etime, which is the elapsed time in minutes since the process began running; pcpu which represents the current percentage of the CPU capacity the process is consuming; and vsize, which shows the virtual-memory size in kilobytes for the process.

The third and fourth fields contain the desired lower and upper thresholds for the indicator you're tracking.

The fifth and final field is the kill option. It is a value from 0 to 3:

0: Send a notification when either the low warning or high error threshold have been crossed, but *don't* kill the process.

1: Send a warning notification when the low threshold has been crossed or an error notification when the high threshold has been crossed, *and* kill the process.

2: Send only a low-level warning notification when either the low or high threshold has been crossed, *and* kill the process.

3: Kill the process without any notification at all.

Note that for safety, if the kill option is not set or is set to anything but one of the values outlined here, processes will not be killed. Notice that there are two levels of notification. I have used alphanumeric paging for the high level (error status) and e-mail for the low level (warning status). You may want to implement the notification method as appropriate for your needs.

The first section of the script sets up a few configuration variables, which alternatively could be stored in a separate configuration file and sourced each time the script runs through the loop. This would allow for live configuration changes to the script. The debug value is for testing and the sleeptime value represents the amount of time to delay between each run. The kill_plist variable is the main configuration value that lets the script know what processes and values it should be watching.

```
#!/bin/sh
debug=1
sleeptime=3
kill_plist="dhcpd:pcpu:15:30:1 sshd:pcpu:15:30:1"
```

The following function performs all notifications and process terminations in the script. It is called with seven sequentially numbered parameters. The positional variables are somewhat difficult to understand and their values could have been assigned to more meaningfully named variables before they were used, for ease of debugging later. To streamline the script a little, I didn't do this.

```
notify ()
{
  case $2 in
    0)
      # Warn/error level and don't kill..
      echo "$1: $3 process id $4 found with $5 $7. Should be less than $6."
    ;;
    1)
      # Warn/error level and kill..
      echo "$1: $3 process id $4 found with $5 $7. Should be less than $6."
      test $debug -eq 0 && kill $4
    ;;
    2)
      # Warning level only...
      echo "Warning: $3 process id $4 found with $5 $7. Should be less than $6."
      test $debug -eq 0 && kill $4
    ;;
    3)
      # Just kill, don't warn at all..
      test $debug -eq 0 && kill $4
    ;;
    *)
      echo "Warning: killoption not set correctly, please validate configuration."
    ;;
  esac
}
```

Here, for ease of reference, I define all of the command-line arguments passed to this function:

$1: Text passed used for building the notification string; used for the difference between warning and error

$2: The kill option, which has a possible value of 0-3

$3: The process name that is being monitored

$4: The process ID of the process being monitored

$5: The current value of the indicator you are tracking

$6: The monitor's lower threshold

$7: The text equivalent of the indicator you are tracking

This is also a good example of how a function can reduce the length and complexity of a script. The body of this function is code that would have to be repeated eight times throughout the script if it were not placed in a function. An older version of this script was written this way. Putting the code into a function reduced the script's length by roughly 40 percent.

The following code is the beginning of the main loop. The script is intended to be run at system startup; it will then be run continuously through an infinite loop. After each iteration completes, the script will sleep for a predetermined time before the next iteration. The first part here is a nested loop that progresses through each record in the configuration string to parse its fields and set up the monitor.

```
while :
do
  for pline in $kill_plist
  do
    process=`echo $pline | cut -d: -f1`
    process="`echo $process | sed -e \"s/%20/ /g\"`"
    type=`echo $pline | cut -d: -f2`
    value=`echo $pline | awk -F: '{print $3}'`
    errval=`echo $pline | awk -F: '{print $4}'`
    killoption=`echo $pline | awk -F: '{print $5}'`
```

The process variable is assigned the first field in the configuration record (pline). It is possible that the process command name you're monitoring will consist of more than one word, separated by spaces. Such spaces are replaced (here using the sed command) with %20, which is a commonly used substitute for the space character, as in URL encoding, for example.

The type variable is the second field in the configuration record. As mentioned, it specifies the performance indicator to watch: cputime (amount of CPU time consumed), etime (elapsed time or age of process), pcpu (current percentage of the CPU consumed), or vsize (virtual-memory size).

The value variable holds the lower warning threshold for the monitored value, taken from the third field.

The errval variable is assigned the value of the upper error threshold for the monitored value, taken from the fourth field.

The killoption variable is assigned the final field of the configuration record and specifies an action to perform when the process deviates from the normal range.

If the kill option was not specified initially, we set it to be the default kill option. This makes sure no processes are killed unless one of the options for doing so is explicitly used.

```
    if [ "$killoption" = "" ]
    then
      killoption=0
    fi
    test $debug -gt 0 && echo "Kill $process processes if $type is greater than
$errval"
```

Next we pare down the full list of processes running on the system to the ones running the command being monitored. Then we start a loop that iterates through the remaining processes.

```
    for pid in `ps -eo pid,comm | egrep "${process}$|${process}:$" | grep -v grep |
awk '{print $1}'`
      do
```

For each process ID, the script has to gather the pertinent information. The embedded ps command gathers only the specific information we want.

```
      test $debug -gt 0 && echo "$process pid $pid"
      pid_string=`ps -eo pid,cputime,etime,pcpu,vsize,comm | \
        grep $pid | egrep "${process}$|${process}:$" | grep -v grep`
```

The following case statement is the heart of the monitor. The script tests for the monitor type (cputime, etime, pcpu, or vsize); the cputime is the first monitor type listed. The code for each type is slightly different, but all are very similar. Here we obtain the process time from the ps output, as well as the number of fields that the proc_time variable contains.

```
      case $type in
        "cputime")
          proc_time=`echo $pid_string | awk '{print $2}'`
          fields=`echo $proc_time | awk -F: '{print NF}'`
          proc_time_min=`echo $proc_time | awk -F: '{print $(NF-1)}'`
```

Both of these are needed because the format of the time value varies depending on the amount of time it represents. The cputime and etime variables have values of the form days-hours:minutes:seconds or hours:minute:seconds. A low value might look something like 00:28 for 28 seconds. A high value could be 1-18:32:29 for 1 day, 18 hours, 32 minutes, and 29 seconds. Both of these types have to be processed and converted to minutes. (Seconds are dropped for simplicity.)

Of the four performance indicators, the logic for handling the cputime and etime values is the most complex because the format used to report them changes depending on the amount of time these values represent.

```
            if [ $fields -lt 3 ]
            then
              proc_time_hr=0
              proc_time_day=0
```

```
      else
      proc_time_hr=`echo $proc_time | awk -F: '{print $(NF-2)}'`
      fields=`echo $proc_time_hr | awk -F- '{print NF}'`
      if [ $fields -ne 1 ]
      then
        proc_time_day=`echo $proc_time_hr | awk -F- '{print $1}'`
        proc_time_hr=`echo $proc_time_hr | awk -F- '{print $2}'`
      else
        proc_time_day=0
      fi
   fi
```

Once all time values have been determined, we convert them to minutes for comparison with the monitor thresholds.

```
      curr_cpu_time=\
       `echo "$proc_time_day*1440+$proc_time_hr*60+$proc_time_min"\
       | bc`
      test $debug -gt 0 && echo "Current cpu time for \
       $process pid $pid is $curr_cpu_time minutes"
```

If the current cputime value is between the warning and error thresholds, we call the notify() function with the appropriate switches. It will handle output and process termination, as described earlier.

```
      if test $curr_cpu_time -gt $value -a \
         $curr_cpu_time -lt $errval
      then
         notify "Warning" $killoption $process $pid \
         $curr_cpu_time $value "minutes of CPU time"
```

If the current cputime is greater than the error threshold, we call the notify() function with a different set of options.

```
      elif test $curr_cpu_time -ge $errval
      then
         notify "Error" $killoption $process $pid \
           $curr_cpu_time $value "minutes of CPU time"
```

The final condition handles the case where there is no issue with the running process: the script just issues a message saying so.

```
      else
         test $debug -gt 0 && echo "process cpu time ok"
      fi
   ;;
```

The `etime` monitor is nearly the same as the `cputime` monitor. The primary difference is the field that is extracted from the `ps` output to get the current process age.

```
"etime")
  proc_age=`echo $pid_string | awk '{print $3}'`
  fields=`echo $proc_age | awk -F: '{print NF}'`
  proc_age_min=`echo $proc_age | awk -F: '{print $(NF-1)}'`
```

Once again, you convert the age of the process to values that will then be used to calculate the age in minutes.

```
if [ $fields -lt 3 ]
then
  proc_age_hr=0
  proc_age_day=0
else
  proc_age_hr=`echo $proc_age | awk -F: '{print $(NF-2)}'`
  fields=`echo $proc_age_hr | awk -F- '{print NF}'`
  if [ $fields -ne 1 ]
  then
    proc_age_day=`echo $proc_age_hr | awk -F- '{print $1}'`
    proc_age_hr=`echo $proc_age_hr | awk -F- '{print $2}'`
  else
    proc_age_day=0
  fi
fi
```

Now expressing the process age in minutes makes the threshold check very simple.

```
curr_age=\
  `echo "$proc_age_day*1440+$proc_age_hr*60+$proc_age_min" \
  | bc`
test $debug -gt 0 && echo "Current age of $process pid \
  $pid is $curr_age minutes"
```

We now perform the comparison checks against the monitor thresholds as before. The first check determines if the current process age is between the low and high thresholds. The second sees if the current age is above the high threshold. In both these cases, call the `notify()` function for end-user output and process termination. The final possibility is that there is no issue, and in this case the script gives a message stating that the process is OK.

```
if test $curr_age -gt $value -a $curr_age -lt $errval
then
  notify "Warning" $killoption $process $pid \
    $curr_age $value "minutes of elapsed time"
elif test $curr_age -ge $errval
```

```
then
  notify "Error" $killoption $process $pid \
    $curr_age $value "minutes of elapsed time"
else
  test $debug -gt 0 && echo "process age ok"
fi
;;
```

The test for percentage CPU usage is quite simple. The value to be compared to the thresholds is obtained directly from the ps output. There is no need for further calculation as was needed in the code for the cputime and etime monitors.

```
"pcpu")
  curr_proc_cpu=`echo $pid_string | awk '{print $4}' | \
    awk -F. '{print $1}'`
  test $debug -gt 0 && echo "Current percent cpu of \
    $process pid $pid is $curr_proc_cpu"
```

Once again, we compare the percentage CPU value with the configured low and high thresholds and call the notify() function to alert the user and perform any required process termination. If the CPU percentage is below either of these values, the code outputs an "OK" message.

```
if test $curr_proc_cpu -gt $value -a \
  $curr_proc_cpu -lt $errval
then
  notify "Warning" $killoption $process $pid \
    $curr_proc_cpu $value "percent of the CPU"
elif test $curr_proc_cpu -ge $errval
then
  notify "Error" $killoption $process $pid \
    $curr_proc_cpu $value "percent of the CPU"
else
  test $debug -gt 0 && echo "process cpu percent ok"
fi
;;
```

The vsize monitor is as simple as the percent-CPU monitor. We obtain the current process's memory footprint directly from the ps output.

```
"vsize")
  curr_proc_size=`echo $pid_string | awk '{print $5}'`
  test $debug -gt 0 && echo "Current size of $process pid \
    $pid is $curr_proc_size"
```

We have to check the current memory size against the monitor thresholds one last time. If they are within a low or high warning status, we call the notify() function for output and termination. If not, the code outputs that the process size is OK.

```
        if test $curr_proc_size -gt $value -a \
          $curr_proc_size -lt $errval
        then
          notify "Warning" $killoption $process $pid \
            $curr_proc_size $value "blocks of virtual size"
        elif test $curr_proc_size -ge $errval
        then
          notify "Error" $killoption $process $pid \
            $curr_proc_size $value "blocks of virtual size"
        else
          test $debug -gt 0 && echo "process virtual size ok"
        fi
     ;;
```

Finally we close the monitor case statement and the two inner processing loops. The script then goes to sleep for the configured amount of time before starting over again. It will then continue its monitoring until the monitor itself dies or is killed or the system is shut down.

```
      esac
    done
  done
  sleep $sleeptime
done
```

■ ■ ■

## CHAPTER 32

Managing File Counts

System administrators have to manage the computing resources available to their users. One resource consists of the directory queues for e-mail and print servers. These directories contain the files waiting to be processed by the server. The number of files in these directories varies depending on the volume of work on the server. There are times when no one is using the service and the queue empties out. There are also times when the server is heavily loaded and the queue will be full. Usually, though, the number of files will stay within stipulated limits.

Of course, from time to time you will have problems with a queue filling up faster than the server can process the requests. This might be due to a bubble of extremely heavy load or because of some type of problem that prevents the server from processing the requests. You will want to monitor the queue directories so you can take the proper measures when a problem arises.

The script presented in this chapter is a simple monitor that counts the files in the specified directories. The script gives you the necessary core functionality; you will, however, want to modify the directory locations and notification methods for your own site and needs.

File-Count Monitor

First we define the directories to be monitored. It would be a bit cleaner to place this definition in a separate file so you don't have to modify the script to make configuration changes. However, to keep the script as simple as possible I have not done that. Each entry in the FILENUM variable is a colon-delimited set of fields. The fields specify the directory name to monitor, the warning threshold, the maximum limit, and finally the e-mail address to which to send notifications.

```
#!/bin/sh
FILENUM="/var/spool/mqueue:50:100:root \
/var/spool/lp:50:100:root@yourdomain.net /:50:100:rbpeters"
```

Now we start looping through each of the configured directories to check the file counts. First sed swaps colons with spaces in the configuration entry; then the set command assigns, to each of the positional parameters $1 through $4, the corresponding element of the output, which consists of the items in the original colon-separated fields. Once the fields are assigned to the variables, the script determines the number of files in the directory.

```
for monitor in $FILENUM
do
  set -- `echo $monitor | sed -e 's/:/ /g'`
  file_count=`ls $1 | wc -l`
```

The script completes by comparing the current file count to the three possible situations:

Everything is normal. The file count is lower than the warning threshold.

A warning state. The count is between the warning threshold and maximum limit.

An error state. The count is above the maximum limit.

In either the warning or error state, the script will send a notification via e-mail specifying the condition of the directory. There is one inherent problem with the e-mail notification type. If you're monitoring a mail queue directory that is filling up, it is likely that the e-mail notification will not be sent. In this case, you may want to change your notification method to use something other than e-mail such as an alpha-numeric pager or phone.

```
  if [ $file_count -lt $2 ]
  then
    continue
  elif [ $file_count -ge $2 -a $file_count -lt $3 ]
  then
    echo "Warning: File count in $1 is $file_count, should be less \
      than $2" | mail -s "Directory file count warning for $1" $4
  else
    echo "Error: File count in $1 is $file_count, should be less \
      than $2" | mail -s "Directory file count error for $1" $4
  fi
done
```

To make this script more useful, you would need to call it with cron or possibly surround the code with an infinite loop that a perpetual process would run to continually monitor your machine. The script's main function is carried out in the assignment of the file_count variable by performing an ls on the target directory and then piping the output to the wc utility. This is one of a number of ways to get queue-status information. Two other ways of determining the file count in a directory are to use the echo and find commands. Here are some possible solutions:

```
file_count=`ls $1 | wc -l`
file_count=`find $1 -type f | wc -l`
file_count=`echo $1/* | wc -w`
```

Note that the wc -l switch has been replaced with -w for the last solution. This is because the result of the shell's expansion of the asterisk will appear in the form of a single line of filenames separated by spaces.

Testing File-Count Methods

The different methods of counting the files in a directory are not all created equal. Some older operating systems cannot handle large numbers of files when the ls or find command is used. Sometimes the find-oriented solution will return incorrect results on directories containing between 12,000 and 15,000 files. Also, I have worked on systems with file counts of more than one million in a single directory; in these cases ls returns an "argument list too long" error. I have not yet found a situation in which the echo solution fails.

On my current Gentoo Linux system, both find and ls seem not to suffer from these earlier limitations, and I have used both to successfully count files in a single directory numbering well above 800,000 files. While testing, I noticed that there is a speed difference between the three solutions.

The find solution is by far the fastest. It took about .4 seconds with just over 300,000 files in a directory. The second fastest is echo *. It took about 1.5 seconds. This measure is most accurate if you work in the directory whose files are to be counted. If a full path is supplied with the asterisk (e.g., /some/full/path/*), the command takes longer because each element in the shell expansion contains the full path and all that extra text needs to be processed. The slowest in my tests was ls. It took about 4 seconds to complete. Both find and ls seemed to take similar amounts of time regardless of whether the full path is supplied.

Realistically speaking, with a current operating system any of these solutions should work fine. It is not very likely that you will deal with this extreme number of files in a single directory, so the performance differences between the solutions will almost surely be insignificant.

CHAPTER 33

■ ■ ■

Processes Running from inittab

In several chapters of this book,[1] I discuss system monitors and some methods of running them on your machine at all times. By automatically starting a process at the system level you can accomplish this task in multiple ways without user interaction. There is cron, the system scheduler, as well as at, another scheduling utility. You also can start a process with an rc (run control) startup script, traditionally located in the /etc/rc directory, which is processed automatically at boot time.

Here I want to discuss the init process. The init man page states that it is "the parent of all processes." Init runs the scripts that, in turn, run the startup scripts living in the /etc/rc directories.[2] It also controls the running system's runlevel. Init is started as the last step in the system boot process. If you are looking for the init configuration parameters, they are kept in the /etc/inittab file.

The main problem with monitors that need to run on the system permanently is that if they die or have to be killed, it is challenging to get them restarted automatically. The methods for automatically starting processes have some limitations on their ability to keep processes running.

System-startup scripts will start a process, but have no notification or recovery method that can be used if a process ends. In addition, these scripts are run only at boot time, and many systems run continuously for long periods between reboots.

Cron and at jobs that start processes can be scheduled to run frequently, but the process code would need to be written so that it recognizes if another instance of itself is already running. As you'll see, scheduled tasks are not a terribly efficient use of system resources. Although a process may run for long periods of time without issues, the scheduler also uses some resources to continuously check and/or start the process. Additionally, if a process does die or get killed, there is a period of time before the next scheduled job when the monitor is not running.

---

1. Log-file monitoring is covered in Chapter 7, process monitoring in Chapter 31, file-count monitoring in Chapter 32, and network monitoring in Chapter 42.
2. The startup scripts may be found in different locations depending on your operating system. /sbin/rc#, /etc/init.d/rc#, and /etc/rc# are some of the locations I have seen.

This is where init comes in. There is an action value among the /etc/inittab entries called *respawn* that is quite useful for certain tasks. When an entry is added to the inittab and the action defined for that entry is *respawn*, init makes sure that a process corresponding to that entry is always running. If the process dies or is killed, init will automatically restart or "respawn" it. The process restart is nearly instantaneous, and the amount of time during which no instance of the desired process is running is negligible. The following are a few example lines from a system inittab file:

```
1:2345:respawn:/sbin/mingetty tty1
2:2345:respawn:/sbin/mingetty tty2
3:2345:respawn:/sbin/mingetty tty3
4:2345:respawn:/sbin/mingetty tty4
5:2345:respawn:/sbin/mingetty tty5
6:2345:respawn:/sbin/mingetty tty6
```

An /etc/inittab entry takes the form of a line with four colon-separated fields. The first field is a unique identifier for the entry, of one to four characters in length. The second field is a list of the runlevels in which the entry should be run. In these examples, each of the entries will be run in runlevels 2 through 5. The third field names the action to be taken, which in this case is respawn. (init can perform a number of actions besides respawn on a process, such as once, off, boot, and wait.) The last field is the script or program that you want to run.

Respawn entries are likely to be part of the default /etc/inittab file for starting the boot-time rc scripts or getty login sessions, as seen in the preceding sample entries.

I have also used init in this way to make sure monitors that are critical to tracking system health are always running. The init process is the top dog of all processes on a running system; if it can't keep processes running, your system is probably fairly "sick" and you are likely to have bigger problems than deficient monitors.

The following is an example of an entry I have used for my system monitors in the /etc/inittab. The im identifier is arbitrary and needs only to be unique in the file as a whole. It simply identifies the entry in the file. The process is run on runlevels 3 and 5 and is respawned if it dies. It executes the MyMonitors script.

```
im:35:respawn:/bin/nice /usr/local/bin/MyMonitors >/dev/null 2>&1
```

Entries can be added to the /etc/inittab file at any time, but init won't automatically reread the inittab file when it is modified. You can manually cause such a rereading by issuing the init q command as root, which will reread the file and implement the current configuration.

One potential issue to watch for if you create a respawn inittab entry is that the script to be called should include code enabling it to run continuously. If you create a script that performs a monitor function and exits when finished, init will assume the program is constantly dying and continuously try to restart the process. On most systems, if this happens you will start receiving messages in the system logs warning you that the process is "respawning too fast." Init will then disable the respawn of the job for a period of time since it recognizes that there is some type of issue with the configured entry. The issue could be that the configured job runs and exits normally whereas respawned jobs should run continuously, or simply that the syntax of the inittab line is incorrect.

CHAPTER 34

■■■

Automatic RCS

The RCS (Revision Control System) is a set of programs used for source-code version control. It is used heavily by programmers to maintain source files and track source-code changes. The script in this chapter[1] was created in an effort to control configuration files on a system without having to perform the manual check-in and check-out process used with the RCS. This is done by replacing your system editor with this script, which in turn calls your editor with the appropriate RCS commands.

The script demonstrates a few useful techniques: it grabs command-line parameters, it calls the script through a link, and finally it demonstrates the use of the check-in and check-out commands in the RCS. Many more features and options are available in the RCS, but they are mostly outside the scope of this discussion.

This script isn't intended to be called specifically as an add-on utility; it is intended as a replacement for the original editor for your environment. I wrote it for use with vi, although other editors could be replaced in the same manner. You would first rename the original vi or vim binary in /usr/bin to something like /usr/bin/vim-rcs. When you move this script to its new location, you would replace the original /usr/bin/vi (or vim) with your script so that when you call vi/vim, you will be running this script instead. The $VI variable refers to the new location of the original vi/vim binary so the script knows where you moved it. This works even when calling vi (now the script) with a wild card such as *, because the shell will expand the wild card before executing the call.

We start out with some configurable system variables. The file locations defined with these variables may vary from installation to installation, so you'll need to make the appropriate changes for your site.

Note You must have the RCS installed on your system; it may not be installed by default.

---

1. The script is based on one given to me by my colleague Brian Grell.

```
#!/bin/sh
CI=/usr/bin/ci
CO=/usr/bin/co
TEST=/usr/bin/test
BASENAME=/bin/basename
ME=`$BASENAME $0`
DIRNAME=/usr/bin/dirname
```

The ME variable is assigned the name with which the script was invoked. If you named this script vi so that it would replace the vi binary, ME would be set to vi. We assign the ME variable its value by using basename to remove any leading path used to call the script. Later in this chapter we will come back to this variable and the way it is used. For now, note that when installing the script on your system, you will also need to create a soft link in a directory in your PATH variable; that soft link should be called vir and point to the script.

When a script is run, environment variables are set that don't directly relate to the script itself since they are part of the shell executing the script and its environment. One example is the variable $@, which is set to the values of all the positional parameters (starting from 1) that were passed to the script. (As you have seen, positional parameter 0 is assigned the name of the script.)

```
ALLTHEFILES=$@
```

To get a little more specific, consider the following:

```
runme a b c d
```

In this example, the value of $0 would be runme, $1 would be a, $2 would be b, and so on. $@ would be set to the combination of all of the positional parameters: a b c d.

This is necessary in our example script because you might want to call your editor with a wild card, such as filename*, or you might want to call the editor to edit a list of files. The variable ALLTHEFILES is set for this purpose.

In the following code we start the main loop that iterates through the list of files passed to the script. First we determine the path and filename of the current file.

```
VI=/usr/bin/vim-rcs
for file in $ALLTHEFILES
do
  # Get some basic info about the file
  PATH=`$DIRNAME $file`
  FILENAME=`$BASENAME $file`
```

Now the script should determine whether the file has already been checked in under the RCS. If it has, we check it out. Then we edit the file as usual.

```
$TEST -f "$PATH/RCS/$FILENAME,v" -o -f "$PATH/$FILENAME,v" && $CO -l $file
$VI $file
```

After each file has been edited, we want to see how the script was called to determine whether it needs to be checked back in. Recall that a soft link to the script was created when the script was installed. If the script was called with this `vir` soft link instead of with a `vi`/`vim` command, which we can find out by examining $ME, then we can assume that even if the file was not under RCS control before, it needs to be checked in so it will be available in the future. The script checks to see if the RCS-controlled version of the file exists. If the controlled version does not exist, the script checks the file into the RCS with the initial check-in (`-i`) switch; otherwise it checks it in as normal.

```
  if [ "$ME" = "vir" ]
  then
    $TEST ! -f "$PATH/RCS/$FILENAME,v" -o ! -f "$PATH/$FILENAME,v" && $CI -i $file
  else
    $TEST -f "$PATH/RCS/$FILENAME,v" -o -f "$PATH/$FILENAME,v" && $CI -u $file
  fi
done
```

You can see that by determining how the script was invoked (using the soft link or using the name of the file), you avoid having to force all of the files you edit into the RCS. Chapter 13 contains further discussion of the technique of using the syntax of the invocation to select a script's behavior.

You could upgrade this script by defining directories for which it is assumed that all files inside those directories should be checked into the RCS even if they weren't originally. (The /etc directory would be a good candidate for this treatment.) Files residing in other directories would be edited as usual, without any version control.

CHAPTER 35

■■■

Colorful /proc Reporting

The proc file system is found on many UNIX and Linux variants and gives a virtual view into the running system. Traditionally the proc file system is attached to the /proc mount point, but proc is not really a file system and mostly contains "files" of zero size. Even though these objects look as if they are empty when they are listed, they actually contain quite a lot of information about the running system. When viewed, they show system information from the kernel's perspective: their contents are based on system resources and characteristics, such as memory, CPU, kernel, and network utilization.

There are several kinds of files in the /proc directory tree on a Linux machine. The first type is a series of directories that have numbers as names, each containing a group of files that hold specific information about the running system. Each numbered directory corresponds to a running process ID. The files in these directories relate to the command that was invoked, the execution environment, parameters passed to the command, memory usage, and other valuable pieces of process information. The other file types and directories found in /proc contain items such as current resource usage, system settings, hardware information, and network usage.

The man page for proc contains far more detail than this chapter, but please note that implementations of the proc file system on different operating systems are by no means identical. I have worked on older versions of Solaris whose /proc contained only numbered directories for running processes, and those directories held files that were different from their Linux counterparts. With this state of affairs, you are certain to profit from exploring the documentation for your specific system.

The script we are about to explore has its origins in a utility that creates a brief system-status report. The script returned a single line of key performance indicators; the information was derived from files located in /proc directories. It displayed all the process-performance values for each system being monitored on a few lines all contained in a single window, using colors to indicate load level, memory, and swap usage (green for normal usage and red for high). The main purpose of this tool was to permit a quick visual check of whether certain machines were overloaded.

Our code extends the functionality of the original script from providing just one line of output per system to displaying a more comprehensive report about the processes running on a single machine. The code itself is not very complex but it does demonstrate some of the /proc system usage data. You will also learn how to add color to your output.

The first function sets up the colors that the script will use. These are standard ANSI color definitions, and each one begins with the string \033. This is the plain-text ASCII code for an escape character. The numerical notation used here is easier to read in text form than the actual escape character. (The escape character happens to be ^[, and if you want to type it in, you must use your editor's mechanism for handling this character—for example, pressing Ctrl+v and then ESC in vi.) Note that these color definitions may not work on all terminal types. I have had no problems with using these values in a simple xterm window.

```sh
#!/bin/sh
def_colors () {
  # Attributes
  normal='\033[0m'; bold='\033[1m'; dim='\033[2m'; under='\033[4m'
  italic='\033[3m'; noitalic='\033[23m'; blink='\033[5m';
  reverse='\033[7m'; conceal='\033[8m' nobold='\033[22m';
  nounder='\033[24m'; noblink='\033[25m'
  # Foreground
  black='\033[30m'; red='\033[31m'; green='\033[32m'; yellow='\033[33m'
  blue='\033[34m'; magenta='\033[35m'; cyan='\033[36m'; white='\033[37m'
  # Background
  bblack='\033[40m'; bred='\033[41m'
  bgreen='\033[42m'; byellow='\033[43m'
  bblue='\033[44m'; bmagenta='\033[45m'
  bcyan='\033[46m'; bwhite='\033[47m'
}
def_colors
```

I did not use all of the colors or attributes defined in the function, but I included them for the sake of completeness. This function would be an excellent addition to a standard library, which is discussed in Chapter 2.

Now that the colors are defined, the script clears the display and then obtains the name of the machine from the /proc/hostname file. Then it displays a header for the report.

```sh
clear
hostname=`cat /proc/sys/kernel/hostname`
echo
echo -e "System Report for $white$hostname$normal on `date`"
echo
```

There are a few noteworthy items in the command that displays the header line: first, echo is used with the -e switch, which translates escaped three-digit number sequences contained in text into the corresponding ASCII character; in our case it translates the ANSI escape-character sequence into the escape character. Other escape values can be used to represent other special characters, such as the carriage return, tab, and backspace.

The second item is the hostname variable, which is surrounded by variables that control color output. The first variable changes the output from the default color to white. Once the hostname variable's value has been presented, the color is reset to the default. Changes to the text color can be accomplished together with and at the same time as modifications to the foreground and background color. Other attributes, such as blinking text, can be changed as well by using the appropriate variable.

ANSI graphics were common on old dial-up bulletin-board systems prior to widespread Internet access. Note that when the blink attribute is used, the action of blinking utilizes network resources when displaying in remote terminals. The bandwidth used is probably minimal, but you should be aware of it. The blink attribute poses more of an issue when it is used over a serial connection with a modem.

The next section of code grabs more data from various files in /proc to get a few more items of information, such as processor type and NIS domain name. The script then determines if the processor is manufactured by Intel or AMD and changes the output color depending on the vendor before printing this portion of the report to the screen.

```
processor=`grep 'model name' /proc/cpuinfo | cut -d: -f2 | cut -c2-`
nisdomain=`cat /proc/sys/kernel/domainname`

cache=`grep 'cache size' /proc/cpuinfo | awk '{print $4,$5}'`
bogomips=`grep 'bogomips' /proc/cpuinfo | awk '{print $3}'`
vendor=`grep 'vendor_id' /proc/cpuinfo`

echo -e "Hostname: $white$hostname$normal NIS Domain: $white$nisdomain$normal"
if [ "`echo $vendor | grep -i intel`" ]
then
  cpu_color=$blue
elif [ "`echo $vendor | grep -i amd`" ]
then
  cpu_color=$green
fi

echo -e "Processor: $cpu_color$processor$normal"
echo -e " Running at $white$bogomips$normal bogomips with\
$white$cache$normal cache"
echo
```

Now the script gathers information about the operating system and kernel, including their versions and release numbers. It also obtains the system uptime and outputs colorized text reporting the results.

```
ostype=`cat /proc/sys/kernel/ostype`
osrelease=`cat /proc/sys/kernel/osrelease`
rev=`cat /proc/sys/kernel/version | awk '{print $1}'`
da_date=`cat /proc/sys/kernel/version | cut -d\ -f2-`
upsec=`awk '{print $1}' /proc/uptime`
uptime=`echo "scale=2;$upsec/86400" | bc`
```

```
echo -e "OS Type: $white$ostype$normal Kernel:\
$white$osrelease$normal"
echo -e " Kernel Compile $white$rev$normal on\
$white$da_date$normal"
echo -e "Uptime: $magenta$uptime$normal days"
```

These lines gather system memory and swap information and calculate the proportion of these system resources currently used by the running processes. One interesting bit is the use of the set command; it uses the result of greping through /proc/meminfo to assign values to positional parameters. This is a convenient way of assigning each item in a space-separated sequence of items to its own variable.

```
set `grep MemTotal /proc/meminfo`
tot_mem=$2 ; tot_mem_unit=$3
set `grep MemFree /proc/meminfo`
free_mem=$2 ; fre_mem_unit=$3
perc_mem_used=$((100-(100*free_mem/tot_mem)))
set `grep SwapTotal /proc/meminfo`
tot_swap=$2 ; tot_swap_unit=$3
set `grep SwapFree /proc/meminfo`
free_swap=$2 ; fre_swap_unit=$3
perc_swap_used=$((100-(100*free_swap/tot_swap)))
```

Once the script has calculated percentages, the color of the output is set depending on the usage value that is being reported. Messages reporting usage levels of less than 80 percent appear in green, values between 80 and 90 percent appear in yellow, and 90 percent utilization or greater values appear in red. I have chosen the percentages somewhat arbitrarily. One improvement to the script would be to replace the percentage values with variables that are initialized using either a command-line switch or a configuration file.

```
if [ $perc_mem_used -lt 80 ]
then
  mem_color=$green
elif [ $perc_mem_used -ge 80 -a $perc_mem_used -lt 90 ]
then
  mem_color=$yellow
else
  mem_color=$red
fi
if [ $perc_swap_used -lt 80 ]
then
  swap_color=$green
elif [ $perc_swap_used -ge 80 -a $perc_swap_used -lt 90 ]
then
  swap_color=$yellow
```

```
else
  swap_color=$red
fi

echo -e "Memory: $white$tot_mem$normal $tot_mem_unit Free: $white$free_mem$normal \
  $fre_mem_unit %Used: $mem_color$perc_mem_used$normal"
echo -e "Swap: $white$tot_swap$normal $tot_swap_unit Free: $white$free_swap$normal \
  $fre_swap_unit %Used: $swap_color$perc_swap_used$normal"
echo
```

In addition to memory and swap utilization, the script determines the system-load averages, again using the set command to assign values to the positional variables. The /proc/loadavg file contains a single line of space-separated fields, where the first three fields are the 1-minute, 5-minute, and 15-minute load averages of the running system.

```
set `cat /proc/loadavg`
one_min=$1
five_min=$2
fifteen_min=$3
echo -n "Load Average:"
for ave in $one_min $five_min $fifteen_min
do
  int_ave=`echo $ave | cut -d. -f1`
  if [ $int_ave -lt 1 ]
  then
    echo -en " $green$ave$normal"
  elif [ $int_ave -ge 1 -a $int_ave -lt 5 ]
  then
    echo -en " $yellow$ave$normal"
  else
    echo -en " $red$ave$normal"
  fi
done
echo
```

When the file's output is applied to the set command, the first three fields become the values of the positional parameter variables $1, $2, and $3. Once these values have been obtained, the script adjusts the color of the text. A load average below 1 will be reported in green, between 1 and 5 in yellow, and any value 5 or greater in red. Keep in mind that the colors for the load averages are assumed to be for single-CPU systems.

The final operation counts the running processes and determines their states. Once the total number of processes is calculated, the script displays the process count. It also gives a breakdown of processes by status type, telling the user how many processes are running, sleeping, stopped, or zombified.

```
running=0; sleeping=0 stopped=0; zombie=0
for pid in /proc/[1-9]*
do
  procs=$((procs+1))
  stat=`awk '{print $3}' $pid/stat`
  case $stat in
    R) running=$((running+1));;
    S) sleeping=$((sleeping+1));;
    T) stopped=$((stopped+1));;
    Z) zombie=$((zombie+1));;
  esac
done
echo -n "Process Count: "
echo -e "$white$procs$normal total $white$running$normal running\
$white$sleeping$normal sleeping $white$stopped$normal stopped\
$white$zombie$normal zombie"
echo
```

The following is a sample report that the script generates while running. I have used boldface wherever the report is supposed to appear in a special color. It is more informative with colorized output, although even without color it is useful for capturing a snapshot of the system state and displaying everything on one screen.

```
System Report for casper on Thu Aug 4 21:33:19 PDT 2005

Hostname: casper NIS Domain: (none)
Processor: Intel(R) Pentium(R) 4 CPU 1.80GHz
Running at 3555.32 bogomips with 256 KB cache

OS Type: Linux Kernel: 2.6.10-gentoo-r7
Kernel Compile #2 on Thu Feb 24 14:38:44 PST 2005
Uptime: 163.70 days
Memory: 514836 kB Free: 183744 kB %Used: 65
Swap: 506036 kB Free: 491324 kB %Used: 3

Load Average: 0.04 0.11 0.05
Process Count: 140 total 1 running 139 sleeping 0 stopped 0 zombie
```

It is possible to retrieve most of the information in the files located in the /proc directory tree using other methods. Programs such as hostname, netstat, top, ps, uptime, and others get their data from /proc. In some cases those programs are easier to use because they condense information and present it in a more readable form. In other cases getting the data directly from the files residing in /proc is easier or faster. This is the situation with our script: there is no data to format and there is no unneeded functionality that may impact performance.

The part of the script that gets the load average provides a good illustration of this; the data in /proc/loadavg is easier to process than data from other sources. Load-average data can be found by running a number of other programs, including uptime, w, or top. The output of these commands contains uptime data as well as load information that would have to be parsed to gather the data you want.

It is fairly simple to extract the load averages from this output with awk, but obtaining load averages directly as demonstrated in our script, without determining the uptime as well, is a bit more economical in terms of system resources.

```
8:33PM up 33 mins, 4 users, load average: 0.00, 0.22, 0.38
9:13PM up 430 days, 0:09, 2 users, load average: 0.01, 0.13, 0.10
```

Another use of the proc file system is to influence the running system by modifying the files located in /proc. A simple example is the system name found in /proc/sys/kernel/hostname; by redirecting a new name into this file, you would end up overwriting the previous entry, thus changing the system name. You can view the change by using the uname -n command. The change lasts only until your next reboot, as the system-configuration files still hold the system's original name.

Other system attributes can be modified in the same way, such as RAID rebuild rates and the way the system handles swap or power-management settings. Bear in mind, however, that the power to modify system settings is dangerous. You might cause the system to hang or even to crash. It would be wise to perform extensive testing on noncritical machines before implementing environment-wide modifications.

■ ■ ■

## CHAPTER 36

Password-Aging Notification

With security concerns reigning supreme, it is wise to keep a tight leash on your user accounts. Unfortunately, it can be difficult to control password aging in an environment with many users. It's definitely preferable to have user passwords set to expire automatically; however, if the account goes unused for a long period of time, even though the password on an account is expired the account will still be active. In some instances an account can still be accessed without the password being updated. Also, if a user logs in to their account infrequently, they may not know that their account is about to expire. Even when a user does use her account regularly, the expiration warning message may go unnoticed among the other items that typically scroll across the screen in the message of the day.

Requiring users to change their passwords after they have aged a certain number of days is a common practice. The logic behind it is that if a password is stolen or found out, it will be useful for only a limited amount of time. Another result of this practice is that users will tend to change their password in a way that least impacts their work so they don't have to learn a new password. One method might be to leave the main password in place but change only one or two characters such as a digit so the password is incremented but still basically the same.

A better solution might be to require strong passwords and then periodically run a utility such as John the Ripper[1] against the encrypted passwords to ferret out any insecure ones. Implementing this solution combined with password aging might be even better albeit annoying to your user base.

The following script watches over the /etc/shadow file to determine how long it's been since the users have changed their passwords. The shadow file contains, among other things, account information such as encrypted user passwords and the day when a password was last changed. When the expiration date of an account approaches, the script starts annoying the user with a canned e-mail message letting them know they need to change their password and that the account will be locked if they don't. The script could easily be modified to support other notification methods.

---

1. http://www.openwall.com/john/

Some NIS and HP-UX environments don't use shadow files to hold encrypted passwords and account-aging information. The users' encrypted passwords are held in the second field of the world-readable password file. If you think this isn't the best method to maintain security, you are correct. Also, without the shadow file, there is no information tracking the age of a password. In Chapter 37 I will demonstrate another script that can be used to create and maintain a pseudo–shadow file on such systems.

Script Initialization

First off, we have to set a bunch of environment variables. Originally these were set in a separate file accessed from our script. This makes configuration a bit more convenient, but to simplify this demonstration, I included the initialization of the variables in the script.

```
#!/bin/sh
HOME=/usr/local/pass_aging
```

The following line of code establishes the number of days that the user's password is valid before the account will be locked. The value could also be set dynamically by pulling the fifth field from the /etc/shadow file if the account has been configured appropriately. However, I have found that accounts on a system often are created by many different people and the fields in the /etc/shadow file are not always filled in correctly to include appropriate account-expiration settings.

```
VALID_DAYS=90
```

The ENVIRONMENT variable is used to customize the notifications with some meaningful information about the affected accounts. For example, you can assign Accounting or Development to the ENVIRONMENT variable. A notification might then read, "Your Development account is about to expire."

```
ENVIRONMENT="Scripting"
```

The following code shows the e-mail addresses used for administrative notification. The reports of account-password aging are sent to the ADMIN_EMAIL address. The DEBUG_EMAIL address is used for testing.

```
ADMIN_EMAIL=root
DEBUG_EMAIL=
```

Since this script has the potential for disrupting your environment by modifying passwd and shadow files, it would be wise to perform a lot of testing prior to running it. However, when the DEBUG_EMAIL variable is non-null, the shadow file will *not* be updated and users will *not* be notified. The notifications that would have been sent to the users will instead be sent to the DEBUG_EMAIL address. This may generate a lot of mail to that address, but this setting prevents potentially major problems and it is worth using.

Next the passwd and shadow files are configured to be used with this script. It would be wise to make backup copies of the real files. These definitions are useful in that you can configure the script to work with NIS since those files don't generally live in /etc.

```
shad=/usr/local/pass_aging/bin/shadow_copy
pswd=/usr/local/pass_aging/bin/passwd_copy
```

The exclude file, shown next, is a flat file containing a list of usernames not to be modified by the script. In some environments there may be userless accounts (such as apache or sendmail, which are associated with applications) that would break if the accounts were suddenly locked. You could improve this script by using a file that associates userless accounts with the e-mail addresses for the users responsible for those accounts. This would allow a notification to be sent to the account owner when expiration is approaching. It would also separate the management of this type of account from the general exclude list.

```
exclude="$HOME/config/exclude_list"
```

The following code shows a few more variables to set up some paths, filenames, and various other items in our script. The ED variable defines the file that will contain editing changes to be made to the shadow file. The max variable represents the number of days a password is permitted to exist without change. The notify variable is used to start notifying users that their accounts are about to expire. The notifications start two weeks (14 days) prior to expiration. The remaining variable assignments specify files that will all contain parts of the final aging report that is sent to the administrator. Nothing too fancy here.

```
ED=ed.script
max=$VALID_DAYS
notify=$(($max-14))
OUTFILE=$HOME/aging
NOTEOUT=$HOME/notes
WARNOUT=$HOME/warnings
REPORT=$HOME/report
ARCHIVE=$HOME/archive
BIN="$HOME/bin"
```

Since this script is going to read and potentially modify the shadow file, it must be run as root. You have to ensure that this is the case when installing the script.

```
if [ "`id -un`" != "root" ]; then
  echo "This script must be run as root - exiting" >&2
  exit 1
fi
```

Then we have to clean up any old transient report files that exist.

```
for file in $OUTFILE $WARNOUT $NOTEOUT $REPORT
do
  if [ -f $file ]
  then
    rm $file
  fi
done
```

Next we determine the number of days that have passed since 1/1/1970. Password-aging information in the /etc/shadow file is held in the third field of each account entry. This field contains an integer that expresses the date on which the password was last changed as a number of days since 1/1/1970. Subtracting this number from the current number of days elapsed since that date gives us the age of the password.

```
seconds_since_epoch=$((`date +%s`))
seconds_per_day=86400
days_since_epoch=$(($seconds_since_epoch/$seconds_per_day))
```

We now back up the shadow file for safety. We want to be able to return to the original file to start over if necessary. Using cp -p will also preserve the original modification time and permissions on the new copy of the file.

```
backdate=`date +%m%d%y%H%M`
cp -p $shad $ARCHIVE/shadow.$backdate
```

The following code lets you clean the archive directory by removing old reports and backup shadow files more than seven days old.

```
find $ARCHIVE -mtime +7 -exec rm {} \;
```

Processing Begins

Now here is where the real script begins. We start a loop that iterates through all the user-names in the passwd file.

```
for user in `cut -d: -f1 $pswd`
do
```

To line up the text in the final report in columns and make it a little more readable, you might like to create some padding spaces based on the length of the username to be reported.

```
  padding=""
  user_length=`echo $user | awk '{print length}'`
  padding_len=$((15-$user_length))
  counter=1
```

```
while [ $counter -lt $padding_len ]
do
  padding="${padding} "
  counter=$(($counter+1))
done
```

The code would also benefit from using `printf` to format the report appropriately instead of inserting spaces manually to line up the columns. The `printf` command is a print function that gives you a lot of control over how the output is formatted.

Next we populate some variables with the values from the current user's `shadow` entry. First is the number of days after which the user must change his password. The second is the number of days since January 1, 1970 that the password was last changed. These will be used to determine when an account should expire.

```
exp_days=`grep "^${user}:" $shad | cut -d: -f5`
pass_days=`grep "^${user}:" $shad | cut -d: -f3`
```

Depending on whether the encrypted password is located in the `passwd` or the `shadow` file, you have to use one of the following two lines:

```
#pass_word=`grep "^${user}:" $pswd | cut -d: -f2`
pass_word=`grep "^${user}:" $shad | cut -d: -f2`
```

Our implementation uses the second (uncommented) line; it gets its data from the `shadow` file. You probably think the script could simply check for the existence of the `shadow` file; in case it isn't there, it should default to the `passwd` file. This would work in most—but not all—situations. I have worked on some machines that have both files but use only the `/etc/passwd`. I have also seen systems that will use the `/etc/passwd` file unless an `/etc/shadow` exists. In that case the `shadow` file will be used. This script will, of course, need to be customized to fit your environment.

You also need to check for a special case: if the encrypted password consists of a single asterisk (*) character, you have to escape it with a backslash (\). If the asterisk isn't escaped, it will be evaluated later as a wild card denoting all filenames residing in the current working directory (the traditional meaning of *). In a shell environment, another method to get around this problem would be to set `noglob`, which turns off that type of evaluation.

```
if [ "$pass_word" = "*" ]
then
  pass_word="\*"
fi
```

If the user account is incorrectly configured with a null password, the script creates a message explaining this state of affairs and appends it to the warning-output file. The contents of this file will be added to the final report at a later stage.

```
if [ "$pass_word" = "" ]
then
  echo "$user $padding WARN: $user has null password set, \
    set password or lock account" >> $WARNOUT
fi
```

Then we determine by checking the exclude file whether the current user is one of those exempted from password expiration. If the user is not exempt from password expiration, the script continues on to the core of the program.

```
exempt=`grep "^${user}$" $exclude`
if [ "$exempt" = "" ]
then
```

Before proceeding we have to make sure the user's password has an expiration date set. If it doesn't, the else clause that follows will create a notification for the final report.

```
if [ "$pass_days" != "" -a "$exp_days" != "" ]
then
```

Determine Password Age

This is the beginning of the core of the script. First we determine how many days have passed since the password was last changed. Then we evaluate this number to determine if the user should start receiving notifications that his account is about to be disabled.

```
days_since_change=$(($days_since_epoch-$pass_days))
if [ $days_since_change -lt $notify ]
then
```

A locked account is indicated by the first character of the password; when the script locks an account, it changes the user's encrypted password string to a string of the form *CLOSED_${the_date}*. If the password is still young, no action needs to be taken against the account. However, we should check to see if the account has already been locked, and if so, append a notice to the report.

```
first_char=`echo $pass_word | cut -c1`
if [ "$first_char" = "*" ]
then
  echo "$user $padding $days_since_change Already locked"\
    >> $OUTFILE
else
  echo "$user $padding $days_since_change OK" >> $OUTFILE
fi
```

The following code checks whether the password is still valid but the user-notification period has begun. If so, we determine how many days it will be before the account is locked. (The length of the notification period is configurable; recall that at the beginning of the script I set it to start 14 days prior to the password expiring.)

```
elif [ $days_since_change -ge $notify -a $days_since_change -le $max ]
then
  exp=$(($max-$days_since_change))
```

We then report warning notifications to the output file and to the debugging e-mail address, provided it has been configured.

```
if [ "$DEBUG_EMAIL" != "" ]
then
  echo "$user $padding $days_since_change Expires in $exp days ; \
    Would have sent mail ; sent mail to $DEBUG_EMAIL" >> $OUTFILE
else
  echo "$user $padding $days_since_change Expires in $exp days ; \
  sending mail" >> $OUTFILE
fi
```

Finally, we notify the user that the password will expire in the determined number of days. Please recall that if the DEBUG_EMAIL variable is *not* null, notifications will be sent only to the debug address specified in the configuration section. Only when this variable is null will notifications be sent to the specified user. This is handled in the send_email script called earlier; it also checks whether the debug e-mail address has been set. At a first glance it may seem that the notifications should always be sent to the user, but this is not the case. (The send_email script is not included here, but it should be simple to implement.)

```
$BIN/send_email $user $days_since_change about_to_expire
```

In the following example the password has expired and the account needs to be locked. We first set some variables in anticipation of changing the user's password to a CLOSED string showing the date on which the user account was locked, as described earlier.

```
else
  first_char=`echo $pass_word | cut -c1`
  the_date=`date +%y%m%d`
  CLOSED="*CLOSED_${the_date}*"
```

If the account has already been locked in the following conditional statement, the echo statement reports that fact to the output file. (The logic for account-checking could be reorganized so that the same checks wouldn't have to be done multiple times; here I have broken down the cases for easier understanding, at the cost of some repeated code.)

```
if [ "$first_char" = "*" ]
then
  echo "$user $padding $days_since_change Already locked"\
    >> $OUTFILE
else
```

To lock the account, we will construct and run an ed script that modifies the passwd or shadow file. First we remove any existing ed scripts created from previous runs.

```
if [ -f $HOME/$ED ]
then
  rm $HOME/$ED
fi
```

Once again, if the debug e-mail address has been set, we only append to the output file a report that the account is expired.

```
if [ "$DEBUG_EMAIL" != "" ]
then
  echo "$user $padding $days_since_change \
    Would have locked account ; sent mail to\
    $DEBUG_EMAIL" >> $OUTFILE
else
```

Otherwise we append to the output file the notification that the user account is now being locked.

```
echo "$user $padding $days_since_change Locking account\
  *CLOSED_${the_date}*" >> $OUTFILE
```

The ed script contains instructions to substitute the user's encrypted password with the CLOSED string. When you construct this code, you have to use a backslash to escape all occurrences of the following special characters in the encrypted password string: ., /, $, and *. See Chapters 24 and 25 for more information on escaping special characters. These sed statements check for the specified special characters in the password string and replace all instances with the same character preceded with a backslash. This is so the shell ignores their special meanings and treats them simply as any other character.

```
pass_word=`echo $pass_word | sed -e s/\\\./\\\\\\\\./g`
pass_word=`echo $pass_word | sed -e s/\\\*/\\\\\\\\*/g`
pass_word=`echo $pass_word | sed -e s/\\\$/\\\\\\\\$/g`
pass_word=`echo $pass_word | sed -e s/\\\\\//\\\\\\\\\\\//g`
```

We now have to cut off the last two characters of the modified password string. These are extraneous and were introduced by the preceding transformations. The $ character, which is a valid character in an encrypted password string, also denotes the special end-of-line character in a string. This is the nature of strings on a UNIX or Linux system. Since all of the $ characters of the encrypted string were replaced with \$, the replacement action also included the end-of-line character that is now escaped and shouldn't be included in the encrypted string; both the trailing \ and $ characters need to be removed. This form of the sed command is explained in more detail in Chapter 24.

```
pass_word=`echo $pass_word | sed -e 's/\(.*\)\(.\)\(.\)$/\1/'`
```

Now we create the ed script that will replace the encrypted password string with the CLOSED string.

```
echo "/$user:$pass_word/s/$pass_word/$CLOSED" > $HOME/$ED
echo "w" >> $HOME/$ED
echo "q" >> $HOME/$ED
```

To run the ed script, use one of the following two lines, depending on whether your password entries live in the passwd or the shadow file. The same ed script can be used to replace the encrypted password within the passwd or shadow file—whichever applies. As you can see, my example uses the shadow file. More information on how to modify files using ed can be found in Chapter 25.

```
# ed -s $pswd < $HOME/$ED > /dev/null
  ed -s $shad < $HOME/$ED > /dev/null
fi
```

Now we send an e-mail notification to the account stating that it has been locked. Once again, if the debug e-mail is set, the message will go to that address and not to the real user.

```
if [ "$DEBUG_EMAIL" = "" ]
then
  $BIN/send_email $user $days_since_change account_locked
fi
  fi
fi
```

The next else matches the line far earlier in the loop, where the check was performed to see whether the user account is exempt from expiration. If that test fails, we append a message about the nonexpiring account to the output file for the final report. This completes the main loop.

```
else
  echo "$user $padding WARN: $user password not set to expire. \
    Fix shadow entry" >> $WARNOUT
fi
else
  echo "$user $padding Note: $user is exempt from password\
    expiring" >> $NOTEOUT
fi
done
```

The script then collects all notification output files and sorts them by the age of the passwords. Then all transient files are removed. The final report will list any warnings in order of importance; for example, users without a password will appear first.

```
for file in $WARNOUT $OUTFILE $NOTEOUT
do
```

```
    if [ -f $file ]
    then
      sort -rn +1 $file >> $REPORT
      rm $file
    fi
  done
```

Finally, the report is sent to the administrator and archived for later reference.

```
cat $REPORT | mail -s "$ENVIRONMENT password aging report" $ADMIN_EMAIL
mv $REPORT $ARCHIVE/report.$backdate
```

Here is a sample of the output from a final report:

```
fred           122 Already locked
rbpeters       105 Locking account *CLOSED_041124*
yabbadmin      14  OK
xfs            14  OK
webalizer      14  OK
vinmaster      14  OK
vcsa           14  OK
uucp           9   OK
```

CHAPTER 37

■ ■ ■

A Pseudo–shadow File

Some environments do not use a shadow file for maintaining passwords. These environments keep encrypted passwords in either a local passwd file or one that is handled through NIS. I have seen this mode of operation in several versions of HP-UX and NIS. NIS can support using a shadow file, but not all NIS clients have this capability.

The script in this chapter, which is intended to be run daily, creates and maintains a pseudo–shadow file to track the age of user passwords and their change history. The script does not, however, remove the encrypted password from the already-existing passwd file.

I intend this contrived shadow-file generator to be run in conjunction with the password-aging script in Chapter 36. The script in that chapter relies on information contained in a shadow file to determine the date of the last password change.

The first section of the script sets up several environment variables to be used later. The variables originally were taken from a separate configuration file, but for the sake of simplicity I have included them at the beginning of the script.

```
#!/bin/ksh
HOME=/usr/local/pass_aging
ARCHIVE=$HOME/archive
BIN="$HOME/bin"
DEBUG=duh
shad=/usr/local/pass_aging/bin/shadow_nis
pswd=/var/yp/src/passwd
PERL=/usr/bin/perl
ED=ed.script
```

The only interesting variables being set here are the debug flag and the variables storing the locations of the passwd and shadow files. The DEBUG variable just needs to be set to anything non-null to generate some debugging output while the script is running, so that you can see what it is doing when you are testing.

The shad variable holds the location of the shadow file. Since the shadow file is a regular file that the system itself doesn't actually use, you can call it anything you want. The pswd file definition is the real master passwd file that the machine relies on. This script only ever has read access to that file, so there is no danger in possibly modifying the live file even when testing. If your anxiety level is high, you could copy the original and run the script against the copy.

In the following code we determine the number of days since 1/1/1970, the start of the UNIX epoch. The number in the third field of a shadow-file entry represents the date that the password for that account was last changed, expressed as a number of days since the beginning of the epoch. This value can be determined in a number of ways. Please refer to Chapter 3 for more discussion on this topic.

```
seconds_since_epoch=`$PERL -e 'print time'`
seconds_per_day=$((60*60*24))
days_since_epoch=$(($seconds_since_epoch/$seconds_per_day))
```

If this is the first time the script is run and there is no existing shadow file, the script will create one based on the specified passwd file. Since the age of the password was probably not tracked before the first time this script is run, the script assumes that *today* is the day the password was last changed, and enters that value in the new shadow file. This gives users the benefit of the doubt.

```
if [ ! -f $shad ]
then
  test "$DEBUG" != "" && echo DEBUG: $shad does not exist, creating
  cat $pswd | awk -v days=$days_since_epoch -F: \
    '{print $1 ":" $2 ":" days ":0:90:7:::"}' > $shad
fi
```

Even though this file isn't used by any system process, we want to back it up to be able to retrace our steps in case something goes wrong. I have used saved files many times to restore account information without having to use a system backup. We also want to be able to remove the older files in the backup directory.

```
backdate=`date +%m%d%y%H%M`
test "$DEBUG" != "" && echo DEBUG: Backing up $shad to $ARCHIVE/nis_shadow.$backdate
cp -p $shad $ARCHIVE/nis_shadow.$backdate
find $ARCHIVE -mtime +7 -exec rm {} \;
```

Like the script in Chapter 36, this script will construct and run an ed script, which allows us to edit the shadow file in place when changes need to be made. This is discussed in more detail in Chapter 25. First we have to remove any previously created ed script files that may be lying around.

```
if [ -f $HOME/bin/$ED ]
then
  test "$DEBUG" != "" && echo DEBUG: Cleaning up old ed.script
  rm $HOME/bin/$ED
fi
```

Now we're in the core of the program. The loop iterates through the current passwd file and updates the corresponding entries in the new shadow file.

```
for user in `cut -d: -f1 $pswd`
do
```

First you have to determine whether the user's name appears in the shadow file. If he has a new account, he may not have been entered into it yet. If this is so, you have to create an entry in the shadow file.

```
user_exist=`grep "^${user}:" $shad | cut -d: -f1`
if [ "$user_exist" = "" ]
then
  echo "$user:$cur_pass_word:$days_since_epoch:0:90:7:::" >> $shad
  test "$DEBUG" != "" && echo DEBUG: Missing $user, adding to $shad
fi
```

Now the script gathers the user's encrypted password from the passwd file and its age from the shadow file.

```
cur_pass_word=`grep "^${user}:" $pswd | cut -d: -f2`
old_pass_word=`grep "^${user}:" $shad | cut -d: -f2`
pass_days=`grep "^${user}:" $shad | cut -d: -f3`
test "$DEBUG" != "" && echo DEBUG: \
  $user, $cur_pass_word, $old_pass_word, $pass_days
```

The shadow file is updated only when this script is run. If the password saved in the shadow file isn't the same as the current one in the passwd file, some updates need to be made to the shadow file.

```
if [ "$old_pass_word" != "$cur_pass_word" ]
then
  test "$DEBUG" != "" && echo DEBUG: $user password has changed,\
    updating $shad
```

Now we have to make sure the encrypted passwords are handled correctly. These passwords contain special characters (., /, *, and $) that need to be escaped with a preceding backslash where they appear in the ed script. This operation will ensure that the correct password string is entered in the shadow file.

```
old_pass_word=`echo $old_pass_word | sed -e s/\\\./\\\\\\\\./g`
old_pass_word=`echo $old_pass_word | sed -e s/\\\*/\\\\\\\\*/g`
old_pass_word=`echo $old_pass_word | sed -e s/\\\$/\\\\\\\\$/g`
old_pass_word=`echo $old_pass_word | sed -e s/\\\\\//\\\\\\\\\\\//g`

cur_pass_word=`echo $cur_pass_word | sed -e s/\\\./\\\\\\\\./g`
cur_pass_word=`echo $cur_pass_word | sed -e s/\\\*/\\\\\\\\*/g`
cur_pass_word=`echo $cur_pass_word | sed -e s/\\\$/\\\\\\\\$/g`
cur_pass_word=`echo $cur_pass_word | sed -e s/\\\\\//\\\\\\\\\\\//g`
```

These sed commands look pretty ugly, but that's because a lot of escape slashes have to be evaluated and in turn the following escape slash needs to be escaped itself. For more coverage of sed commands for updating encrypted password strings, refer to Chapter 36.

With all the characters being replaced, there is one character that gets escaped but should not be part of the final password string. The special $ character is the "end of line" character for all strings on UNIX and Linux systems, and normally is not visible. When all the special characters were escaped in the previous sed commands, this trailing \$ became visible at the end of the string. It wasn't part of the original encrypted password, so the last two characters (\$) need to be removed from the string. This use of sed is discussed in more detail in Chapter 24.

```
old_pass_word=`echo $old_pass_word | sed 's/\(.*\)\(.\)\(.\)$/\1/'`
cur_pass_word=`echo $cur_pass_word | sed 's/\(.*\)\(.\)\(.\)$/\1/'`
```

Now we create an instruction in the ed script that will replace the old encrypted password and its *days since last change* value with the new encrypted password and the current *days since epoch* value. We do this by taking the new values from the current passwd file. One such instruction is appended to the ed script using double greater-than signs (>>) for each user account, and then all shadow-entry updates are made at once by running the ed script.

```
  test "$DEBUG" != "" && echo DEBUG: Creating ed file to change\
    $old_pass_word:$pass_days to $cur_pass_word:$days_since_epoch
  echo "g/$user:$old_pass_word/s/$old_pass_word:\
    $pass_days/$cur_pass_word:$days_since_epoch/g" \
    >> $HOME/bin/$ED
else
  test "$DEBUG" != "" && echo DEBUG: No changes for $user
  continue
fi
done
```

Now that the loop is complete for all the users, you should add the final two lines to the ed script and process the shadow file with all its changes.

```
# Complete and process the file with the ed.script
echo "w" >> $HOME/bin/$ED
echo "q" >> $HOME/bin/$ED
test "$DEBUG" != "" && echo DEBUG: Running ed.script for $user on $shad
ed -s $shad < $HOME/bin/$ED > /dev/null
```

You might want to make one refinement: once the modifications are complete, you could check the line counts of the passwd and shadow files to see whether they match. If they don't match, it is possible that an account has been removed and the account is not present in the passwd file; the entry is still visible in the shadow file, though. The script should then remove the old usernames from the shadow file to keep both files synchronized.

CHAPTER 38

■■■

Linux Gold-System Build

Building a system manually can be fun. Building many systems manually is tedious and prone to error, especially when all systems should be built in exactly the same way. For this reason, Kickstart by Red Hat, Jumpstart by Sun, and other utilities were created to automate a network-based system build that is based on preset parameters. These utilities work well when you are building new systems on a regular basis. The downside of this method is that a client is required to be on the network and it needs to have access to the server to do a system build. Also, a build server needs to be set up and maintained, but if you are building only a moderate number of systems, it may not be worth the extra effort to set up a build server.

The build script in this chapter has a small image size and can be run from a bootable CD. The CD boots and then automatically calls a script that partitions and formats the hard disk. The script then proceeds to install a preconfigured OS image to the system hard disk. This method has the advantage of having no network or build-server requirements. The newly built system can also have site-specific configurations that may not be part of a standard installation. The script has the added advantage that it can install applications that may not be in a proprietary format, such as an RPM (Red Hat Package Manager).

The process I used was to find a Linux live distribution on a single boot CD that was designed to be customizable. I chose the "Roll your own Linux Rescue or Setup CD."[1] There are now many distributions like this, including live DVD images for larger installations, but at the time this one seemed to be the best choice.

You install this distribution on a hard disk on a running system, from which you can customize the final CD image. The gold image file and this script are placed into the distribution directory tree, and the final modification is to change the live CD startup script to call your build script. The last task is to run the script that came with the distribution to create the final .iso file, which you would then burn to a CD. The resulting CD automatically boots and runs this install script, prepares the hard drive, and installs the customized system image. I refer to the image as the *gold image* because it is the master copy of the system being installed.

The process of building a master gold system is basically manual. Once the template system is built, fully customized, and tuned to your environment, you should create an image

---

1. http://www.phenix.bnl.gov/~purschke/RescueCD

file from that disk. The gold system will then mount an NFS server (at /mnt/nfs) with sufficient space for the image and run the following command to create the image file.

This command creates a compressed tar file of the whole disk on the running gold
system. It excludes the contents of the /proc and /mnt/nfs directories because they are
specific to the gold system, and you can't use the contents if they are propagated to subsequent builds.

```
tar cvfz /mnt/nfs/wholedisk.tar.gz / --exclude /proc/* \
  --exclude /mnt/nfs/*
```

Most of the build script is for preparing the hard disk to accept the final image created
from the gold system. The process determines the hard-drive geometry parameters and
bases the partitioning on those values, since the disk model and manufacturer are likely
to vary from system to system. Once the disk has been prepared, the script creates the file
systems and unarchives the gold image.

First we assign a bunch of variables that determine and store the architecture parameters
of the hard disk; we will use them to create the input file for sfdisk, which is a Linux partition-table manipulator. Additionally, they determine the amount of memory on the system
and then use double the memory value for the swap partition. It is safe to calculate swap
memory as double the amount of base memory. The value in /proc/cpuinfo that contains
the total amount of memory on a system may vary depending on the live CD image that is
being used. To deal with this case, the egrep command checks for two of the possible values.
If you choose a different live CD, you may want to check that these are valid.

```
#!/bin/sh
bytes_per_cyl=`sfdisk -l /dev/hda | grep Units | awk '{print $5}'`
tracks_per_cyl=`sfdisk -l /dev/hda | grep Disk | awk '{print $5}'`
sectors_per_track=`sfdisk -l /dev/hda | grep Disk | awk '{print $7}'`
sectors_per_cyl=$(($tracks_per_cyl*$sectors_per_track))
bytes_per_sector=$(($bytes_per_cyl/$sectors_per_cyl))
cyl_count=`sfdisk -l /dev/hda | grep Disk | awk '{print $3}'`
usable_cyl=$(($cyl_count-4))
disk_in_sectors=$((($sectors_per_cyl*$usable_cyl)-$sectors_per_track))
mem_in_bytes=`cat /proc/meminfo | egrep "MemTotal:|Mem:" | awk '{print $2}'`
swap_in_bytes=$(($mem_in_bytes*2))
```

The input file that is sent to sfdisk specifies the size of each partition in sectors. The
following function (sector_calc) takes its input in bytes and converts the number of bytes
into sectors. It also determines whether the file system fits evenly on cylinder boundaries.
If not, the function rounds up the value to the next cylinder.

```
sector_calc () {
  size=$1
  slice_in_sectors=$(($size/$bytes_per_sector))
  slice_in_cyl=$(($slice_in_sectors/$sectors_per_cyl))
  slice_rem=$(($size%$bytes_per_sector))
  if [ $slice_rem -ne 0 ]
```

```
    then
      slice_in_cyl=$(($slice_in_cyl+1))
      slice_in_sectors=$(((($slice_in_cyl*$sectors_per_cyl)-$sectors_per_track))
    else
      slice_in_sectors=$(((($slice_in_cyl*$sectors_per_cyl)-$sectors_per_track))
    fi
}
```

Now the script determines the size in sectors for each of the file systems that will be on the final build by sending the file-system size values to the sector_calc function.

```
sector_calc $swap_in_bytes
swap_in_sectors=$slice_in_sectors

sector_calc 250000000
root_in_sectors=$slice_in_sectors

sector_calc 30000000
boot_in_sectors=$slice_in_sectors

sector_calc 1000000000
var_in_sectors=$slice_in_sectors

sector_calc 512000000
home_in_sectors=$slice_in_sectors

sector_calc 512000000
tmp_in_sectors=$slice_in_sectors
```

A lot of file systems were part of this build, but it would be trivial to modify the code to remove unnecessary ones or to add your own file systems to match your gold build.

The last two file systems split in half whatever is left over after the other file systems are allocated. This was done in my environment because we used these two partitions more heavily than the rest and wanted to distribute the remainder of the space evenly. Their sector calculations are slightly different because they are based on the size of the whole disk minus the other file systems.

```
rest_of_disk_in_sectors=$(($disk_in_sectors-$swap_in_sectors-\
  $boot_in_sectors-$root_in_sectors-$var_in_sectors-$home_in_sectors-\
  $tmp_in_sectors))
usr_in_sectors=$(($rest_of_disk_in_sectors/2/$sectors_per_cyl*\
  $sectors_per_cyl))
usrlocal_in_sectors=$usr_in_sectors
```

We need to define and write the partition-table file that will be used to format the new system's hard disk. We begin by reproducing the partitioning output from sfdisk -d /dev/hda. That command dumps the partition table in a format that can be used as input to subsequently partition another disk. You would want to do this on your gold

system to make sure the script output and the gold partition table match while accounting for any hard drive–architecture variations.

```
PARTTAB=/tmp/parts.out
double_sectors_per_track=$((2*$sectors_per_track))

cat > $PARTTAB <<SOMETAG
# partition table of /dev/hda
unit: sectors
```

The interesting scripting technique here is the use of the cat command to enter text in
a free format. Here cat takes input from the code up to the tag SOMETAG and then redirects
that output to the output file specified by $PARTTAB. This code structure is called a here-
document. A here-document is where free-format text, opened and closed by a delimiter
(SOMETAG) in this case, is used as input to another code structure, such as a loop or, in this
case, a variable. The previous version of this code had each of the lines of text individually
redirected to the output file. This technique makes the code less cluttered and easier to
read; you can find more details about this in Chapter 28.

This code may be somewhat daunting to read and comprehend because of the formatting and the length of each line. With a bit of close examination, however, you'll see it isn't
quite as complex as it might seem.

```
/dev/hda1 :\
start=$sectors_per_track,size=$boot_in_sectors,Id=83,bootable
/dev/hda2 : start=$(($sectors_per_track+$boot_in_sectors)),size=$\
(($disk_in_sectors-$boot_in_sectors)),Id=5
/dev/hda3 : start=0,size=0,Id=0
/dev/hda4 : start=0,size=0,Id=0
/dev/hda5 : start=$(($double_sectors_per_track+$boot_in_sectors)),\
size=$usr_in_sectors,Id=83
/dev/hda6 : start=$\
(($double_sectors_per_track+$boot_in_sectors+$usr_in_sectors)),\
size=$usrlocal_in_sectors,Id=83
/dev/hda7 : start=$\
(($double_sectors_per_track+$boot_in_sectors+\
$usr_in_sectors+$usrlocal_in_sectors)),size=$var_in_sectors,Id=83
/dev/hda8 : start=$\
(($double_sectors_per_track+$boot_in_sectors+\
$usr_in_sectors+$usrlocal_in_sectors+$var_in_sectors)),\
size=$home_in_sectors,Id=83
/dev/hda9 : start=$\
(($double_sectors_per_track+$boot_in_sectors+\
$usr_in_sectors+$usrlocal_in_sectors+$var_in_sectors+\
$home_in_sectors)),size=$tmp_in_sectors,Id=83
/dev/hda10 : start=$\
(($double_sectors_per_track+$boot_in_sectors+\
```

```
$usr_in_sectors+$usrlocal_in_sectors+$var_in_sectors+\
$home_in_sectors+$tmp_in_sectors)),size=$swap_in_sectors,Id=82
/dev/hda11 : start=$\
(($double_sectors_per_track+$boot_in_sectors+\
$usr_in_sectors+$usrlocal_in_sectors+$var_in_sectors+\
$home_in_sectors+$tmp_in_sectors+$swap_in_sectors)),\
size=$root_in_sectors,Id=83
SOMETAG
```

Each line is simply a partition definition. They are all part of the cat output that is being written to the file that will build the file-system structure on the hard disk. Each line is of the following form:

```
/dev/partition : start={start sector},size={sectors},Id={partition type},[bootable]
```

The start (start=) and size (size=) calculations are very long and may get a little confusing. If you read these lines in order starting at /dev/hda5, you'll see that the calculation just increments the start position of the file system by the size of the previous file system.

Finally you are able to install the newly created partition table to the disk.

```
sfdisk -f /dev/hda < $PARTTAB
```

Now you can create all ext2 file systems on disk. Of course, you may want to use other file-system types.

```
for slice in 1 5 6 7 8 9 11
do
  echo Making file system on slice $slice...
  mke2fs /dev/hda$slice
done
```

We create a mount point in /tmp for accessing the hard drive and mount the root partition to it. Note that when this script is running, the /tmp directory is part of a ramdisk from the live CD. Once the root partition has been mounted, the script creates all other drive mount points on the physical disk.

```
mkdir -p /tmp/root
mount /dev/hda11 /tmp/root

for dir in boot usr var home tmp
do
  mkdir -p /tmp/root/$dir
done
```

Since there is some dependency between the file systems, the mounting process needs to happen in the proper order: the lowest-level partitions should be mounted first.

```
mount /dev/hda1 /tmp/root/boot
mount /dev/hda5 /tmp/root/usr
if [ ! -d /tmp/root/usr/local ]
```

```
then
  mkdir /tmp/root/usr/local
fi
mount /dev/hda6 /tmp/root/usr/local
mount /dev/hda7 /tmp/root/var
mount /dev/hda8 /tmp/root/home
mount /dev/hda9 /tmp/root/tmp
```

Here is where the prepared disk is populated. We unarchive the whole disk-image file onto the newly formatted hard drive. All the files should land in the correct file system, since the file system has been partitioned in exactly the same way as the original gold system.

```
cd /tmp/root
tar xvfzp /usr/wholedisk.tar.gz
cd /
```

Once that is complete, you need to create the swap partition and install the boot loader. The chroot command runs the lilo boot loader installation based on the hard drive /root directory, and not from the root of the CD. Of course, if you choose to use grub instead of lilo, you'll need to modify this command.

```
mkswap /dev/hda10
chroot /tmp/root lilo -C /etc/lilo.conf
```

We have reached the end of the installation process. The script dismounts all partitions in the proper order. Partition 6 should be dismounted first since /usr/local is attached to /usr, and partition 11 should be dismounted last since it is /root. Now when the newly built system is rebooted, it should be an exact duplicate of your original gold system except for any hard-drive size differences. All that is left to do is to make system-specific changes, such as entering your IP address and a system name, and then you can connect the finished system to the network.

```
for slice in 6 1 5 7 8 9 11
do
  umount /dev/hda$slice
done
```

CHAPTER 39

■ ■ ■

System Snapshots

Disk snapshots are a way of taking backups of files and directories at given time intervals. By accessing the specific snapshot interval, you can go back in time and find the version of a file from its snapshot backup. The script in this chapter backs up a list of directories that is configurable within the script; the backup is either at another location on the same disk, or on a separate disk altogether.

This script takes a copy of the original source directories and backs them up as the first snapshot. Any subsequent snapshot backups use hard links for any files that have *not* changed, and any changed files are copied. Like a soft link, a hard link allows multiple points of access to a single file, but a soft link is just a pointer to the original file whereas a hard link is a secondary or tertiary file that points to the same data as the original. Once a hard link is established, there is no distinction between it and the original file except for name and path. The benefit in using a hard link is that you have the same file (since it was not modified) in multiple snapshot locations, but it is not taking up any extra disk space. This is all performed with the rsync command.

If you have a directory tree that contains an archive of something like digital photos, where there isn't much change in the files, you will need only the room to back up the space the photos take up. This is the minimum amount of space required. If you have a directory that contains a lot of source code that gets modified regularly, the space required will be the same as the original code plus the space required to contain all the changed files. The amount of change that occurs in the files you back up determines the amount of space required.

This script is a heavily modified form of one I found on the Internet.[1] The main difference between this script and the original is that the original saved backup sets based on the schedule by which that the job was run, whereas this one saves many snapshot types, decreasing in granularity as they age.

For example, with the original script, if you were to create a cron job for an hourly snapshot, it would run every hour, make a complete backup of the specified directories in the first hour, and then back up any changes to that original backup for each subsequent hour following. Also, the current HOURLY.0 directory is moved up one hour to HOURLY.1 along

---

1. The original author of the script is Mike Rubel. At http://www.mikerubel.org/computers/rsync_snapshots/ index.html he goes into great detail about how his script works and any updates that have been made.

with any older snapshot, and the new snapshot is created as HOURLY.0. If you then wanted to create a daily snapshot of the same directories as the hourly backups, you'd have to schedule another cron job that would run once a day. The downside of this method is that each backup type (hourly, daily, etc.) will take up another 100 percent of the originally backed-up disk space, plus any changes.

This version of the script should be configured and then scheduled as a cron task to run hourly, much the same as the original. In the destination directory specified, it creates snapshot directories in the form of HOURLY.0, HOURLY.1, ...HOURLY.23, ...DAILY.0, DAILY.1, etc. The main difference here is that the script automatically rolls the oldest hourly snapshot to the current daily snapshot. The daily snapshots roll to weeklies, then monthlies, and finally yearlies. This is all done while consuming only the original space from the source files, plus any changes.

In the snapshot destination directories are the locations where the configured source directories to be backed up are rooted. In other words, if you are backing up /etc and /usr/local/bin, there will be an HOURLY.0/etc and an HOURLY.0/usr/local/bin directory containing your backed-up files.

The default script behavior is as follows:

- Hourly snapshots occur every time the job is run. Presumably this will be an hourly scheduled job.

- Daily snapshots are created from the oldest hourly snapshot rolled to the newest daily snapshot every time the job is run *and* it is 1am.

- Weekly snapshots are created from the oldest daily snapshot rolled to the newest weekly every time the job is run *and* it is 1am on Monday.

- Monthly snapshots are created from the oldest weekly snapshot rolled to the newest monthly every time the job is run *and* it is 1am on the 1st of the month.

- Yearly snapshots are created from the oldest monthly snapshot rolled to the newest yearly every time the job is run *and* it is 1am on the 1st of the year.

With this method, you need only one job to keep snapshots for a long period of time, so you don't take up extra disk space with multiple jobs. I noticed when running this script on my system that the snapshot destination directories didn't keep their creation date when moved. Instead the date would be modified to the time the move happened. This is noted on the web page from the original script, as are some hints for workarounds. I converted my ext2 file system to ext3 using the tune2fs command, which can be done while the system is running; the problem was resolved.

Snapshot Script

The first part of the script sets some configuration variables.

```
#!/bin/sh
SEPARATE_MOUNT=1
SYNCDIR="/root /etc /home /var/www /usr/local /var/spool/cron \
/var/mail /var/named /var/lib/squirrelmail"
MOUNT_DEVICE=/dev/hdb1
SNAPSHOT_RW=/snapshot
DEST=/$SNAPSHOT_RW
```

The SEPARATE_MOUNT variable is specified when you are saving your backups to a separate physical disk. A value of 1 will use a different disk and a value of 0 will not. It's a good idea to keep your backups on a separate disk, but it's not always feasible. The MOUNT_DEVICE value is the disk device that you are going to use. This is required only if you are going to use a separate mount. The SNAPSHOT_RW value is the mount point that you'll use to mount the separate device if you are using one. The DEST directory is the destination directory that all the snapshots will be written to.

The next group of variables sets the values that will be tested against for determining whether to roll a specific snapshot up to the next-oldest group. These variables also set the number of snapshots to keep for each type as well as define the types of snapshots. The BACKUPS variable is the list of backup types that you will be looping through. The order of this list is important and should move from least to most granular.

```
MONTHLY_STAMP=`date +%e`
WEEKLY_STAMP=`date +%u`
DAILY_STAMP=`date +%k`
HOURLY_STAMP=`date +%k`
MONTHLY=11
WEEKLY=3
DAILY=6
HOURLY=23
BACKUPS="MONTHLY WEEKLY DAILY HOURLY"
```

The following group of variables defines the binaries that will be used in the script. Most of these could be removed and the actual binary could be used in the code—except fuser, which wouldn't be in the path of a cron job.

```
ID=`which id`
ECHO=`which echo`
MOUNT=`which mount`
UMOUNT=`which umount`
FUSER=/sbin/fuser
```

```
RM=`which rm`
BC=`which bc`
MV=`which mv`
TOUCH=`which touch`
RSYNC=`which rsync`
DATE=`date +%m.%Y`
```

Since this script is backing up system files as well as potentially mounting and dismounting separate disks, you must make sure you're running as root. Otherwise, exit and echo a warning message.

```
if [ `$ID -u` != 0 ]
then
  $ECHO "Sorry, must be root. Exiting..."
  exit 1
fi
```

If you are using a separate disk device, check to see if it is already mounted. If it is, use the fuser command to kill any processes that are active on that device and then dismount the disk. If the dismount is not successful, echo a warning stating that fact, and exit.

```
if [ $SEPARATE_MOUNT -ne 0 ]
then
  mounted=`mount | grep $SNAPSHOT_RW`
  if [ "$mounted" != "" ]
  then
    $FUSER -k $SNAPSHOT_RW
    $UMOUNT $SNAPSHOT_RW
    if [ $? -ne 0 ]
    then
      $ECHO "snapshot: could not umount $SNAPSHOT_RW"
      exit 1
    fi
  fi
```

Now that the disk is dismounted, perform a file-system check on it using fsck.

```
/sbin/fsck -y $MOUNT_DEVICE
if [ $? -ne 0 ]
then
  $ECHO "snapshot: had problems fsck\'ing $SNAPSHOT_RW"
  exit 1
fi
```

Since we are dismounting and remounting the disk every hour, the file system likes to make sure it is clean. If we didn't perform the fsck here, eventually we would start receiving messages stating that the device has been mounted too many times without an fsck. Additionally, corruption of the file system can occur in this state; that happened to my system before I added this check.

Once the file system checks out, you can mount the disk in a read-write mode. If the mount is unsuccessful, issue a warning.

```
$MOUNT -o rw $MOUNT_DEVICE $SNAPSHOT_RW
if [ $? -ne 0 ]
then
  $ECHO "snapshot: could not mount $SNAPSHOT_RW"
  exit 1
  fi
fi
```

Now check to see if the destination directory exists. If it doesn't, create it.

```
if [ ! -d $DEST ]
then
  mkdir -p $DEST
fi
```

Snapshot Promotion

This is where we prepare to roll up the previous snapshots to the next least-granular. This starts a loop through all the backup types and determines the maximum number that should be kept. Do this for each snapshot type (hourly, daily, etc.). For example, you could roll the DAILY.7 backup to the WEEKLY.0.

```
for BU in $BACKUPS
do
  eval max_count=\$$BU # Maximum to keep
  eval stamp=\$${BU}_STAMP # The timestamp for that type
```

The two eval lines here make this function for each snapshot type. The eval command evaluates the line once before it is evaluated for the script. Take the backup type ($BU) of MONTHLY as an example. First it sets the max_count variable to the value of $MONTHLY. It might appear that it would use $BU instead. Because of the eval, it was using the value of $BU to set the name of the variable that we want the value from. In this case the backup type was $MONTHLY. This is a method of using a variable as a variable name (or what might be called *indirect variables*). More on this technique can be found in Chapter 7.

When promoting the backup types we first determine the oldest possible snapshot of a particular type and check for the existence of that type.

```
oldest_one=`echo $max_count+1 | $BC`
if [ -d $DEST/${BU}.0 ]
then
```

If there are previous snapshots of that type, determine which one is the oldest. This may not be the highest number you are keeping. For example, if you have configured the script to save eleven monthly backups and it has been running for only three months, the eleventh monthly directory won't exist yet to be promoted. In this case, the oldest monthly would be the third, and that one would be promoted.

```
    current_oldest=`ls -td $DEST/${BU}* | tail -1 | cut -d. -f2`
  fi
```

This test condition seems somewhat complex. Here's what it does: if the oldest possible snapshot of the type specified exists *and* it is 1am *and* this snapshot type meets its criteria to be promoted *and* this is the first time through the loop, then remove the oldest possible snapshot. This is so you can clean up the oldest of this snapshot type on your system to maintain the retention policy.

```
  if [ -d $DEST/$BU.$oldest_one -a $HOURLY_STAMP -eq 1 -a \
    $stamp -eq 1 -a "$PREV_BU" = "" ]
  then
    $RM -rf $DEST/$BU.$oldest_one
  fi
```

The script will remove only the oldest snapshot on the system, because the PREV_BU variable is set when the loop for rolling up the old snapshots completes its first iteration. This is so you won't remove the oldest of each type of snapshot—just the oldest one of them all.

Prepare to roll up the oldest backup of this snapshot type to the next least-granular type .0 backup if necessary. For instance, you could move the DAILY.4 snapshot to the WEEKLY.0 snapshot.

```
  if [ $HOURLY_STAMP -eq 1 -a "$PREV_BU" != "" -a ! -d \
    $DEST/$PREV_BU.0 -a ! -d $DEST/$PREV_BU.1 ] || [ \
    $HOURLY_STAMP -eq 1 -a $stamp -eq 1 -a \
    "$PREV_BU" != "" -a $DEST/$PREV_BU.0 ]
  then
    if [ "$current_oldest" != "" ]
    then
```

Check again for any pre-existing snapshot .0 backup that would get in the way of moving the oldest of this type up to the next least-granular type. If the code does find one, remove it.

```
      if [ -d $DEST/$PREV_BU.0 ]
      then
        $RM -rf $DEST/$PREV_BU.0
      fi
      $MV $DEST/$BU.$current_oldest $DEST/$PREV_BU.0
    fi
  fi
```

This check should never find a directory to remove, but it is a safety net. Once that is complete, move the oldest snapshot of this type ($current_oldest) to the .0 snapshot of the next least-granular type.

Now that the oldest snapshot of this type has been moved out of the way, determine if you should roll up all the rest. This should always be done for hourly snapshots. The other types of snapshots should have this done only if their time-stamp criteria are met.

```
if [ $HOURLY_STAMP -eq 1 -a $stamp -eq 1 ] || \
   [ $HOURLY_STAMP -eq 1 -a "$BU" = "DAILY" ] || \
   [ "$BU" = "HOURLY" ]
then
  while [ $max_count -ge 0 ]
  do
    count_plus=`echo $max_count+1 | $BC`
    if [ -d $DEST/$BU.$max_count ]
    then
```

Now determine if you have more snapshots of a type you want to keep than you have configured. If you do, you should remove the oldest one. Otherwise just move the oldest one up an iteration.

```
      if [ -d $DEST/$BU.$count_plus ]
      then
        $RM -rf $DEST/$BU.$count_plus
      fi
      $MV $DEST/$BU.$max_count $DEST/$BU.$count_plus
    fi
    max_count=`echo $max_count-1 | $BC`
  done
fi
```

This loop iterates through all the snapshots of a particular type from the oldest to the newest and moves them up one. For clarity, if you have daily snapshots 0, 1, and 2, you would first move 2 to 3, then 1 to 2, and finally 0 to 1.

The PREV_BU variable needs to be set so the next time this loop iterates it knows what the next least-granular type is. This is why the order for the $BU variable is important.

```
PREV_BU=$BU
Done
```

Creating the Latest Snapshot

The following loop is where the real magic happens. The rsync command copies from each of the source locations into the latest .0 snapshot. It also creates the hard links for any unchanged file to the next oldest hourly .1 snapshot while simply copying any files that have been changed since the last rsync was performed.

```
for dir in $SYNCDIR
do
  final_location=`dirname $dir`
    mkdir -p $DEST/HOURLY.0/$final_location
  $RSYNC -a --delete --link-dest=$DEST/HOURLY.1/$final_location \
    $dir $DEST/HOURLY.0/$final_location
done
```

Now determine if the rsync completed successfully. Since this is the heart of the script, you want to validate that it had no issues.

```
if [ $? -ne 0 ]
then
  $ECHO "$RSYNC error, sync did not complete correctly, aborting"
  exit 1
fi
```

Finally the script remounts the separate disk device as a read-only file system.

```
if [ $SEPARATE_MOUNT -ne 0 ]
then
  $MOUNT -o remount,ro $MOUNT_DEVICE $SNAPSHOT_RW
  if [ $? -ne 0 ]
  then
    $ECHO "snapshot: could not remount $SNAPSHOT_RW readonly"
    exit 1
  fi
fi
```

The idea here is that you want access to the files you are backing up, but you don't want to run the risk of having the backups removed accidentally. (This happens only if you are saving your snapshots to a separate disk.)

Final Thoughts

You could make a couple of modifications to this code to suit your needs. For instance, the following bit of code can replace the section where the rsync is performed by the cp command, in the event you don't have the required version available.

```
if [ -d $DEST/hourly.0 ]
then
  $CP -al $DEST/hourly.0 $DEST/hourly.1
fi
```

The extended rsync options are a bit cleaner, though. These four lines should not be included in this script and are here only for example. They are part of the original script this one is based on and can be found at the link provided earlier.

Another modification that could enhance this script would be to use rsync's remote capabilities. This would allow you to save your snapshots to a separate machine.

CHAPTER 40

■ ■ ■

Removing Large Files and Log Rolling

This chapter gives a few tips relating to moving or removing files that are consuming large amounts of disk space. In some cases you may have a file system that's filling up because a process adds copious amounts of entries to a log file. When you run into a large log file that is found to be the primary cause of a full file system, your first inclination may be to remove the file to reclaim space. However, this may not work as you might intend.

Before I go into why, let me first talk a little about files and their structure. The file name is the visible representation of an inode that allows you to access the data in the file. The inode contains all the important information about a file, such as its ownership, permissions, modification times, and other items of interest. An inode also holds information about the location of the data on the hard disk. A file name is a user-friendly way of accessing an inode, which is represented by a number. You can determine the inode number of any file by running the command `ls -i filename`.

Here is an example of a full directory:

```
$ ls -i
474322 3715152.pdf          214111 rsync.tar.gz
474633 770tref.pdf          215939 yum-2.0.5-1.fd.fr.noarch.rpm
215944 openbox-3.1-1.i386.rpm
```

Note that the inode number precedes each of the five files listed here. As just mentioned, part of the data contained in an inode is a pointer to the data on the physical disk. If the file has been opened by a process for writing, the process writes to this location on the hard disk.

The potential problem with removing a large file to clean up disk space is that if a user or an administrator removes the file, the inode may still be kept open by a process that is writing the data, and the disk space will not be returned to the system. The operating system won't realize it should release the disk space for reuse until the process closes the file. At that time the disk space will definitely be reclaimed.

One way of finding out if a process is keeping a file open is to use the `fuser` command, which will display a list of process IDs that are accessing a given file. You also can use the `lsof` command to find this information. `lsof` is designed to list open files and the processes that are accessing them. Once you know the processes that are using the file, you can stop them before deleting the file. However, you may not be able (or want) to do this. The other problem with needing to stop a process that is holding a file open is that doing so may be against existing site policies. The process or application that is holding the file open might be production-critical and impact business needs if it is halted.

Another way to clean up the space used by a file is to zero out the file by redirecting /dev/null into the file. This trims the file down to zero bytes while leaving the file itself in place. The file remains open and accessible to any process that might be using it. However, the operating system will release the disk space in a timely fashion. Keep in mind that some processes may keep a file open for writing for a very long time.

Here is a sample of a directory listing, including an offending log file that is consuming large amounts of disk space. We have a choice of several possible commands that will zero out the file.

```
$ ls -l
total 113172
-rw-rw-r-- 1 rbpeters rbpeters    1057862  Jun  7 18:21 3715152.log
-rw-rw-r-- 1 rbpeters rbpeters     449184  Jun  7 18:21 770tref.log
-rw-rw-r-- 1 rbpeters rbpeters 1104249096  Jun  7 21:22 really_big.log
```

The following command is one, cp /dev/null really_big.log is another, and echo > really_big.log is yet another. All of these commands overwrite a large file with nothing.

```
$ >really_big.log
```

This is the resulting directory listing after the file has been zeroed out:

```
$ ls -l
total 1484
-rw-rw-r-- 1 rbpeters rbpeters 1057862 Jun 7 18:21 3715152.log
-rw-rw-r-- 1 rbpeters rbpeters  449184 Jun 7 18:21 770tref.log
-rw-rw-r-- 1 rbpeters rbpeters       0 Jun 7 21:25 really_big.log
```

This procedure can be used to rotate log files. For example, you may have an application for which you would like to keep one week's worth of log information. You would then rotate it to an older version to keep up to one month. After a month, you would delete the file. One solution includes the logrotate command, which is part of multiple Linux distributions.

The following is a simple script that copies the existing log file to a backup with a version number and then zeroes out the file. During the time the script is being run, any existing processes that are writing to the file can still access it.

The code first defines the file in question and then checks whether it exists. If it does exist, execution continues.

```
#!/bin/sh
LOGFILE=./my.log
if [ ! -f $LOGFILE ]
then
  echo "Nothing to do... exiting."
else
```

You've already seen the use of the redirect (>) to zero a file. The main addition to this idea here is the cp -p command.

```
cp -p $LOGFILE ${LOGFILE}.0
> $LOGFILE
fi
```

This command preserves the original file's ownership and time stamp for the new copy. Thus the new copy maintains the attributes of the original file and it appears as if the file had been moved. This is also a useful technique when modifying scripts, configuration files, or any other file for which preserving the original file's attributes would be valuable.

CHAPTER 41

■ ■ ■

Core Finder

In a production environment, it is a good idea to know whether your applications are dumping core often. It is also considered good housekeeping to know about your core files so your hard disk won't fill up with unnecessary files. The small script in this chapter tracks down and cleans up core files. The script was intended to be run as an hourly `cron` job, although you could change the schedule to fit your needs. The job also has its priority lowered using the `nice` command so that it won't interfere with the performance of regular processes on the machine. The notifications I've received from this script have characterized chronic issues with applications on more than one occasion. Without the script, I would have never seen the patterns.

This script steps through each of the locally mounted file systems and finds all core files. It determines the applications that created the core files and moves the core files to a central location for later examination. The script also logs its actions and cleans up old saved files.

First we have to set up some straightforward variables.

```
#!/bin/sh
HOWOLD=30
FSLIST="/ /boot"
UNAME=`uname -n`
DATE=`date +%m%d%I%M`
DATADIR="/usr/local/data/cores"
LOGFILE="$DATADIR/cor_report"
```

The HOWOLD variable is used as the maximum age, in days, for saved core files. Any files older than this will be removed.

The FSLIST variable contains the list of file systems that will be checked for core files. The list will vary from system to system. You could set FSLIST dynamically by using the df command to determine the locally mounted file systems. The command might look something like this: FSLIST=`df -l | grep '^/dev' | awk '{print $6}'`, which gathers the lines starting with /dev and then prints the field containing the file-system name.

The other four variables contain the name of the system that the script is running on (UNAME), the current date (DATE), the directory to which the core files will be saved (DATADIR), and the name of the log file (LOGFILE).

Now we determine whether the data directory exists. This is the directory where the core files will be saved. If it doesn't exist, you have to create it. The -p option to mkdir adds any omitted parent directories to the path of the directory being created.

```
if [ ! -d $DATADIR ]
then
  mkdir -p $DATADIR
fi
```

Then you need to find all previously saved core files that don't need to be kept around anymore, and remove them.

```
find $DATADIR -name \*\.core\.\* -mtime +$HOWOLD -exec rm {} \;
```

The following is the script's main loop. It finds all the core files created since the last time the script was run.

```
find $FSLIST -mount -type f -name core -print | while read file
do
  if [ -s $file ]
  then
    coretype=`file $file | cut -d\' -f2`
    mv $file $DATADIR/$UNAME.core.$coretype.$DATE
    echo "$coretype $UNAME $DATADIR/$UNAME.core.$coretype.$DATE" | \
      tee -a $LOGFILE | mailx -s "core_finder: $coretype core file \
      found on $UNAME" sysadmins
  else
    rm $file
  fi
done
```

If a core file's size is zero bytes, we remove it. If it is larger than zero bytes, we use the file command to determine the application that created the core file. Then the core file is saved in the archive directory and its name is changed to include the type of core and the date when the file was found. Then we add an entry to the log file noting the action that was taken, and send an e-mail notice to the administrators.

■ ■ ■

Network Adapter Failover

The script in this chapter provides network redundancy. It monitors the network accessibility of the local machine for issues. When there is a problem detected with a primary network interface, it reverts its configuration to a backup interface. We are assuming a network architecture where two network interface cards (NICs) are installed in the machine that runs the script. We're also assuming there are network connections running to both interfaces, which are configured in the same fashion (subnet/vlan, speed, duplex, and so on). Each interface should be physically connected to a different network switch for the sake of redundancy.

The goal is that if the primary network hardware fails for any reason, the system will recognize the lack of connectivity and switch the network settings to a backup interface. This script probably wouldn't be very useful in a small environment, as redundant network hardware can get expensive. However, it is a good tool for use in an environment where high availability and redundancy are key.

This script performs very well. In testing, I was logged into the system through the network and, after executing some commands validating connection, I disconnected the primary interface cable. The failover of the interface occurred in less than 10 seconds and my command-line session carried on as if nothing had happened.

Depending on when the interface failure occurs, the maximum time for a failover to complete would be about 15 seconds. The script first checks network availability, sleeps for 10 seconds, wakes up and checks again, and continuously repeats this process. The shortest amount of time the script could take to recognize and execute a failover is probably less than 5 seconds. Most systems can take that amount of interruption without much impact.

Like in many scripts in this book, the configuration of variables happens in the script itself. It would probably make for cleaner code to save the configuration information in a separate file, which can then be sourced from the script. If this were done, you could change the values without interfering with the code.

```
#!/bin/sh
LOG=/var/log/messages
PRIMARY=eth0
SECONDARY=eth1
ME=`uname -n`
```

This first group of configuration variables sets up the log file where log entries for any potential network failures will be entered. The primary and secondary interface names are also defined. These names will change depending on your hardware and operating system. For instance, network interfaces on most Linux machines have names like eth0 or eth1. Other UNIX variants might use names such as iprb0 or en1. We also determine the system name so that failover messages can indicate the machine that had the problem.

The following code sets the networking information. These are the settings that will be switched when a failure occurs:

```
IP=`grep $ME /etc/hosts | grep -v '^#' | awk '{print $1}'`
NETMASK=255.255.255.0
BROADCAST="`echo $IP | cut -d\. -f1-3`.255"
```

The networking information will be specific to your implementation. You will need to determine your IP address appropriately. The address could be located in the local hosts file (as shown here) or the NIS or DNS information locations. The IP address could also have been set manually. The subnet mask and broadcast address are also system-specific.

The next set of configuration variables determines the way the script monitors for network availability.

```
PINGLIST="Replace with a space-separated list of IP addresses"
PING_COUNT=2
SLEEPTIME=10
MAILLIST=sysadmins
```

The PINGLIST variable holds a list of IP addresses situated in a route architecturally beyond the switches to which the redundant interfaces are attached. All PINGLIST addresses should refer to systems that are always running, such as core network routers. The variable can specify any number of IP addresses. Having a single address doesn't give enough redundancy, whereas two or three do. I used three router addresses outside our local subnet.

The PING_COUNT and SLEEPTIME variables describe the number of pings to use for each of the addresses in the PINGLIST and the amount of time to sleep between network checks. The MAILLIST variable is a comma-delimited list of mail addresses that will be sent a notification when any failover takes place.

The ping utility has operating system–dependent command-line switches that are used when sending specific numbers of ping packets to a system. This check determines the OS of the system the script is running on. It then sets a variable containing the appropriate ping switch.

```
if [ "`uname | grep -i hp`" != "" ]
then
  ping_switch="-n"
elif [ "`uname | grep -i linux`" != "" ]
then
  ping_switch="-c"
fi
```

Now we have to determine the currently active network interfaces.

```
NICS=`netstat -i | awk '{print $1}' | \
  egrep -vi "Kernel|Iface|Name|lo" | sort -u`
NIC_COUNT=`netstat -i | awk '{print $1}' | \
  egrep -v "Kernel|Iface|Name|lo" | sort -u | wc -l`
```

The script needs to know which interface is the primary interface prior to entering the main loop. This is so that it will be able to switch interfaces in the correct direction. The commands may need to be validated on your specific operating system. There may also be other values that you'll want to filter out with the egrep command. For instance, on my FreeBSD box, there is a point-to-point interface that I wouldn't want involved, and I'd filter it out here.

Now we have the list of currently active interfaces on the system. If there is only one interface, we of course assume it to be the primary interface. If there are more interfaces, we loop through all the active ones to find the interface with the specified primary IP address and make it the current interface.

```
if [ $NIC_COUNT -gt 1 ]
then
  for nic in $NICS
  do
    current=`ifconfig $nic | grep $IP`
    if [ "$current" != "" ]
    then
      CURRENT_NIC=$nic
    fi
  done
else
  CURRENT_NIC=$NICS
fi
```

If the initial active primary interface is the specified SECONDARY interface, you have to reverse the variables so the script won't switch interfaces in the wrong direction.

```
if [ "$CURRENT_NIC" = "$SECONDARY" ]
then
  SECONDARY=$PRIMARY
  PRIMARY=$CURRENT_NIC
fi
```

This starts the main loop for checking the network's availability. It starts by sleeping for the configured amount of time and then initializes the variable for the ping response.

```
while :
do
  sleep $SLEEPTIME
  answer=""
```

Check the Network

The core of the script can be found in the following loop. It iterates through each of the IP addresses in the PINGLIST variable and sends two pings to each of them.

```
for node in $PINGLIST
do
   if ping $node $ping_switch $PING_COUNT > /dev/null 2>&1
   then
     answer="${answer}alive"
   else
     answer="${answer}"
   fi
done
```

The answer is based on the return code of the ping. If a ping fails, its return code will be nonzero. If the ping is successful, the answer variable will have "alive" appended to it. Under normal conditions, if all router addresses are replying, the answer variable will be in the form of "alivealivealive" (if you have, say, three addresses in the PINGLIST).

If the answer from the pings is non-null, we break out of the loop because the network is available. Thus all IP addresses present in the PINGLIST variable must fail to respond for a failover to occur.

```
if [ "$answer" != "" ]
then
   echo network is working...
   continue
```

This allows us to avoid moving the network settings unnecessarily in the event of one IP address in the PINGLIST being slow to respond or down when the network is in fact available through the primary interface.

If all pings fail, you should use the logger program to put an entry in the LOG file. Logger is a shell interface to syslog. Using syslog to track the failover in this way is simpler than creating your own formatted entry to the log file.

```
else
   logger -i -t nic_switch -f $LOG "Ping failed on $PINGLIST"
   logger -i -t nic_switch -f $LOG "Possible nic or switch \
     failure. Moving $IP from $PRIMARY to $SECONDARY"
```

Switch the Interfaces

Now we perform the actual interface swap.

```
ifconfig $PRIMARY down
ifconfig $SECONDARY $IP netmask $NETMASK broadcast $BROADCAST
ifconfig $SECONDARY up
```

First we need to take down the primary interface. Then we have to configure the secondary interface. Depending on your operating system, the final command to bring up the newly configured interface may not be required. With Linux, configuring the interface is enough to bring it online, whereas Solaris requires a separate command for this.

In Solaris the interface remains visible with the `ifconfig` command after it is brought down. To remove the entry, we have to perform an `ifconfig INTERFACE unplumb`. The same command used with the `plumb` option makes the interface available prior to being configured. FreeBSD will work with the same command options, although that option has been provided only for Solaris compatibility. The native `ifconfig` options for FreeBSD are `create` and `destroy`.

We now need to send out an e-mail notification that the primary interface had an issue and was switched over to an alternate NIC. An additional check here to verify that the network is available would be wise. This way, if both interfaces are down, mail won't start filling the mail queue.

```
echo "`date +%b\ %d\ %T` $ME nic_switch[$$]: Possible nic or \
    switch failure. Moving $IP from $PRIMARY to $SECONDARY" | \
    mail -s "Nic failover performed on $ME" $MAILLIST
```

Now that the interfaces have been switched, the script will swap the values of the `PRIMARY` and `SECONDARY` variables so any subsequent failovers will be performed in the right direction.

```
    place_holder=$PRIMARY
    PRIMARY=$SECONDARY
    SECONDARY=$place_holder
  fi
done
```

APPENDIX A

▪▪▪

Test Switches

One of the fundamental elements of programming is the ability to make comparisons: you test for certain conditions to be able to make decisions. You can use the test command to evaluate many items, such as variables, strings, and numbers. I keep the information in this appendix close at hand since I haven't memorized all of the parameters. I often use these switches for checking files and strings, and this is a simple quick reference for easy lookup. Note that in Table A-1 the "test" column refers to the system command test such as /usr/bin/test. The "bash" and "ksh" columns refer to the built-in test command for those shells.

Table A-1. *Test Switches*

Switch	test	bash	ksh	Definition
-a FILE		✔	✔	FILE simply exists.
-b FILE	✔	✔	✔	FILE exists and it is a block special file such as a disk device in /dev.
-c FILE	✔	✔	✔	FILE exists and it is a character special file such as a TTY device in /dev.
-d FILE	✔	✔	✔	FILE exists and it is a standard directory.
-e FILE	✔	✔	✔	FILE simply exists.
-f FILE	✔	✔	✔	FILE exists and it is a standard file such as a flat file.
-g FILE	✔	✔	✔	FILE exists and it is set-group-ID. This is the file permission that changes the user's effective group on execution of the file.
-G FILE	✔	✔	✔	FILE exists and its group ownership is the effective group ID of the user.
-h FILE	✔	✔	✔	FILE exists and it is a symbolic link. This is the same as -L.
-k FILE	✔	✔	✔	FILE exists and it has the sticky bit set. This means that only the owner of the file or the owner of the directory may remove the file.
-l STRING	✔			Length of STRING is compared to a numeric value such as /usr/bin/test -l string -gt 5 && echo.
-L FILE	✔	✔	✔	FILE exists and it is a symbolic link. This is the same as -h.

Table A-1. *Test Switches (Continued)*

Switch	test	bash	ksh	Definition
-n STRING	✔	✔	✔	STRING has nonzero length.
-N FILE		✔	✔	FILE exists and has been modified since it was last read.
-o OPTION		✔	✔	True if shell OPTION is enabled, such as set -x.
-O FILE	✔	✔	✔	FILE exists and its ownership is determined by the effective user ID.
-p FILE	✔	✔	✔	FILE exists and it is a named pipe (or FIFO).
-r FILE	✔	✔	✔	FILE exists and it is readable.
-s FILE	✔	✔	✔	FILE exists and its size is greater than zero bytes.
-S FILE	✔	✔	✔	FILE exists and it is a socket.
-t [FD]	✔	✔	✔	FD (file descriptor) is opened on a terminal. This is stdout by default.
-u FILE	✔	✔	✔	FILE exists and it has the set-user-ID bit set.
-w FILE	✔	✔	✔	FILE exists and it is writable.
-x FILE	✔	✔	✔	FILE exists and it is executable.
-z STRING	✔	✔	✔	STRING has a length of zero.

APPENDIX B

■ ■ ■

Special Parameters

Shell special parameters are variables internal to the shell. These variables reference various items, such as the parameters passed to a script or function, process IDs, and return codes. It is not possible to assign a value to them since they can only be referenced.

This appendix is a compilation of the parameters available in bash, ksh, pdksh, and Bourne sh. All of these variables are accessible in each of the shells mentioned, except for $_, which is not available in the Bourne shell.

It isn't necessarily obvious from the shell man pages that you would need to prepend the variables with a $ sign to reference them. For instance, to find the value of the previous command's return code, you would use a command like this:

echo $?

or

RETURN_CODE=$? ; echo $RETURN_CODE

Table B-1. *Shell Internal Special Parameters*

Parameter	Definition
*	Complete list of all positional parameters, starting at 1. If double quoted, becomes a single word delimited by the first character of the IFS (internal field separator) value.
@	Complete list of all positional parameters, starting at 1. If double quoted, becomes individual words for each positional parameter.
#	The number of positional parameters, in decimal.
?	The return code from the last foregrounded job. If the job is killed by a signal, the return code is 128 plus the value of the signal. Example: Standard kill is signal 15, which would result in a return code of 143.
-	All of the flags sent to the shell or provided by the set command.
$	The shell's process ID. If in a subshell, this expands to the value of the current shell, not the subshell.
!	The process ID of the most recently backgrounded command.
_	Expands to the last argument of the previous command.

Table B-1. *Shell Internal Special Parameters (Continued)*

Parameter	Definition
0	Expands to the name of the shell or shell script.
1...9	The positional parameters provided to the shell, function, or script. Values larger than 9 can be accessed with ${number}.

APPENDIX C

■ ■ ■

Other Shell-Scripting Resources

Whenever I'm shell scripting I keep a number of resources close at hand. I may run into odd problems or have specific needs for the current working project. The following are the resources I use for my work.

Manual Pages

When you are working on a Linux or UNIX system, the resources you will nearly always have at hand are your system man pages. This means a copious amount of free and detailed information regarding your specific system is available, and man pages are highly recommended. With that said, although man pages usually are accurate, they are not always understandable or easy to read. In all, I would advise you to take the rough with the smooth.

I would also recommend looking at similar man pages from different system types to gain differing views of the same utility. For example, the proc man page on one version of Linux is not as complete as that of another Linux version, but the more complete version is applicable to the other. Another example is the date man page on Linux that contains many formatting options, whereas a Solaris man page does not even though the formatting syntax still functions on Solaris. If you have a variety of systems available to you, the comparison is worth your time.

Books

The titles in the "Scripting Books" section relate to the nuts and bolts of shell scripting; they teach you how to script and use various shell types. The "Supplementary Books" section lists titles that are not necessarily related to shell scripting directly but are an excellent resource for enhancing your scripting capabilities.

Scripting Books

Olczak, Anatole. *The Korn Shell User and Programming Manual*. Addison-Wesley, 1997.

Kochan, Stephen and Patrick Wood. *UNIX Shell Programming, Third Edition*. Sams, 2003.

Burtch, Ken O. *Linux Shell Scripting with Bash*. Sams, 2004.

Supplementary Books

Dougherty, Dale and Arnold Robbins. *sed & awk, Second Edition*. O'Reilly, 1997.

McCarthy, Martin. *The Procmail Companion*. Addison-Wesley, 2001.

Libes, Don. *Exploring Expect*. O'Reilly, 1994.

Friedl, Jeffrey E. F. *Mastering Regular Expressions, Third Edition*. O'Reilly, 2006.

Frisch, Æleen. *Essential System Administration, Third Edition*. O'Reilly, 2002.

Nemeth, Evi, Garth Snyder, Scott Seebass, and Trent R. Hein. *UNIX System Administration Handbook, Third Edition*. Prentice Hall, 2000.

Taylor, Dave. *Wicked Cool Shell Scripts*. No Starch Press, 2004.

Shell Resources

The following sites are the primary sources of shell-scripting wisdom. They contain various levels of information, including documentation, man pages, FAQs, and download instructions.

The bash shell site: `http://www.gnu.org/software/bash/bash.html`

The korn shell site: `http://www.kornshell.com/`

The pdksh shell site: `http://www.cs.mun.ca/~michael/pdksh/`

Online Resources

There are endless resources on the Internet relating to shell scripting. Carefully selected search criteria are only a search engine away. The following resources represent a selection of what I have used over the years:

Advanced Bash Scripting Guide (`http://www.tldp.org/LDP/abs/html/`). This is a complete how-to shell-scripting guide that starts from the beginning and assumes no previous expertise, and then works up to advanced scripting.

An Introduction to the UNIX Shell (`http://www.softlab.ece.ntua.gr/facilities/documentation/unix/docs/sh.txt`). I haven't found an official bourne shell site, but this is a good start. There are also plenty of other bourne shell programming guides available.

Heiner's SHELLdorado—Your UNIX Shell Scripting Resource (`http://www.shelldorado.com`). This site is an excellent resource for all sorts of shell-related topics. There are articles, best practices, tutorials, tips, scripts, and more.

SysAdmin Magazine (`http://www.samag.com`). This publication does not focus specifically on shell scripting; it is mainly focused on system administration, but it usually has some excellent shell-programming articles discussing useful procedures or problem solutions.

LiveFire Labs (`http://www.livefirelabs.com`). This is a hands-on UNIX-training company. The site has an e-mail list you can sign up for to receive the UNIX tip, trick, or shell script of the week.

Usenet comp.unix.shell group (`http://groups.google.com/group/comp.unix.shell`). Though not a web site, this resource is one of the best I have found relating to shell scripting. It is a news discussion group that focuses on everything to do with shells. There are incredibly talented people hanging out in this Usenet group who are willing to answer your shell-related questions. There is also a vast amount of history that can be searched and an FAQ maintained by the group's members.

Index

You Need the Companion eBook

Your purchase of this book entitles you to buy the companion PDF-version eBook for only $10. Take the weightless companion with you anywhere.

We believe this Apress title will prove so indispensable that you'll want to carry it with you everywhere, which is why we are offering the companion eBook (in PDF format) for $10 to customers who purchase this book now. Convenient and fully searchable, the PDF version of any content-rich, page-heavy Apress book makes a valuable addition to your programming library. You can easily find and copy code—or perform examples by quickly toggling between instructions and the application. Even simultaneously tackling a donut, diet soda, and complex code becomes simplified with hands-free eBooks!

Once you purchase your book, getting the $10 companion eBook is simple:

1. Visit www.apress.com/promo/tendollars/.

2. Complete a basic registration form to receive a randomly generated question about this title.

3. Answer the question correctly in 60 seconds, and you will receive a promotional code to redeem for the $10.00 eBook.

THE EXPERT'S VOICE™

2855 TELEGRAPH AVENUE | SUITE 600 | BERKELEY, CA 94705

Offer valid through **6/09**.